D0834526

Writing in the
Social Sciences
English 202A

Second Custom Edition for
The Pennsylvania State University

Taken from:
Writing and Thinking in the Social Sciences
by Sharon Friedman and Stephen Steinberg
and
Writing Research Papers in the Social Sciences
by James D. Lester and James D. Lester, Jr.

Cover Art: Providence, by George Delany.

Taken from:

Writing and Thinking in the Social Sciences
by Sharon Friedman and Stephen Steinberg
Copyright © 1989 by Pearson Education, Inc.
Published by Prentice Hall
New York, New York 10036

Writing Research Papers in the Social Sciences
by James D. Lester and James D. Lester, Jr.
Copyright © 2006 by Pearson Education, Inc.
Published by Pearson Longman
Upper Saddle River, New Jersey 07458

All rights reserved. No part of this book may be reproduced, in
any form or by any means, without permission in writing from the
publisher.

This special edition published in cooperation with Pearson Learning
Solutions.

All trademarks, service marks, registered trademarks, and registered
service marks are the property of their respective owners and are used
herein for identification purposes only.

Pearson Learning Solutions, 501 Boylston Street, Suite 900, Boston,
MA 02116
A Pearson Education Company
www.pearsoned.com

Printed in the United States of America

1 2 3 4 5 6 7 8 9 10 V0ZN 17 16 15 14 13

0002000010271802882

AM

ISBN 10: 1-269-41731-2
ISBN 13: 978-1-269-41731-0

To Danny and Joanna

CONTENTS

INTRODUCTION: THE INTERPLAY BETWEEN WRITING AND THINKING

The purpose of any composition course is to teach students "how to write." Yet writing specialists have come to realize that one does not learn to write simply by acquiring a set of abstract skills. Rather, one begins to write effectively when there is a desire to develop and communicate ideas. We write *about* something, and in doing so, we deepen our understanding of our subject. We write to learn, and in the process we learn to write.

This is what is meant by the term "composition with content." The premise is that students will improve their writing through a process of reading and thinking in conjunction with writing on a regular basis with feedback from instructors and peers. This premise has changed how writing is taught. In addition to general composition courses designed to upgrade writing skills, specialized courses are offered where students read, write, and think within their chosen field of inquiry—the humanities, the natural sciences, or the social sciences. In these courses students are discouraged from inventing topics "off the cuff," or from speculating about issues by parroting conventional opinions. Instead, students are asked to write on topics that they have studied to some extent, so that their writing will be informed by prior reading and thought.

Writing and Thinking in the Social Sciences draws upon six disciplines: anthropology, economics, history, political science, psychology, and sociology. Although each discipline has its own characteristic research tradition, it is also the case that there is much common ground in terms of subject and method, and in terms of writing as well.

Our goal is to teach you, as social science students, how to make use of your background knowledge and interests to become effective writers in your chosen field of study. We hope to demonstrate how the act of writing clarifies the subject matter, and conversely, how mastery of a subject helps to produce coherent writing. This is our overall purpose. We approach it through three related steps, corresponding to the three major divisions of this book:

In Part I (Chapters 1 to 5) we provide general instruction on the writing process and the distinctive character of social science writing. An underlying rationale of these chapters is that before students can write social science they have to grasp how social scientists think.

In Part II (Chapters 6 to 9) we examine the tools that are commonly employed in social science research—the experiment, observation, the interview, and the document—and explore the implications that research method has for the writing process. In each instance we present a sample essay drawn from the social science literature.

These sample essays are taken from the disciplines of educational psychology, history, and sociology. Note, however, that the chapters are organized not by discipline, but by method—the experiment, observation, the interview, and the document. It is true that each method tends to be associated with a particular discipline—the experiment with psychology, observation with anthropology, the interview with sociology and political science, the document with history. But it is also the case that all these methods are used, to a greater or lesser extent, in each discipline. For example, although interviews are most identified with sociology and political science where they are used to gauge popular attitudes and opinion, psychologists use "depth interviewing" to probe the inner states of mind of subjects, and anthropologists engaged in field studies routinely use informants who are "interviewed" in order to elicit information about the people or community under study. Even historians have recently developed a field of "oral history," which is based on detailed interviews with individuals who have firsthand knowledge of some historical event or phenomenon. Thus, it would hardly be possible to represent the broad spectrum of research and writing in any one discipline with a few sample essays. By focusing on method rather than on discipline, however, we are able to illustrate the general *forms* that govern research and writing in the social sciences.

Each of the four chapters in Part II begins with a general introduction to the method, presents the sample essay, and ends with a critical analysis of this essay in terms of both "composition" and "content." Through a close reading and analysis of these four sample essays, you will begin to acquire a basic literacy in "the language of social research," a literacy that is indispensable for your writing as students in social science courses.

Perhaps we should add that these sample essays, which were written by leading scholars, do not represent the kind of original research and writing that is expected of undergraduates. Our purpose in including these essays is to demonstrate the ways in which professional social scientists frame research questions and gather, organize, and interpret evidence in an attempt to answer these questions. These are mental operations that you will need as students even if you do not conduct original research. Papers assigned in courses typically require you to synthesize information gathered by others who *have* conducted original research. To do this effectively, you need to know what kinds of strategies are appropriate for addressing certain kinds of questions, and how these strategies are useful in collecting and analyzing research material. As we emphasize throughout this book, reading, writing, and thinking are interrelated skills. To write well, one needs to know how to read and interpret what *others* have written.

Moreover, even if you are not expected to undertake full-fledged research projects, it is likely that you will be asked to carry out simplified exercises that employ social science methods. For example, you may be asked to work with original documents, to conduct a survey of students on campus, or to observe, record, and interpret a situation or event. David Hamilton, a composition theorist, calls these research exercises "serious parodies of science." Although they are done with fairly simple means, they require exacting thought. In the following passage Hamilton suggests the range of possibilities:

> One can move toward the social sciences by framing and assessing the behavior of people much as you might describe the movement of wind or of stars. Traffic patterns, study habits, the way people behave on elevators or in other stylized situations all present problems. If you introduce a variable [a new factor], say a stuck elevator, there is more to describe. You can treat a common local event such as a homecoming parade as an exotic native rite in order to study the terms "exotic," "native," "rite," and so on. It helps to force distance on these latter problems.[1]

Unlike scholars who do research in order to advance the frontiers of knowledge, students typically carry out these more limited research projects in order to advance their understanding and appreciation of a particular subject, or to learn more about a method by putting it into practice. With this in mind, research exercises are provided at the end of Chapters 6 to 9. However, whether you are actually doing research, or writing about research conducted by others, it is essential that you have an understanding of how social scientists go about addressing problems.

In Part III (Chapters 10 to 13) we examine the forms of academic writing that students are likely to encounter in social science courses—the summary, the critical paper, the research paper, and the essay exam.

All of these papers require that you be an analytical reader as well as a skillful writer. That is, you must be able to understand and interpret the writing of professional social scientists. Again, this was our rationale for presenting and analyzing the four sample essays in Part II. As students enrolled in social science courses, you will be expected to develop your own point of view on a topic or issue, based upon your reading, and to effectively communicate it in writing. You must be able to distill an argu-

---

[1]David Hamilton, "Interdisciplinary Writing," *College English*, 41 (March 1980), 786.

ment, comprehend its parts, and make judgments about its validity and significance.

Thus, skillful writing is based on skillful reading. However, this process also works in reverse. Writing a paper, or even an exam, will sharpen your understanding of a work, and force you to develop ideas about it. You may balk at the prospect of writing papers and essay exams, but this is the surest way to master the material in your courses.

Finally, we would like to make one observation about student attitudes toward writing. For most students writing is a difficult and even painful process. Students are all too willing to admit that they "hate to write." In our view, this is a symptom, not a cause, of poor or defective writing. As you improve your writing skills, you will begin to take pleasure in writing—not necessarily because writing is intrinsically satisfying, but because you will find yourself thinking more clearly and communicating your ideas with greater conviction.

Sharon Friedman
Stephen Steinberg

ACKNOWLEDGMENTS

One's development as a writer is necessarily interwoven with one's life. Each of us would like to acknowledge our appreciation to individuals who inspired and tutored us in the craft of writing.

Stephen Steinberg:
As a fledgling graduate student, I collaborated on a research project, resulting in a book, with Gertrude Jaeger. It fell upon me to crank out a rough first draft, which Gertrude would then overhaul. My education as a writer came as I observed my purple prose transformed into writing that was lucid and polished, and like its author, free of affectation. Gertrude always respected the immortality of the written word, and this is how I remember her.

My next lesson came from Ileene Smith who, as a young editor at Atheneum, was assigned to copyedit my book, *The Ethnic Myth*. She had the cheek, at our very first meeting, to tell me that I was wordy. I was taken aback since I had always thought of myself as terse. By the time we completed the editing several months later, I conceded the point. Her scrupulous and unrelenting editing made me a better writer. As I have come to understand, to write is to write again.

Sharon Friedman:
My interest in the teaching of writing began in graduate school. The Department of English Education at New York University has been a pioneer in the theory and pedagogy of composition. Its faculty encouraged graduate students to pursue research in a field that traditionally was considered tangential to literature and language study. This experience prepared me for a unique opportunity to work as a graduate fellow in an innovative composition program at Queens College.

The chief architects of this program were Robert Lyons and Donald

McQuade. They assembled a dynamic group of doctoral students from universities in the New York metropolitan area. To their credit, they did not simply march us into classrooms to teach composition. With other faculty members, they organized workshops around a broad range of topics dealing with both theory and practice. As a group we produced exciting syllabi, new approaches to the pedagogy of writing, and a rich file of ideas that "worked" in the classroom. We had a genuine sense of mission that we could help students see the value of learning to write well. More than a few of these graduate fellows went on to make the teaching of writing central to their careers, and several of them—Lennard Davis, Janice Forman, Bella Mirabella, Anne Schotter, and Joanna Semeiks—are still my friends as well as intellectual compatriots.

We want to thank Phil Miller, executive editor at Prentice Hall, for his faith in this project and his infinite patience. The raw manuscript fell into the competent hands of Fred Bernardi, our production editor, whose editorial skills and judgment are especially appreciated. A number of people served as readers at different stages in the writing of this book: Pat Belanoff (State University of New York at Stony Brook); Joseph Bensman (City College and Graduate Center, CUNY); John T. Harwood (Pennsylvania State University); William B. Julian (Central College); Kate Kiefer (Colorado State University); William G. Roy (University of California, Los Angeles); and Dean Savage (Queens College and Graduate Center, CUNY). We received much thoughtful criticism that we heeded as we revised the manuscript.

We also want to thank our friends "across the disciplines" who provided us with useful source material: Lisa Fleisher (educational psychology); Floyd Hammack (education); Michael Krasner (political science); William Muraskin (history); Jon Peterson (history); Alice Sardell (political science); and Andrew Schotter (economics).

As is customary, we would like to end by thanking our respective spouses. In this case it can truly be said that without them this book would not have been possible.

Part I
COMPOSITION WITH CONTENT

Chapter 1
SOCIAL SCIENCE AS A DISTINCT FORM OF INQUIRY

SOCIAL SCIENCE AND COMMON SENSE[1]

Knowledge about "man and society" did not wait upon the establishment of social science in institutions of higher learning, which is mostly a twentieth-century phenomenon. Throughout history sages, mystics, and poets in their various guises have pondered the human condition, often with extraordinary insight. Who can deny that Shakespeare comprehended the complex machinations of the unconscious long before psychology emerged as a discipline? Or that Machiavelli's astute analysis of how a prince might enhance his power is as relevant to the modern nation-state as it was to sixteenth-century Florence? Certainly Herodotus, the ancient Greek scholar who is regarded as the father of history, is an inspiration to present-day historians, despite the fact that he wrote his history of the Persian Wars in the fifth century B.C.

What, then, is unique about social science? How is knowledge obtained through social science different from knowledge obtained by individuals relying on intuition or common sense? Clearly, the truth or falsity of a proposition cannot be gauged by who is advancing it—whether a social scientist or a social seer. Notwithstanding their claim to scientific objectivity, social scientists have been known to make grievous errors. One noto-

---

[1]The first two sections of this chapter were influenced by Ernest Nagel, *The Structure of Science* (New York: Harcourt, Brace & World, Inc., 1961) chapters 1 and 2.

rious example is the considerable body of research and writing early in this century that "proved" the inferiority of certain races. As this example shows, the scientific method is less than a perfect safeguard against error. On the other hand, social seers at times have advanced ideas that may be profoundly true, even if they lack scientific rigor.

But how are we to determine whether or not a proposition is true? It is this concern with *verification* that defines social science and distinguishes it from other kinds of knowledge. The characteristic refrain of the social scientist is, "Yes, but how do we *know* that?" It is well and good to speculate that the Republicans will go down to defeat in the next election, or that the poor will one day rise in revolt, or that the economy is heading for another depression, or that Hitler was a madman, or that human beings are innately good or innately evil, and so on. There has never been a dearth of pundits to issue opinions on such matters, often with a passion that can be quite compelling. But social scientists, by profession, are skeptics. They need to be convinced. For the passion and conviction of the seer, they substitute dispassionate inquiry and a willingness to suspend belief. Evidence becomes something of an obsession, for it is through evidence, systematically garnered in accordance with fixed procedures, that social scientists arrive at "truth." This insistence on evidence is the hallmark of social science—the single most important factor that distinguishes it from knowledge derived from other sources.

This does not mean that social seers are indifferent to evidence. Even the fortune teller who dazzles her clients with her "uncanny powers" has mastered the art of detecting and interpreting such social indicators as dress, speech, and body language. For social scientists, however, observation is less an art than a craft—one that is practiced in accordance with strict rules designed to minimize the chances of error. And unlike the fortune teller who jealously guards her trade secrets, the social scientist is obliged to present all the evidence, thereby dispelling any aura of mystery.

In short, contrary to knowledge based on intuition, abstract thought, or revelation, knowledge in the social sciences is based on the scientific method. The essence of the scientific method is *controlled inquiry*, or the systematic collection and analysis of evidence. Thus, before a proposition is accepted as true, it must be demonstrated to be consistent with the available evidence, and must withstand the critical scrutiny of other researchers and critics.

In this respect social science is also different from the "conventional wisdom," a term that is applied to the common sense explanations of social phenomena that enjoy wide popular currency. The trouble with these everyday beliefs is that they are typically accepted uncritically, and held irrespective of the evidence. Often the conventional wisdom consists of empty platitudes or vague generalizations that do not even lend themselves to an empirical test, and thus cannot be either confirmed or disconfirmed.

For example, according to one familiar tenet of conventional wisdom, "Prejudice is fear." Undeniably, this statement has a kernel of truth. However, the blanket statement that "prejudice is fear" is so ambiguous as to be virtually useless as an explanation of prejudice. It does not specify what people are afraid of, why they should be afraid, or why these assumed fears afflict some people and not others. Nor can the conventional wisdom explain why some groups are singled out for hostility, or why prejudice that is dormant one year can erupt into mass violence in the next. On closer examination, the assertion that "prejudice is fear" raises more questions than it answers.

As this example suggests, the commitment to controlled inquiry often pits social science against the conventional wisdom. There is a "debunking motif" running through sociological writing, as Peter Berger noted in his *Invitation to Sociology*.[2] Rooted in an insistence on hard evidence, this debunking motif manifests itself in a tendency to question and, if necessary, to challenge prevailing opinion, which all too often is selective, biased, self-serving, simplistic, or merely trendy—certainly not based on deep thought or careful investigation.

Thus one assumption underlying social science is that the world is not always as it appears or as we are told it is. Aside from the pitfalls of commonsense explanation alluded to above, every society propagates myths that gloss over its contradictions and failures. Promulgated as they are at the highest levels of society, these myths are not easily resisted, least of all by people who are not inclined to question basic values and assumptions. But part of the mission of social science is to get behind the facade of official society, and to adopt a critical stance toward established institutions and prevailing beliefs. Thus, if social science has a credo, it is that nothing is to be accepted on faith alone, that even the most cherished assumptions must be subjected to critical scrutiny. This is what Max Weber, one of the pioneers of modern sociology, meant when he wrote that the social scientist should be a "disturber of the intellectual peace."[3]

It should come as no surprise, therefore, that social science is a field where there is much intellectual ferment, where different writers and schools engage in spirited debate, sometimes in classrooms and symposia, more often in print. Compared to the natural sciences, knowledge in the social sciences is not given to absolute and fixed answers, and notwithstanding all attempts to marshal evidence and establish proofs, social science is fraught with ambiguity. It is not a field for people who tend to view the world in black and white terms, or who are wedded to simple dichotomies—between right and wrong, truth and error. On the other hand, those with a high tolerance for ambiguity, who are willing to question

[2]Peter Berger, *Invitation to Sociology* (New York: Doubleday, 1963), p. 38.

[3]Max Weber, "Science as a Vocation," in Hans Gerth and C. Wright Mills, *From Max Weber* (New York: Oxford University Press, 1946), pp. 129–56.

the conventional wisdom, and who can break with the equation that "whatever is, is good," will find social science to be provocative and illuminating.

As noted earlier, much social science deals with subjects that are more or less familiar, though imperfectly understood. The excitement of learning comes not from discovering previously unknown terrain, but rather from reassessing old assumptions and gaining new insight into aspects of social life previously taken for granted. Thus, even for students in a first encounter with social science, the moment of discovery is not likely to evoke a shout of, "Eureka!" (which, in Greek, means "I have found"). Rather it is apt to take a more sobering and reflective expression as one realizes, "I never thought of it that way before."

Again, the unique character of social science is perhaps best understood against the background of the natural sciences. By comparison, there are few, if any, obvious frontiers in social science; few, if any, breakthroughs that call into question whole systems of thought or open up entirely new vistas. There is nothing in social science to compare with the discovery of the atom, or the cure for polio, or the development of genetic engineering. However, it is in the best tradition of social science to shed new light on old problems, to establish relationships among apparently disconnected events, and to find deeper meaning in aspects of social life that are only superficially understood.

Given these objectives, it is all the more important that social scientists communicate their findings effectively. Muddled thinking can hardly be remedied with turgid or unintelligible prose. If social science is to fulfill its mission of bringing greater clarity to our understanding of the world around us, then it must uphold standards of excellence in writing as well as research.

THE MANY MEANINGS OF "WHY"

All science, indeed all knowledge, attempts to answer the question, "Why?" However, this question assumes different meanings, which in turn yield different answers. Therefore, it should not be surprising that the various social sciences typically approach the same general question from vastly different perspectives, employ different research strategies, and reach different conclusions.

As an illustration, let us turn again to the question, "Why prejudice?" This question can be approached on two different levels of analysis. The one most commonly employed in social research asks, "Why are some individuals prejudiced and others not?" Even this question has multiple meanings. It can be construed to mean, "How do *individuals* acquire their prejudiced beliefs?" Attention is thus directed to the socialization process, and the role of various institutions—the schools, the mass media, the state—in either propagating prejudice or upholding norms of tolerance. On the other hand, concern with the sources of prejudice in the individual may lead to an exploration of the psychological needs that are served by prejudice, for example, in blaming innocent minorities for one's own frustrations or failures. Or the search for individual motives may be directed toward the material interests that are served by prejudice, for example, in reducing competition for jobs. Indeed, there is an enormous body of research in each of the social sciences that has explored the gamut of historical, social, economic, and psychological factors that help to determine whether or not individuals are prejudiced in their beliefs and actions.

The question, "Why prejudice?" can be approached on a second, more abstract level of analysis. In this instance what is being explained is not individual variations in prejudice, but the entire *system* of prejudice. Implicitly, it is assumed that prejudice will have special appeal to certain individuals, depending on such factors as their upbringing, their values, and their personalities. But where do prejudiced beliefs come from in the first place? What are their historical sources? What is the constellation of societal forces that explains their persistence down to the present? Why has racial and ethnic prejudice been so pronounced in the United States, as compared to other nations?

What is involved here is a difference between *microscopic* and *macroscopic* levels of analysis, a distinction that can be applied to virtually any area of social inquiry. A microscopic approach focuses on *individual* manifestations of a particular phenomenon. In the case cited above, prejudice is treated as an attribute of discrete individuals, and thus the "causes" of prejudice are presumed to reside within individuals—their personalities, their cultural values, or their social milieu.

In contrast, a macroscopic approach treats prejudice as an attribute of a social system, and thus looks for systemic rather than individual factors that account for the level and intensity of prejudice. On this view, individual prejudice is but a last link in a long chain of causation, reaching back to factors that have little or nothing to do with individuals. To be sure, there could be no prejudice if there were no bigots. Nevertheless, from a macroscopic perspective individual beliefs and actions are influenced and constrained by factors over which they, as individuals, have little or no control. Individuals may be held morally responsible for their prejudice, but from a macroscopic perspective the "root causes" or "ultimate sources" lie far outside the individual.

For example, according to one macroscopic theory of slavery, Africans were not enslaved because of some preexisting or spontaneous racial hatred on the part of whites toward blacks. Rather, slavery was a system that was instituted in order to provide cheap labor—the cheapest of all labor, slave labor—to southern agriculture, which produced the raw cotton that was essential to the textile industry both in the north and in Britain. Racial prejudice, as we know it, evolved in order to give moral justification and political legitimacy to what at bottom was a system of labor exploitation. Thus, blacks were not enslaved because they were hated; it would be more accurate to say that they were hated so that they might be enslaved. How does the individual fit into this model? Not only slaveholders, not only southerners, but the entire nation had a stake in slavery. Even after slavery was abolished, a caste system was instituted that nourished and reinforced belief in black inferiority. The end result was a pervasive racism that was reflected in white beliefs, feelings, and actions, and that was passed down from one generation to the next. From a macroscopic perspective, the individual is but the last link in a long chain of causation.

Clearly, microscopic and macroscopic approaches are both useful, although they address different questions and yield different insights. Furthermore, the various social sciences, and different schools within a particular discipline, have tended to focus on one or another of the meanings of "why" alluded to above. The following breakdown does not attempt to summarize the large and diverse body of research in each discipline, but only to suggest a main thrust or emphasis in terms of the specific questions that have governed research on prejudice.

Psychology.   The emphasis in psychology is on the role that psychological factors play in the formation of prejudice, and in determining how individuals respond to established systems of prejudice. The psychological classic on this subject is *The Authoritarian Personality*, which was undertaken in the aftermath of the Second World War in order to better understand the genocide of European Jews.[4] The authors concluded that prejudice is an integral part of a much larger syndrome of psychological traits, comprising an "authoritarian personality." In their view, individuals acquired a predisposition for an authoritarian personality in early childhood, partly as a result of repressive childrearing practices. As this example suggests, psychologists tend to treat prejudice as a problem of the individual, resulting from deep inner conflicts that are "acted out" on defenseless minorities. Consistent with this view, some psychologists have actually proposed mass therapy as the only means of eliminating prejudice.

Sociology.   Unlike psychologists, sociologists tend to treat prejudice not as a personal aberration, but as "normal" behavior, in the sense that it is often granted political and social legitimacy, and is acquired through routine processes of social learning. The sociological classic in this area is Gunnar Myrdal's *An American Dilemma*.[5] Myrdal viewed racism as representing a glaring contradiction between American ideals and practices. Blacks, he argued, were trapped in a vicious circle, in that they were forced to live under degrading conditions, which reinforced racist attitudes among whites, thus forming the basis for further discrimination. According to Myrdal, this vicious cycle can be broken either by convincing whites, presum-

---

[4]Theodor Adorno and others, *The Authoritarian Personality* (New York: Harper, 1950).
[5]Gunnar Myrdal, *An American Dilemma* (New York: Harper, 1944).

ably through educational programs, to abandon their prejudice, or by upgrading the condition of the black minority. Though this model has its critics, it has dominated sociological thinking on prejudice for over three decades.

History.   As a discipline history has been preoccupied with questions concerning the origins and evolution of different systems of prejudice, and their impact on the groups involved. For example, in *White Over Black* Winthrop Jordan traced the development of racism from the earliest encounter between Englishmen and Africans in the sixteenth century to the establishment of slavery in the United States.[6] There is also a large canon of studies that document the history of particular groups in meticulous detail, often focusing on specific places and periods. For example, in *Harlem: The Making of a Ghetto*, Gilbert Osofsky traced the history of blacks in New York City between 1890 and 1930, and in *The Promised City*, Moses Rischin conducted a similar study of Jews in New York between 1890 and 1914.[7]

Political Science.   The distinctive focus of political science is not on individual prejudice, but on the state and its role in fomenting or legitimating prejudice. For example, in his 1950 study of *Southern Politics in State and Nation*, V. O. Key documented the various contrivances that southern states employed to circumvent the Fifteenth Amendment which granted blacks the vote.[8] These included the poll tax, literacy tests, and the white primary, not to mention intimidation and outright violence, which resulted in the disfranchisement of virtually the entire black population. As race history has changed, so has the research focus. More recently, political scientists have conducted studies on the civil rights movement, the ghetto "uprisings" of the 1960s, and the various public policies designed to combat racism and to reduce racial inequality.

Economics.   The chief contribution that economists have made to the study of prejudice has been to establish the key role that economic factors play in producing and maintaining inequalities among racial and ethnic groups. Some economists—for example, Gary Becker in *The Economics of Discrimination*—have focused on the factors that either provide an economic rationale for discrimination in the marketplace or make it unprofitable.[9] Others, like William Tabb in his book *The Political Economy of the Black Ghetto*, have analyzed the broad economic forces that relegate blacks to impoverished ghettos, and deny them access to the more desirable jobs that would allow them to break out of the "cycle of poverty."[10]

[6]Winthrop D. Jordan, *White Over Black* (Baltimore: Penguin Books, 1969).

[7]Gilbert Osofsky, *Harlem: The Making of a Ghetto* (New York: Harper, 1966). Moses Rischin, *The Promised City: New York's Jews, 1870–1914* (Cambridge: Harvard University Press, 1962).

[8]V. O. Key, *Southern Politics in State and Nation* (Knoxville: University of Tennessee Press, 1977).

[9]Gary Becker, *The Economics of Discrimination* (Chicago: University of Chicago Press, 1957).

[10]William Tabb, *The Political Economy of the Black Ghetto* (New York: Norton, 1970).

Economists have also played a leading role in formulating and evaluating public policies designed to provide assistance and opportunity to disadvantaged groups.

Anthropology. Through countless cross-cultural studies, anthropologists have documented the great variability that race relations assumes in different parts of the world. In some countries—South Africa is the most notorious example—racial difference is the basis of the utter subjugation of one race by another. But in other countries—Brazil and Mexico, for example—intermarriage between settlers and natives was commonplace, resulting in a racially mixed population where racial distinctions are relatively unimportant. In still other countries—Cuba is a recent example—racial differences persist but are no longer a basis for domination and hierarchy. From an anthropological perspective, there is little support for the popular notion that prejudice and conflict are inevitable in racially mixed societies.

As can be gleaned from this discussion, there is no single or simple answer to the question, "Why prejudice?" Prejudice is a complex, multidimensional phenomenon. It can be, and has been, studied from many different vantage points, and instead of a single all-encompassing theory, there are numerous partial explanations that pertain to different facets of the problem.

Recognition of this principle has one major implication for both research and writing. It is extremely important to be clear about exactly what questions are being addressed. Confusion on this point is the source of much muddled thinking and writing. Professional social scientists, not to speak of less skilled practitioners, too often engage in fruitless debate over which of two competing theories is correct when, on closer examination, they are not inconsistent or contradictory, but are merely addressing different facets of a problem.

SUGGESTIONS FOR WRITING AND THINKING

1. It was once generally accepted that women were by nature passive and emotional, and suited only for domestic labor and childrearing. Discuss how the prevailing wisdom on this issue has changed. In what ways do you think social science has contributed to this change?

2. In the section of this chapter titled "The Many Meanings of 'Why'" we showed how different disciplines approach the question of why prejudice exists. Think of another social phenomenon or event, and show how it would be approached differently by an economist, a historian, a psychologist, a political scientist, and a sociologist. You might consider an issue such as teenage pregnancy or the war on drugs, or an event such as a presidential election or the closing of a factory.

Chapter 3
WRITING AND RESEARCH IN THE SOCIAL SCIENCES

Academic writing or discourse generally involves the communication of research findings that address stated problems, and hence is intended to advance the frontier of knowledge. Students, too, are often called upon to conduct original research, or to address some problem in terms of their life experience, personal observation, or library research. Not all writing in social science, however, involves original research. Students and scholars alike often write about research conducted by others. Sometimes this involves reporting on and evaluating a specific study or a body of research. A more common format is the book review, and every discipline has a number of journals that routinely publish reviews of recent books in the field.

More will be said about these different forms of writing in later chapters. The main point here is that whether one is reporting one's own research or attempting to interpret and evaluate the research of others, it is imperative that the writer be familiar with the research process. This is the underlying rationale for Chapters 6 to 9 of this book, which deal with the various methods that are commonly employed in social science research and the implications that each has for composition. As a preliminary step, however, let us consider the role that writing plays in the research process generally.

THE ROLE OF WRITING IN THE RESEARCH PROCESS

Writing is an integral part of the research process because it is through words on paper that we explore questions, define problems, interpret evidence, and communicate insights.

Just how integral the relationship is between research and writing is not always appreciated. To be sure, they are separate operations in the sense that social scientists first carry out the research and then "write up the results." Rarely, however, does writing consist merely of a rote presentation of research findings. In the first place, it is necessary, through writing, to develop a *context* in which evidence will be presented and interpreted. Its meaning becomes clear only in terms of a frame of reference, the question it purports to answer, the problem it attempts to solve, the body of knowledge to which it contributes. Facts rarely speak for themselves. They need to be interpreted, explained, communicated. It is through establishing connections and relationships with other facts and observations that the full significance of otherwise isolated facts is brought out.

As an example, suppose that a researcher found that there has been a sharp rise in ethnic intermarriage. Taken at face value, this fact speaks for itself. Placed in context with other observations and concerns, however, this "isolated fact" assumes great significance as an indicator of much larger trends, and is subject to very different meanings and interpretations. The upswing in intermarriage may be viewed as a sign that groups once stigmatized as undesirable are enjoying greater social acceptance. From another standpoint, however, it may be viewed as a sign that ethnic bonds have so eroded that the future of these groups may be imperiled. Though not necessarily incompatible, these are two very different interpretations of the raw data. Which interpretation is advanced or emphasized depends on the purposes of the research, the questions posed, and the background information introduced as the context for the investigation.

Thus, the act of writing frames the investigation as researchers wrestle with the statement of the problem, their purpose in pursuing this topic, and the strategies they will use to gather evidence, interpret findings, and communicate a point of view. As Chapter 2 suggested, we use writing to discover our ideas; to learn the full meaning of these ideas by seeing them in relation to each other; and finally, to communicate our understanding in clear, precise language, within a context that is meaningful to our readers. In short, writing clarifies and organizes thought.

WHAT IS A RESEARCH PROBLEM?

At this juncture it will be useful to give more formal definition to what is meant by a *research problem,* as well as a number of related terms that will be encountered in later chapters: *hypothesis, data, research procedures, sample, instrument,* and *argument.*

When social scientists speak of a *research problem,* they do not necessarily refer to facets of social life that are deemed problematic or troublesome, such as racism, poverty, or crime. Social scientists are equally interested in "the problem of order," that is, how societies regulate social relations, curb aggression, and maintain civic peace. Broadly speaking, a research problem involves any question or issue around which there is uncertainty or doubt, and that will be addressed or resolved by the research. In framing the research problem, the investigator must specify exactly where the uncertainty or doubt lies, since this gives justification to the research—why it is being undertaken. Once the rationale for the research is established, the writer has both a point of departure and an overriding objective or thrust for the research report.

In pursuing a research problem, researchers often, though by no means always, put forward a *hypothesis,* or a statement of the expected findings. The next step is to collect evidence, or *data,* that will test the hypothesis, or provide answers to the research questions. Data are collected through the use of one or another *research procedure,* such as library or archival research, direct observation, or the collection of statistical data. Social scientists draw a distinction between *quantitative data,* which involve numerical or statistical information, and *qualitative data,* which refer to the nonnumerical observations typical of most historical research and field studies. In quantitative studies it is rarely possible to survey the entire population, and therefore a *sample,* or subgroup, is selected, usually through a scientific sampling procedure that assures that the sample is *representative* of the larger population. Finally, the term *instrument* refers to the data-collection procedure—whether an interview or a self-administered questionnaire.

Like *research problem,* the term *argument* has popular connotations that easily lead to misunderstanding. "Argument" does not necessarily mean that the writer is disagreeing with someone else. In developing an argument the writer is setting forth a point of view, a result, or an interpretation—one that is supported by the data that have been collected. The argument may or may not explicitly challenge an opposing set of facts or assumptions. However, not unlike a defense attorney who presents a case to the jury, writers are well advised to anticipate opposing facts or interpretations that are likely to be advanced by critical readers. In this sense a research paper is more than a simple statement of findings: It is an "argument" in defense of a particular conclusion. This is yet another reason why social science demands writing that is clear, precise, and convincing.

THE RHETORICAL STANCE: SUBJECT, AUDIENCE, AND VOICE

Like all writing, academic discourse is motivated by a desire on the part of the writer to communicate with the reader. Effective communication involves the use of *rhetoric.* This term refers to the means of persuasion, sometimes construed as the "art of writing." The three major elements of rhetoric are *subject, audience,* and *voice.* Writers must always consider the information and/or point of view that they wish to present (subject); the needs and expectations of their readers (audience); and the tone that most clearly reflects their disposition toward both audience and subject (voice).

Wayne C. Booth, a leading writing theorist, refers to the balance among these elements—subject, audience, and voice—as the *rhetorical stance*.[1] In calling for a balance, Booth admonishes the writer not to ignore the reader while expounding on the subject. On the other hand, he warns against concentrating on "pure effect" at the cost of "undervaluing" the subject.

Although subject, audience, and voice are interrelated, it will be helpful if we discuss them separately in the pages that follow.

Subject

The subject is more than an accumulation of facts or ideas on a given area of study. As we suggested in the previous chapter, through an interactive process of reading, thinking, and writing, the subject is refined to a focused statement that contains the purpose of the writer in communicating specific information. This purpose can be simply a statement of intent—for example, to summarize, report on, or expound on a topic. Or the purpose might contain a full-fledged thesis statement, which develops a dominant idea and a point of view. To fulfill this purpose, the writer needs to organize the material with the audience in mind.

As scholars, social scientists are more intent on presenting their subject clearly and logically than they are on affecting readers' senses and emotions. This does not mean that there is no interaction between writer and reader. Both writer and reader are engaged in a collaborative pursuit of knowledge. The emphasis is on the subject and how we understand it, and thus by presenting a subject clearly and logically, the writer is engaging the reader on the basis of a shared concern for truth.

This kind of writing is called "referential writing," according to a schema classifying the aims of discourse proposed by James Kinneavy.[2] According to Kinneavy, referential writing has three related aims: (1) to explore a question, (2) to argue for an answer, and (3) to provide information. In contrast to his other categories—to express oneself, to entertain, to persuade to an action—referential writing is more oriented to the research question than to the audience. Let us briefly consider each of the three aims of referential writing.

Exploratory discourse asks a question, diagnoses a problem, proposes a solution to a problem, or provides a "tentative definition" of some term or concept. This is typically the aim of seminars, symposia, and preliminary studies.

---

[1]Wayne C. Booth, "The Rhetorical Stance," in *The Writing Teacher's Sourcebook*, eds. Gary Tate and Edward P. J. Corbett (New York: Oxford University Press, 1981), p. 111.

[2]James Kinneavy, "The Basic Aims of Discourse," in *The Writing Teacher's Sourcebook*, eds. Tate and Corbett, pp. 95–96.

Scientific discourse attempts to answer a research question either by arguing from accepted premises or by generalizing from particular examples. This is the inherent aim of research, whether it is based on original data or on studies conducted by other investigators.

Informative discourse answers a question by reporting on events, facts, and ideas. This is generally the aim of abstracts, reports, and news articles.

Of course, these aims commonly overlap. We cannot prove or argue a point without first exploring an issue, diagnosing a problem, and reporting on what others have said about that problem. Even if our aim is simply to report, without advancing our own point of view, we select and organize information according to some plan or perspective that we hope will make the material clear to the reader.

Audience

The audience, your intended readers, also influences your selection and arrangement of material, as well as your style of writing. As students, however, you should not write solely for an instructor, even if that person will be the only reader of your paper. The danger is that you will neglect to include enough background information, or to elaborate on key points, because you assume that the instructor already has this knowledge. Even if this is the case, most instructors expect students to demonstrate their understanding of the subject by providing appropriate background information and developing arguments fully. It would be better, therefore, to assume that you are writing not only for your instructor but also for your classmates and others who have an interest in your subject.

There are certain conventions dictated by audience that apply to virtually all writing. For example, readers expect an introduction that conveys the writer's purpose and that provides enough background material to allow the reader to make sense of that purpose. In content and style, the introduction will depend on the audience. If the audience consists of other scholars in the field, the writer will want to place his or her study within the context of the existing literature on the subject. Typically, academic writers begin their articles by pointing to an assumption or understanding that has been put forward by previous writers, and is presumably shared by many readers. The writer's aim is to reaffirm, extend, qualify, or oppose this assumption. If the audience consists of general readers, the writer may also begin by citing a common assumption, but it is likely to be one rooted in public opinion rather than in previous research.

To illustrate how an introduction depends on the intended audience, let us take an article that was initially published in a scholarly journal, and later revised for publication in a popular journal. The research on which these articles were based was designed to test whether the expectations that teachers have of their students influences how well these children actually perform in school. The results were first published in *Psychological*

Reports under the bland title, "Teacher's Expectancies: Determinants of Pupils' IQ Gains." It began as follows:

> Experiments have shown that in behavioral research employing human or animal S's [subjects], E's [the experimenters] expectancy can be a significant determinant of S's response (Rosenthal, 1964, in press). In studies employing animals, for example, E's led to believe that their rat S's had been bred for superior learning ability obtained performance superior to that obtained by E's led to believe their rats had been bred for inferior learning ability (Rosenthal & Fode, 1963; Rosenthal & Lawson, 1964). The present study was designed to extend the generality of this finding from E's to teachers and from animal S's to school children.[3]

About a year later the authors published their findings in a popular journal, *Scientific American,* under the less pedantic title, "Teacher Expectations for the Disadvantaged." This version began as follows:

> One of the central problems of American society lies in the fact that certain children suffer a handicap in their education which then persists throughout life. The "disadvantaged" child is a Negro American, a Mexican American, a Puerto Rican or any other child who lives in conditions of poverty. He is a lower-class child who performs poorly in an educational system that is staffed almost entirely by middle-class teachers.
> The reason usually given for the poor performance of the disadvantaged child is simply that the child is a member of a disadvantaged group. There may well be another reason. It is that the child does poorly in school because that is what is expected of him. In other words, his shortcomings may originate not in his different ethnic, cultural and economic background but in his teachers' response to that background.[4]

This example illustrates how the audience influences not only the style but form and content as well. In the case of the scholarly article, the study is presented entirely within the context of earlier research conducted on animals. If expectations that experimenters have of rats influence their performance, the authors argue, then perhaps the expectations of teachers have similar bearing on the performance of children. Thus, their research is justified in terms of earlier research, and conceived in terms of the theoretical relationship between expectations and performance.

In the case of the *Scientific American* article, the research is introduced and justified on a far more pragmatic level—the academic problems of disadvantaged children—which was a subject that was widely debated at the time the article was published. Thus, the introduction is designed to engage general readers, and to raise their interest in the results. The previous research, which is given such prominence in the scholarly article, is mentioned only in passing (in subsequent paragraphs not quoted here).

[3]Robert Rosenthal and Lenore F. Jacobson, "Teachers' Expectancies: Determinants of Pupils' IQ Gains," *Psychological Reports,* 19 (1966), 115–18.

[4]Robert Rosenthal and Lenore F. Jacobson, "Teacher Expectations for the Disadvantaged," *Scientific American,* 218 (April 1968), 19.

Another difference between the two versions has to do with language. The writing in the scholarly article is admittedly arid, but precise. By comparison, the writing in the *Scientific American* article is undeniably more engaging, though less detailed. As this example suggests, scholars must sometimes forsake lively writing for technical precision and thoroughness.[5]

As students, your writing usually falls between these two poles, since you are implicitly addressing a mixed audience of professionals and peers. Although you are not likely to have the background to reel off a series of studies that lay the groundwork for your own paper, you can still refer to important works on a topic that have influenced your own thinking. Many instructors expect students to emulate the conventions of a scholarly journal. Whether or not this is the case, you should attempt to adapt your language not just to the general reader but to those who are being schooled, as you are, in the language of social science.

Voice

Your success in engaging the audience largely depends on your ability to project a voice that is trustworthy. Aristotle referred to this as "ethos," the ethical appeal of someone who has demonstrated that he or she is a person of good sense, good moral character, and good will. In academic discourse, this means the voice of reason, objectivity, and fairness.[6]

Reason, here, is paramount. The "honest face" is not enough, as Mina Shaughnessy and others have contended.[7] The academic voice conveys good sense and worthy intentions through an ability to elucidate, validate, order information, and above all, to extend an argument.

The "ethos" of the social scientist is based on values of reason, objectivity, fairness, and caution in asserting large claims. Some forty years ago, when social science was in its infancy, the sociologist William Ogburn wrote an essay on "scientific writing" in which he argued that emotive language was inappropriate to scientific discourse. For Ogburn clarity and verification were the distinguishing characteristics of scientific writing. As he wrote:

> The object of scientific exposition is to transmit knowledge, not feelings. Words that arouse emotion are generally more suitable to persuasion and entertainment than they are to science. . . . [The scientist's] report should be in such language that his findings are verifiable. . . . Opinion is often a characteristic of unverifiable statements.[8]

[5]The *Scientific American* article is reprinted in its entirety in Chapter 6.

[6]Patricia Bizzell, "The Ethos of Academic Writing," *College Composition and Communication,* XXIX (December 1978), 351–55.

[7]Mina Shaughnessy, *Errors and Expectations* (New York: Oxford University Press, 1977), p. 206.

[8]William F. Ogburn, "On Scientific Writing," *American Journal of Sociology,* 52 (March 1947), 385–86.

Ogburn's point is that "the scientist should not try to implant attitudes in readers which the facts do not convey."[9] Indeed, one of the hallmarks of social science is to insist upon sufficient evidence to substantiate a claim. It is this reliance on evidence that imparts the voice with authority. As writers, we rely on evidence to make our arguments convincing. As readers, we listen because the evidence compels us to.

In most scholarly writing, there are a number of organizational features that contribute to the authority and clarity of the writer's voice:

- An *initial overview* of the problem to be discussed, usually at the very beginning of a book or article.
- A *pattern* or *plan* evident through the use of divisions, with appropriate headings and subheadings. A common format for research papers includes the following divisions: Introduction, Previous Research, The Present Study, Findings, Conclusions.
- *Emphasis on important points* either by stressing their importance or by repeating them (perhaps in different language) at appropriate junctures, especially when summarizing key findings, interpretations, and conclusions.

Social scientists also employ certain stylistic features to convey a sense of objectivity:

- Words and phrases that indicate relationships between researcher and subject or among facts, events, and ideas. For example: "On the basis of these observations, we can infer . . ." or: "If we compare X to Y, then we see that . . ." or: "It would therefore appear that X is one cause of Y. . . ."
- Restricted use of the personal pronoun *I*. Instead, the passive voice is common. For example: "It was found that . . ." or: "In order to address this question, survey data were employed. . . ."

Note the objective tone in the following passage, which is taken from an article that analyzed the ideological character of Little Orphan Annie. In the very first paragraph, the author provides an overview of the problem, verifies a claim, and states the study's purpose, all in a tone that conveys seriousness and impartiality:

A CONTENT ANALYSIS OF "LITTLE ORPHAN ANNIE"

Verification of claim The most significant characteristic associated with comic strips is their huge audience which includes four-fifths of all adult newspaper readers. If, in the *Overview* face of this popularity, modern comic strips show a tendency to deal with events and issues of the real world, then cognizance must be taken of the *Passive voice* emergence of the comic strip as an important mass communication medium. *Purpose of study* In view of these conditions an analysis was made to determine the nature and extent to which a measurable social, political, and economic ideology was contained in "Little Orphan Annie," a nationally syndicated strip.[10]

[9]Ibid.

[10]Donald Auster, "A Content Analysis of 'Little Orphan Annie'," in *Sociology: Progress of a Decade*, eds. Seymour Martin Lipset and Neil J. Smelser (Englewood Cliffs, N.J.: Prentice-Hall, 1961), p. 241.

Note the use of the passive voice. The author has conducted a study of ideological bias in a comic strip, and seems to be going out of his way to establish his own impartiality, which is accented by the use of the passive voice. We hasten to add that the passive voice is often frowned upon, especially by writing teachers. Let us therefore examine this thorny issue further.

Without doubt, the passive voice is unappealing and cumbersome. Nevertheless, there is some rationale for using it in scientific discourse. The tacit assumption in scholarly writing is that although an author is at work, it is the evidence that provides ultimate authority. The writer is behind the scene, as it were, and irrelevant to the truth or falsity of a proposition. Thus, the passive voice helps to create a tone that is formal, authoritative, and impersonal, and is meant to inspire trust in the reader.

However, we do not wish to give the impression that the use of the personal pronouns *I* or *we* is proscribed under all circumstances. On the contrary, the use of the personal pronoun is sometimes appropriate and even necessary. This is especially true of field studies, where the investigator is engaged in personal observation of some social setting. Perhaps because these studies are inherently subjective, at least compared to studies based on "hard data," researchers are often willing to discuss the value premises that they brought to their study. For example, in her observational study of an old-age community, Arlie Hochschild wrote the following:

> Most of my goals concerning Merrill Court coincided with most of theirs. However, as a person of a different age and social class, and as a sociologist, my perspective differed from theirs. I thought that, as welfare recipients, they were poor; they thought they were "average." I initially felt that there was something sad about old people living together and that this was a social problem. They did not feel a bit sad about living together as old people, and although they felt that they *had* problems, they did not think that they *were* one.[11]

This is more than a statement of refreshing candor. Through use of the first person Hochschild creates analytical distance between her subjects and herself. Paradoxically, by openly discussing how her preconceptions changed in the process of doing the research, Hochschild establishes her objectivity.

THE LANGUAGE OF SOCIAL SCIENCE

As with all fields of specialized knowledge, social science has evolved its own "language." The use of this vocabulary lends authority to the writer's voice in that it demonstrates a working knowledge of one's field. However, when the writer uses this vocabulary imprecisely or as a way of impersonat-

[11]Arlie Russell Hochschild, *The Unexpected Community* (Berkeley: University of California Press, 1973), p. 5.

ing the scholar, the results can be disastrous. Instead of technical precision, we get a tangle of phrases that bore and confuse the reader.

Social scientists have gained a certain notoriety for their use of "jargon." Some of the most trenchant criticism has come from humanists who are appalled by what they regard as a perversion of the English language. Fowler's *Dictionary of English Usage* even has an entry on "sociologese," which includes the following uncharitable comment on why sociologists are given to overblown language:

> Sociology is a new science concerning itself not with esoteric matters outside the comprehension of the layman, as the older sciences do, but with the ordinary affairs of ordinary people. This seems to engender in those who write about it a feeling that the lack of any abstruseness in their subject demands a compensatory abstruseness in their language.[12]

Nor has criticism come only from guardians of the English language. A good many social scientists complain about the obscure and often tortuous prose found in most professional journals and books. In a caustic essay entitled "The Smoke Screen of Jargon," Stanislav Andreski lampooned his fellow sociologists for using "impressive-sounding opaque jargon" that tells us nothing we did not know before.[13] Andreski compares the sociologist to a character in one of Molière's plays who answers the question about why opium makes people sleep by saying that it is because of its soporific power.[14] (The dictionary definition of "soporific" is "causing or tending to cause sleep.")

Because the issue of "jargon" has excited so much criticism of social science writing, let us confront the issue squarely. Is jargon merely a smoke screen for banality, as Andreski and others have claimed? Or is it a legitimate and valuable "tool of the trade," as its practitioners would like to think?

To begin with, let us be clear about what jargon is. The *Random House Dictionary* provides two meanings that are often confused.[15] One meaning is "the language, especially the vocabulary, peculiar to a particular trade, profession, or group." Social scientists can hardly be assailed for using this specialized language in their research and writing. When people complain of "jargon," however, they usually have the second meaning in mind: "unintelligible talk or writing, gibberish." Obviously, gibberish is indefensible,

---

[12]H. W. Fowler, *A Dictionary of Modern English Usage* (New York: Oxford University Press, 1965), p. 570. For a recent analysis of the "ills that afflict sociologists' writing," see Hanan C. Selvin and Everett F. Wilson, "On Sharpening Sociologists' Prose," *Sociological Quarterly*, 25 (Spring 1984), 205–22.

[13]Stanislav Andreski, *Social Sciences as Sorcery* (London: Andre Dent, 1972), p. 55.

[14]Ibid., p. 68.

[15]*The Random House Dictionary of the English Language* (New York: Random House, 1973).

even in the name of science. Thus, what needs to be addressed is the difference between legitimate jargon and academic gibberish. The issue is not whether jargon is aesthetically pleasing—it is not—but whether it enhances or detracts from understanding.

When Jargon IS Jargon

As an example of jargon that clearly detracts from understanding, let us take a passage from a book by Talcott Parsons, who has earned a reputation as the profession's worst jargonmongerer:

> Skills constitute the manipulative techniques of human goal attainment and control in relation to the physical world, so far as artifacts or machines especially designed as tools do not yet supplement them. Truly human skills are guided by organized and codified *knowledge* of both the things to be manipulated and the human capacities that are used to manipulate them. Such knowledge is an aspect of cultural-level symbolic processes, and, like other aspects to be discussed presently, requires the capacities of the human central nervous system, particularly the brain.[16]

What does all this verbiage mean? Andreski offers a simple interpretation:

> As every schoolboy knows, a developed brain and acquired skills and knowledge are necessary for attaining specifically human goals. . . .[17]

In fairness to Parsons, his intended audience was not the general reader, but professional social scientists. Furthermore, as Dennis Wrong has pointed out, Parsons sought to identify what was unique and universal about the human experience, and this forced him to write on a high level of abstraction.[18] Still, the writing in this passage is atrocious. It is not just that the prose is confusing and almost unreadable. To make matters worse, the reader who takes up the challenge and translates the passage into simple English will discover what is already obvious.

It would be easy for us to cite other glaring examples of the misuse of jargon and to join the chorus of critics who decry the debasement of the English language. To do so, however, would beg a larger and more difficult issue: When is jargon legitimate? When does it enhance understanding?

When Jargon Is NOT Jargon

As we suggested earlier, the first principle of writing is clear, direct, unembellished prose. Generally speaking, it is preferable to use common language over jargon. In other words, jargon should be avoided whenever

---

[16]Quoted in Andreski, pp. 60–61. The original source is Talcott Parsons, *Societies: Evolutionary and Comparative Perspectives* (Englewood Cliffs, N.J.: Prentice-Hall, 1966).

[17]Ibid., p. 60.

[18]Dennis H. Wrong, "Professional Jargon: Is Sociology the Culprit?" *University* (Publication of New York University), 2 (March 1983), 7–8.

the same idea can be expressed with common language. However, there are at least five occasions when the common language is problematic and the use of jargon is justified:

1. *The common language is often too ambiguous to be useful in social science discourse.*

Precisely because social scientists do not concern themselves with esoteric matters outside the comprehension of the layperson, it is often necessary to find language that is more precise and discriminating than the common language. Everybody knows what it means to "fall in love," but this term is so imprecise, and given to so many different meanings, that it would be useless in any serious study of this phenomenon. As a result, psychological studies are peppered with words such as "affectual systems," "libido," "erogenous needs," and "oedipal substitution." The layperson may scoff at the use of such abstruse language to describe familiar emotions, but the social scientist would not get very far employing the nebulous words, clichés, and euphemisms that are used in common parlance.

Even when social scientists use common words, they often do so in uncommon ways. Thus, when economists speak of "capital," or political scientists of "democracy," or psychologists of "personality," or anthropologists of "culture," or sociologists of "community," they mean more than what is meant or understood when laypeople use these terms. To a layperson, "democracy" probably conjures up a single salient observation, such as popular elections. But to a political scientist the term is associated with a whole constellation of interrelated factors, and embedded in a large body of scholarship concerning the history, theory, and dynamics of democratic systems. Thus, even when social scientists use common words, they often give them technical definition.

2. *Occasionally no words exist in the common language that adequately express a new idea or describe a new phenomenon.*

At times a writer may not be able to find words to express a new idea or insight, and is forced to coin a new term (these are called "neologisms"). This is a perilous step, to be taken only as a last resort.

On the other hand, some neologisms are justifiable, so much so that they eventually make their way into common parlance. Freud, for example, coined the term "narcissism," building on the Greek myth of Narcissus, the youth who fell in love with his own image reflected in a pool. David Riessman coined the term "inner-directed personality," which involved a juxtaposition of familiar words to form a new concept. While Emile Durkheim did not coin the word "anomie," he was the first to introduce it into the sociological lexicon. All three of these words have made their way into the general language.

For example, a recent edition of the *Random House Dictionary of the English Language* defines "inner-directed" as follows:

Guided by internalized values rather than external pressures. Cf. other-directed.[19]

To the extent that social science jargon is incorporated into the common language, then jargon can be seen not as a debasement of language, but as part of the ongoing evolution of language.

Also to be considered is the fact that a body of social science writing is concerned with *change*, and new developments often require new names. For example, in her book *The Origins of Totalitarianism*, Hannah Arendt was among the first to use the term "totalitarianism" to refer to regimes, like that of Nazi Germany, that seek monolithic control over all major social institutions. "Mass society" is another term invented by social scientists to refer to the tendency of modern society to weld its population into a single undifferentiated mass.

3. *The common language is sometimes too concrete to be useful in theoretical analysis.*

All of the social sciences have theoretical branches whose goal is to develop large concepts on the basis of complex patterns of observation. Often the common language is on too low a level of abstraction to denote these large concepts, and social theorists occasionally feel compelled to coin new terms. This is when critics are most likely to inveigh against the mutilation of language.

For example, Talcott Parsons sought to develop a simple schema for classifying all human societies. He began by identifying two traits defined by dichotomies: universalism-particularism and achievement-ascription. Parsons held that all societies could be classified in terms of these two traits, which were found in different combinations, thus producing four distinct types of societies. According to this schema, all modern industrial societies conform to the "universalistic-achievement pattern," whereas traditional societies organized around kinship belong to the "particularistic-ascriptive pattern." Granted, these are jarring terms, and their usefulness can be debated. Their purpose, however, is to raise the analytical focus above the empirical level, and to transcend the limits of the common language.

4. *The common language is sometimes so riddled with value judgments that it thwarts objectivity.*

Consider the following example. After the assassination of Martin Luther King in 1968, there were outbreaks of violence in dozens of American cities. These were termed "riots" by government officials, the media, and the public at large. On closer examination, however, "riot" is anything but value-free. It conjures up images of wanton violence, and of "rioters" bent on looting and mindless destruction. Indeed, the term virtually implies a the-

[19]*The Random House Dictionary of the English Language* (New York: Random House, 1987).

ory by suggesting that these are the acts of aberrant and antisocial individuals. Insofar as these value judgments are consonant with prevailing views, the bias inherent in the term "riot" easily escapes notice. The social scientist who uncritically accepts the prevailing wisdom will not hesitate to use the term, as Edward Banfield did in an essay titled "Rioting Mainly for Fun and Profit."[20]

Other social critics, however, interpreted the "riots" as a form of protest against ghetto conditions.[21] While not condoning violence, they argued that "riots" were the inevitable byproduct of smoldering resentments within the ghetto population. These writers insisted that it would be more accurate to refer to these events as "revolts" or "uprisings," as Robert Blauner did in his essay "Internal Colonialism and Ghetto Revolt."[22] Clearly, more is involved here than a quibble over word choice.

The Kerner Commission that was commissioned by Congress to study the "riots" sought a middle ground, and adopted the term "civic disorders."[23] At first blush, one is inclined to wince at such stilted language. Its virtue, of course, is that it is neutral and avoids making prejudgments one way or another. After all, whether violence was wanton or selective, whether its participants were driven by antisocial impulses or expressing rage over their condition—these and other such issues must be resolved through empirical research, not assumed in the very terms of discourse. As this example shows, when the common language is so value-laden that it compromises objectivity, the use of jargon is not only permissible, but probably advisable.

5. *Compared to the common language, jargon is often more concise.*
When adolescents refer to a person as "cool," the term embodies a whole welter of ideas and assumptions shared by those who partake of adolescent subculture. By the same token, social science jargon often functions as a shorthand or a code for much larger ideas. Take the term "sex-role socialization," for example. Admittedly, it is cumbersome. Its virtue is that it compresses into a few words shared assumptions about gender and the social character of gender that would otherwise require elaborate explanation. By obviating further discussion, this shorthand term allows the writer to get on with the argument, thus allowing for greater economy of speech and more cogent writing.

In this chapter we presented the best defense of jargon that we could muster. On the whole, however, we agree with critics who contend that social science writing is marred by an excessive use of jargon. As students in

[20]Edward Banfield, *The Unheavenly City Revisited* (Boston: Little, Brown, 1974), chap. 9.

[21]For example, Robert M. Fogelson, *Violence as Protest* (New York: Doubleday, 1971).

[22]Robert Blauner, *Racial Oppression in America* (New York: Harper & Row, 1972), chap. 5.

[23]*Report of the National Advisory Commission on Civil Disorders* (New York: Bantam Books, 1968).

social science courses, you will be introduced to key concepts that make up the language of social science, and you should incorporate these concepts into your thinking and writing. Remember, however, that the overriding function of writing is to communicate. If communication is enhanced by scientific terminology, you should not hesitate to use it. On the other hand, if the same idea can be expressed in plain language, then jargon should be avoided.

SUGGESTIONS FOR WRITING AND THINKING

1. The following abstract is from an article by Claude Fischer on "The Effect of Urban Life on Traditional Values," published in *Social Forces* (March 1975). Rewrite it in plain language as though you were writing for a nonacademic journal intended for an educated audience, such as *Scientific American* or *Psychology Today.*

    Three models predict an association between urbanism and nontraditional behavior: (1) that it is a function of the characteristics of individuals found in cities; (2) that it is due to the anomie* of cities; (3) that it is due to the generation of and consequent influence of innovative urban subcultures. Secondary analysis† of American survey data on religiosity, church attendance, attitudes toward alcohol and birth control confirm the general urbanism-deviance association. . . .Some suggestive data point to Model 3 as the more accurate one.

2. How would you characterize the language in the above abstract in terms of subject, audience, and voice? Is the use of jargon legitimate? Are there instances where you think jargon is unnecessary or inappropriate?

---

*This term was coined by Emile Durkheim, the "father" of sociology. Literally it means "normlessness"—a condition where individuals are not well integrated into groups that provide moral authority and regulation over their lives.

†This term refers to research based on data collected for another purpose.

Chapter 4
RHETORICAL STRATEGIES

In Chapter 3 we discussed the importance of purpose in shaping the content of a paper. One might say that purpose refers to a writer's destination. In this chapter we discuss the rhetorical strategies for reaching that destination. By "rhetorical strategies" we mean the different organizational patterns that recur in all expository writing. Eight rhetorical strategies are discussed in this chapter:

1. Definition
2. Classification
3. Description
4. Narration
5. Illustration
6. Comparison-contrast
7. Cause-effect
8. Argument

Before going any further, we want to stress that these rhetorical strategies are not immutable forms. They are not "muffin tins" into which we pour our academic batter, to use the words of one critic.[1] Writers do not make a conscious decision to adopt one or another strategy, and to adhere to its rules. Rather, in exploring a topic or developing an argument, writers intuitively employ whatever rhetorical strategy helps to clarify and communicate their ideas. Furthermore, different rhetorical strategies may be used within the same paper, depending on purpose and need.

For example, when Durkheim wrote his classic study of suicide, he found it necessary at the outset to define suicide. Next, he developed a classification of different types of suicide, in order to distinguish, for exam-

[1]C. H. Knoblauch and Lil Brannon, "Writing as Learning Through the Curriculum," *College English*, 45, no. 5 (September 1983), 468.

ple, between people who sacrifice their life for a cause and those who destroy themselves out of sheer despair. Then he explored differences in the rate of suicide over time and between different countries. In other words, Durkheim used the rhetorical strategies of "definition," "classification," and "comparison-contrast" even though he did not do so as a matter of preconceived design.[2]

Thus, the discussion that follows only makes explicit what is often tacitly understood by writers as they formulate their ideas and commit them to writing. As a self-conscious writer, you will be able to make better use of rhetorical strategies for generating questions, clarifying thought, and organizing material into a coherent exposition.

DEFINITION

Communication is not possible unless we agree on the meaning of the words that we use. A dictionary will usually suffice to clarify the meaning of particular words. However, the meaning of concepts is not so easily resolved. A common form of writing in all academic disciplines is the extended essay that seeks to define key concepts in all of their ramifications. Indeed, whole volumes have been written explicating concepts such as "capital," "narcissism," "community," and "democracy."

As always, the writer's purpose determines the scope and complexity of the definition. However, there are certain stock methods for defining terms:

- Identify the class to which the subject belongs.
- Cite its essential characteristics.
- Isolate the single, most important characteristic.
- Trace the word's roots.
- Find synonyms or terms that are close in meaning.
- Provide a specific illustration of how it is used.

Needless to say, writers do not use all these methods in defining each term, but only the ones suited to their specific purposes.

In the selection below, Brian Wilson, a sociologist of religion, grapples with the problem of defining "sect." His ultimate purpose is to explain how certain sects resist the tendency to become established denominations, thus preserving their original evangelical ideals. Before addressing this larger question, Wilson had to define what sects are and how they differ from denominations:

> Typically a *sect* may be identified by the following characteristics: it is a voluntary association; membership is by proof to sect authorities of some claim to personal merit—such as knowledge of doctrine, affirmation of a conversion

[2]Emile Durkheim, *Suicide* (Glencoe, Illinois: The Free Press, 1951).

experience, or recommendation of members in good standing; exclusiveness is emphasized, and expulsion exercised against those who contravene doctrinal, moral, or organizational precepts; its self-conception is of an elect, a gathered remnant, possessing special enlightenment; personal perfection is the expected standard of aspiration, in whatever terms this is judged; it accepts, at least as an ideal, the priesthood of all believers; there is a high level of lay participation; there is opportunity for the member spontaneously to express his commitment; the sect is hostile or indifferent to the secular society and to the state.[3]

Wilson then identifies *one* defining attribute of sects: "The commitment of the sectarian is always more total and more defined than that of the member of other religious organizations."[4] Having thus established a clear definition of what a sect is, Wilson then differentiates between different kinds of sects. This brings us to the next rhetorical strategy: classification.

CLASSIFICATION

If definition answers the question, What is it?, then classification answers the questions, What are its parts? What forms does it take? How do they work together to make a whole? When we are treating a large and complex subject, classification is a way of bringing greater order and clarity to the subject. We do this by formulating categories that divide the subject into discrete but related parts.

Let us return to Wilson's article on sect development. Wilson wants to distinguish the subtypes of sects, and he does so in terms of different "types of mission." Specifically:

The *Conversionist* sects seek to alter men, and thereby to alter the world. . . . The *Adventist* sects predict drastic alteration of the world, and seek to prepare for the new dispensation. . . . The *Introversionists* reject the world's values and replace them with higher inner values. . . . The *Gnostic* sects accept in large measure the world's goals but seek new and esoteric means to achieve these ends. . . .[5]

With this classification in place, Wilson is in a better position to approach the larger questions that govern his study, which have to do with the conditions under which sects emerge and whether they are able to preserve their original evangelism. Wilson found that different types of sects display different patterns of development, which validates the usefulness of his classification.

---

[3]Brian R. Wilson, "An Analysis of Sect Development," *American Sociological Review*, 24 (1959), 4.

[4]Ibid.

[5]Ibid., p. 5.

DESCRIPTION

Much social science is concerned with describing some facet of human experience. As a discipline, anthropology has provided graphic descriptions of the multitude of cultures and subcultures that exist in the world today. Sociologists, too, often "go out" into the field to observe social settings, ranging from "typical" towns or suburbs to unusual groups like hippie communes or motorcycle gangs. Political scientists write extensively about political events, economists about economic trends, and so on. The overall purpose of this research is to accurately *describe* some aspect of social life. When done effectively, readers are left with a clear mental picture of the event or phenomenon being studied, even if they have never observed it firsthand.

Presumably, the social scientist's description will be different from that of the legendary "casual observer." Of course, social scientists may also disagree among themselves. Indeed, this is the point of departure for many writers who, in one way or another, are challenging popular or prevailing views. For example, a study titled "Fear and Loathing at a College Mixer" began as follows:

> The predominant view expressed in the sociological literature on dating is that the social events and interactions are "fun" for the participants. An adult observer of adolescents at a social gathering would see them dressed up for the occasion, flirting with one another, dancing to loud music, engaging in light conversation, and generally seeming to be enjoying themselves.[6]

The researchers, however, provide a very different assessment of the college mixer. According to them, it is "a serious socialization process with potentially negative consequences for the individual."[7] Contrary to appearances, it is fraught with tension and anxiety, and often destructive of a person's sense of self-worth.

As this example suggests, description is never random or capricious. In the first place, the selection of detail is governed by social science concepts. In this case the concept of socialization led the observer to record the dress, the gestures, and the conversation of adolescents learning to court one another in a social setting. Secondly, in order to create a clear mental picture, researchers must have some principle for organizing and presenting their observations. As McQuade and Atwan have written:

> . . . whether we are picturing something concrete (the furniture or appliances in the kitchen) or something abstract (the spirit in a room during a holiday)— the process of writing an effective description remains essentially the same.

[6]Pepper Schwartz and Janet Lever, "Fear and Loathing at a College Mixer," *Urban Life*, 4 (January 1976), 413.

[7]Ibid., p. 414.

> We should start with an overview of whatever we want to describe. We should then proceed to select the most striking and significant details and develop them in an intelligible sequence that produces the effect we intended to create.[8]

To move from the general to the particular in this manner allows the writer to capture both the essence and the nuance of the event or phenomenon under study—the key to effective description.

Observe this process in the passage below, which is taken from an observational study of singles' bars:

> We observed that people in the singles' bars had a habit of touching each other. It could be a hand or a shoulder, a pat on the head, a hand steadying a hand to light a cigarette, or an entire body touch. Touching happened not only in crowds but also when there was plenty of room to pass without having body contact.
> Touching was often a simple gesture to start a conversation. "What an attractive necklace you're wearing," one man said to a woman, while stroking her neck. "It must have taken you years to grow your hair that long," another man said as he ran his fingers through a woman's hair. The touching seemed to reinforce what they were saying and at the same time establish intimacy.
> Touching might be a sign of approval or a gesture of affection, or of course have sexual connotations. Touching might also be a pompous way of assuring oneself of being noticed.[9]

After the general observation that people in singles' bars "had a habit of touching each other," the authors provide a detailed description of the specific forms of touching—how it is done, what is said, and so on. Then they move to a slightly higher level of abstraction, and comment on the functions of touching—a sign of approval or affection, a sexual gesture, a way of being noticed. Thus, the reader is provided with both a description and an analysis of this particular behavior.

NARRATION

As a rhetorical strategy, narration is a way of telling what happened. For this reason it is most identified with history. Indeed, history has its origins in storytelling—the earliest histories were epic accounts of the Greek wars. Even today, it is frequently commented that every good historian is a good storyteller, and "narrative history" is staunchly defended against those who would apply "scientific" concepts and methods to the writing of history.

The selection on the next page is taken from Oscar Handlin's book, *The Uprooted*. Handlin essentially "tells the story" of immigration, the

[8]Donald McQuade and Robert Atwan, *Thinking in Writing* (New York: Alfred A. Knopf, 1983), p. 280.

[9]Natalie Allon and Diane Fishel, "Singles' Bars as Examples of Urban Courting Patterns," in *Single Life*, ed. Peter J. Stein (New York: St. Martin's Press, 1981), p. 117.

"arduous transplantation" from the Old World to the New. Not unlike a story, his book is organized in terms of a chronological sequence, as is evident from the table of contents:

1. Peasant Origins
2. The Crossing
3. Daily Bread
4. New Worlds, New Visions
5. Religion as a Way of Life
6. The Ghettos
7. In Fellow Feeling
8. Democracy and Power
9. Generations
10. The Shock of Alienation
11. Restriction
12. Promises

Note that some chapters adhere to a strict chronological sequence (especially Chapters 1, 2, 3, 4, and 12). Other chapters interrupt the chronology to analyze particular facets of the immigrant experience, such as economic survival, religion, and politics.

The narrative flavor of Handlin's account is evident in the following excerpt from Chapter 2, "The Crossing":

> Coming away from the village, the emigrant pushed toward a seaport. Surely in the beginning it was a task sufficiently difficult just to know the road. For guides there were only the remembered tales of pilgrims, of beggars, and of peddlers, the habitual wanderers of the peasant world. . . . Conveyances varied with conditions. On the continent, travel was most commodious by river or canal; but few poor folk could pay the heavy tolls. . . . In some places there were public stages. These too were out of reach, prohibitively expensive, meant for the gentry who alone, in more normal times, had occasion to use them. Here and there was a fortunate fellow with a cart. More rare was a beast to pull it; both would be sold at the destination. But not many peasants had been able to hold on to horse and wagon when all else in their world disappeared from around them. Mostly the emigrants relied on the power of their own legs and began the crossing with a long journey on foot.[10]

Note the sequencing of events as the emigrant leaves the village and pushes toward the seaport, beginning the long journey that ends in America. Also note the attention to detail: The only road map consisted of "remembered tales" of pilgrims, beggars, and peddlers; transportation was nonexistent or too expensive; most end up walking long distances to the points of disembarkation. These graphic details, arranged in chronological sequence, are what gives the reader a clear "mental picture" of what the crossing to America was like.

[10]Oscar Handlin, *The Uprooted* (New York: Grosset & Dunlap, 1951), p. 39.

ILLUSTRATION

If there is a single, overriding purpose of social science, it is to *generalize* about the social universe. Yet generalization has its pitfalls. It is all too easy to spin out generalizations that are not adequately supported by the facts. And from the reader's standpoint, generalizations are often difficult to grasp, precisely because they are abstract. For both reasons, illustration is an indispensable rhetorical device. By citing specific examples, writers give substance to their generalizations. These examples also serve to clarify a writer's intentions and meaning. A good illustration, one might say, is worth a thousand words.

Here, too, an example is in order. In the passage below, Ruth Benedict, the anthropologist, is discussing what it means to "grow up" and to be "conditioned" to adult roles. As an illustration, she describes the process whereby children in our culture learn to eat according to adult schedules:

> It will make the point clearer if we consider one habit in our culture. . . . With the greatest clarity of purpose and economy of training we achieve our goal of conditioning everyone to eat three meals a day. The baby's training in regular food periods begins at birth and no crying of the child and no inconvenience to the mother is allowed to interfere. We gauge the child's physiological make-up and at first allow it food oftener than adults, but, because our goal is firmly set and our training consistent, before the child is two years old it has achieved the adult schedule. From the point of view of other cultures this is as startling as the fact of three-year-old babies perfectly at home in deep water is to us.[11]

This specific example helps to clarify and support what is meant by "cultural conditioning." Benedict furnishes more subtle examples as she develops her thesis further.

COMPARISON-CONTRAST

Comparison-contrast is more than a rhetorical strategy. It is the essence of the scientific method itself. The classical experiment involves a comparison before and after some experimental condition has been altered. Whether through systematic research or less structured observation, social scientists are always looking for similarities and differences.

As a rhetorical device, comparison and contrast serves different purposes. One is to clarify a key term. In the example cited earlier, Wilson clarified the meaning of "sect" by placing it in opposition to "denomination." His classification of sects also involved comparisons and contrasts between different kinds of sects.

Second, comparisons are necessary to carry analysis to a higher level of generalization. For example, in a well-known study, anthropologist Marc Zborowski compared different groups in terms of their responses to pain.

[11]Ruth Benedict, "Continuities and Discontinuities in Cultural Conditioning," *Psychiatry*, 1 (1938), 154.

He found that, consistent with stereotype, "old Americans" were the most stoic of all groups. Not only did Italians and Jews exhibit a lower tolerance of pain, but even after a painkiller was administered, Jews continued to worry about the possible side effects of the medication. Through these comparisons, Zborowski was able to demonstrate differences among ethnic groups in their response to pain.[12] The very fact that groups were different suggests that pain is more than a physiological reaction, but a matter of cultural conditioning as well.

Third, comparisons and contrasts provide a frame of reference. It is not uncommon to hear bald statements like, "America is a racist country," to which someone is bound to retort, "Compared to what?" Only through comparisons and contrasts can we fully assess the significance of otherwise isolated facts or observations. For example, if we were to compare racist patterns in the United States with those in South Africa, we would come away with a better understanding of racism in both countries.

Indeed, this was precisely the purpose of George Fredrickson's historical study, *White Supremacy*. Here is a brief excerpt:

> The term "segregation" came into common use in both South Africa and the American South at about the same time—in the early years of the twentieth century. South African white supremacists may in fact have borrowed the term from their American counterparts. But a close examination of the two modes of legalized discrimination reveals some major differences in how they worked and in the functions they performed. Both, of course, were necessarily based on separatism; but the specific kinds of separation that were stressed and regarded as crucial for maintaining white privilege and furthering white interests were not the same. . . .[13]

Fredrickson's point is that despite obvious similarities, there are fundamental differences between segregation in America and apartheid in South Africa. In the case of South Africa, separation involves an extreme *territorial* division that relegates most blacks to remote and desolate "homelands." Pushed to the brink of starvation, men are forced to travel hundreds of miles to find work, for which they are paid subhuman wages. Comparatively, blacks in the United States are far more integrated into major social institutions. From a writing standpoint, the two cases cast each other in bold relief, enhancing our understanding of both.

CAUSE-EFFECT

It is often held that causal analysis is the ultimate goal of all science. To establish the facts (description) is only a partial or preliminary step to explaining them (explanation). Indeed, as a rhetorical strategy, cause-effect

---

[12]Marc Zborowski, "Cultural Components in Responses to Pain," *Journal of Social Issues*, 8 (1953), 16–31.

[13]George M. Fredrickson, *White Supremacy: A Comparative Study in American and South African History* (New York: Oxford University Press, 1981), p. 241.

is probably the primary mode in social science writing. It is not that the other rhetorical strategies are used any less frequently, but rather they are used within the context of, or in conjunction with, a cause-effect mode.

For example, in his book *The Black Family in Slavery and Freedom*, Herbert Gutman explored the effects of slavery on the black family (an excerpt from this book is found in Chapter 9). Within this context, Gutman had to ascertain what the raw facts were about the condition of black families (description). To accomplish this, he employed slave narratives of various kinds (narration). Classification, comparison-contrast, and other rhetorical strategies were also employed in other parts of his study. However, the *primary* rhetorical mode—the one that was of overriding significance in terms of substance and organization—was cause-effect.[14]

Causal analysis may focus on either causes or effects, or both. For example, some economists have dealt with the causes of unemployment; others, with the effects; still others, with both causes and effects. Of course, dealing with both causes and effects within the same study is likely to become unwieldy. The reason is that causal analysis is never simple. Typically, there are multiple causes and multiple effects that must be sorted out. We also have to think about the relationship that exists among the various causal factors. They may operate more or less independently of each other. Thus, there may be a *convergence* of factors leading to some outcome—say, the Second World War. Or causal factors may be related to each other in a *causal chain*. For example, it might be held that widespread unemployment in the 1930s led to political unrest which undermined public confidence in elected officials, which culminated in Roosevelt's elevation to the presidency.

Whenever we deal with multiple causes, we must try to sort out the *sequence* of events or circumstances that lead to a given outcome. The sequence might be conceived as a movement from *proximate* causes to *ultimate* causes. For example, in the mid-1960s New York City was on the brink of bankruptcy. A proximate cause—the one highlighted in the mass media—was that the city's politicians busted the budget with "liberal spending programs." Another view, however, was put forward by Matthew Edel, an economist. Edel traced the city's fiscal crisis to changes in the global economy that resulted in a massive loss of industries and jobs in New York. This, in turn, sharply reduced the city's tax revenues at the same time that it increased expenditures for social welfare programs. Thus, the *ultimate* causes of the city's fiscal crisis were associated with sweeping changes in the international economy over which the city's politicians had little or no control.[15]

[14]Herbert Gutman, *The Black Family in Slavery and Freedom, 1750–1925* (New York: Pantheon Books, 1976).

[15]Matthew Edel, "The New York Crisis as Economic History," in *The Fiscal Crisis of American Cities*, eds. Roger E. Alcaly and David Mermelstein (New York: Random House, 1977).

Another way of sorting out the relationship among causal factors is in terms of their "explanatory significance"—that is, whether they are seen as having relatively great weight or relatively little weight. For example, social scientists with a Marxist perspective are often accused of placing too much emphasis on economic factors, and underestimating the operation of non-economic factors. The counterargument, however, is that economic factors are not the *only* factors that matter, but the most *important* ones, not only because they directly influence behavior, but also because they condition the effects of noneconomic factors as well.

These controversies underscore the importance of clear, logical writing. It is crucial that studies that posit cause-effect relations be unambiguous about what causal claims are being made, and what relationship exists among the various causal factors.

The example of causal explanation presented below deals with adolescent culture. Observe how the author, James Coleman, develops a causal chain from more remote, or ultimate, causes to more proximate ones, and then speculates about the effects of adolescent culture for the family system:

> Industrial society has spawned a peculiar phenomenon, most evident in America but emerging also in other Western societies: adolescent subcultures, with values and activities quite distinct from those of the adult society. . . . Industrialization, and the rapidity of change itself, has taken out of the hands of the parent the task of training his child, made the parent's skills obsolescent, and put him out of touch with the times—unable to understand, much less inculcate, the standards of a social order which has changed since he was young.
>
> By extending the period of training necessary for a child and by encompassing nearly the whole population, industrial society has made of high school a social system of adolescents. It includes, in the United States, almost all adolescents and more and more of the activities of the adolescent himself. . . .
>
> In effect, then, what our society has done is to set apart, in an institution of their own, adolescents for whom home is little more than a dormitory and whose world is made up of activities peculiar to their fellows. They have been given, as well, many of the instruments which can make them a functioning community: cars, freedom in dating, continual contact with the opposite sex, money and entertainment, like popular music and movies designed especially for them.[16]

The thrust of this passage concerns the sources or "causes" of adolescent culture. Its ultimate sources are in industrial society, which extends childhood and defines children and adults as occupying different spheres. The next link in the causal chain is the school system, which has been delegated many of the socializing functions that once were fulfilled by parents. Other factors—cars, popular culture, changes in sexual mores—

[16]James S. Coleman, "The Adolescent Subculture and Academic Achievement," *American Journal of Sociology*, 65 (1960), 337–38.

also contribute to the development of an adolescent culture that is more or less independent of parental control. The end result is that "home is little more than a dormitory."

Even in this brief excerpt, Coleman presents a sweeping causal analysis, beginning with the emergence of industrial society and ending with changes in the family system. The causal links are clearly spelled out. However, causal analysis is susceptible to a number of fallacies. Let us consider three of the most common ones.

1. *Inverting cause and effect.* This is the logical version of putting the cart before the horse. For example, a number of studies have found that black families where husband and wife are living together have more stable employment and higher incomes. From these facts, some analysts have concluded that a "weak family" is the cause for many of unemployment and poverty. Critics, however, have turned this proposition around, arguing that it is unemployment and poverty that cause families to break up in the first place. The implication here is that broken families are the effect, not the cause, of unemployment and poverty.

2. *Confusing correlation and cause.* Just because two factors vary together, this does not mean that one is the cause of the other. The correlation may be an accidental one. For example, it is known that the population of California has been increasing every year by about five hundred thousand people. It is also known that the California coastline has been disappearing into the Pacific Ocean at a rate of about nine inches every year. The unwary observer might conclude that the California coastline is sinking from the sheer weight of people. Obviously, however, it is not correct to infer a causal relationship since population increase and land erosion are totally unrelated events.[17]

A more serious example is suggested by a recent news story in the *New York Times.* A small town in Florida that was suffering from a mosquito infestation also reported an unusually high rate of AIDS. People speculated that the AIDS virus might be transmitted by mosquitoes. Upon investigation, however, it was found that there were no cases of AIDS among children under 10 or adults over 60. Obviously, if mosquitoes transmitted the AIDS virus then all age groups would be affected. Thus, the investigation dispelled fears that there was any causal connection between mosquitoes and AIDS.[18]

3. *Positing a causal relationship that turns out to be spurious.* A correlation between two factors may be a by-product of a third factor. For example, it would not be difficult to show a correlation between the number of storks in an area and the number of births in a given year. This hardly

[17]This example is taken from Lucy Horwitz and Lou Ferleger, *Statistics for Social Change* (Boston: South End Press, 1980), pp. 285–86.
[18]*New York Times,* January 8, 1988, p. B6.

proves that storks bring babies. What it does reflect is the fact that storks thrive in rural areas, and rural areas have higher birth rates than urban areas. Thus, we would say that the relationship between storks and babies is *spurious*.

To take a less frivolous example, it is known that drivers of small cars have a higher death rate than do drivers of large cars. However, automobile manufacturers contend that this does not constitute proof that small cars are more dangerous. They argue that small cars are more likely to be driven by young people who tend to be more reckless as drivers. In other words, the contention is that the relationship between car size and death rate is spurious, because it masks the effect of a third factor—the age of drivers. In the event that the automobile manufacturers were correct (and there is no reason to suppose that they are), then young drivers of large cars would be equally at risk.

ARGUMENT

As we suggested in Chapter 1, social research is inherently argumentative, in that researchers must convince others of their conclusions. They do so on the basis of evidence and solid reasoning, and by anticipating objections likely to be raised by critics. As a rhetorical form, however, "argument" has a more restricted meaning. To quote McQuade and Atwan:

> In rhetoric, argument is a special form of discourse, one that attempts to convince an audience that a specific claim or proposition is true wholly because a supporting body of logically related statements is also true. In a well-constructed argument, once we establish the truth of statements A, B, and C, and so forth, then we can reasonably be expected to assent to the principal claim or assertion. In other words, the truth of a statement is entirely dependent on the previously acknowledged truth of the other statements.[19]

Like a trial lawyer pleading a case, the writer establishes certain facts (premises) which lead ultimately to a conclusion. Thus, argument conforms to the following thought pattern: If A, B, and C are correct, then X will follow. This leaves two possible sources of error that the writer must guard against: (1) the premises may not be correct, or (2) the premises may be true, but they may not necessarily lead to the stated conclusion. It requires clear thinking and sound reasoning to establish the linkages between premises and conclusions.

Consider the following excerpt from Charles Beard's pioneering study, *An Economic Interpretation of the Constitution*, first published in 1913. As the title itself suggests, Beard is advancing a bold interpretation of the Constitution, one that challenges the conventional view that our founding fathers drafted the Constitution in order to advance the ideals of life, liberty,

---

[19]Donald McQuade and Robert Atwan, *Thinking in Writing* (New York: Alfred A. Knopf, 1983), p. 417.

and the pursuit of happiness. Beard's argument is that the Constitution was basically an economic document, one that was conceived, drafted, and ratified by certain entrenched classes, and designed to protect their property interests. At the outset of his book, Beard presents his argument in capsule form:

> It will be admitted without controversy that the Constitution was the creation of a certain number of men, and it was opposed by a certain number of men. Now, if it were possible to have an economic biography of all those connected with its framing and adoption—perhaps about 160,000 men altogether—the materials for scientific analysis and classification would be available. Such an economic biography would include a list of the real and personal property owned by all of these men and their families: lands and houses, with incumbrances, money at interest, slaves, capital invested in shipping and manufacturing, and in state and continental securities.
>
> Suppose it could be shown from the classification of men who supported and opposed the Constitution that there was no line of property division at all; that is, that men owning substantially the same amounts of the same kinds of property were equally divided on the matter of adoption or rejection—it would then become apparent that the Constitution had no ascertainable relation to economic groups or classes, but was the product of some abstract causes remote from the chief business of life—gaining a livelihood.
>
> Suppose, on the other hand, that substantially all of the merchants, money lenders, security holders, manufacturers, shippers, capitalists, and financiers and their professional associates are to be found on one side in support of the Constitution and that substantially all of the major portion of the opposition came from the nonslaveholding farmers and the debtors—would it not be pretty conclusively demonstrated that our fundamental law was not the product of an abstraction known as "the whole people," but of a group of economic interests which must have expected beneficial results from its adoption?[20]

Observe the structure of Beard's argument. *If* we had the biographies of all 160,000 men who had a hand in the writing or ratification of the Constitution (premise 1), and *if* it were found that supporters and opponents of the Constitution were no different in terms of their social class (premise 2), *then* this would suggest that economics had nothing to do with the Constitution (the conclusion). If, on the other hand, most supporters were men of property (women could not vote), and most opponents were small farmers or debtors, would this not suggest the opposite conclusion? With this rhetorical question, Beard has set the stage for his study. The rest of the book may be seen as an attempt to substantiate his premises and to argue his conclusion regarding the economic basis of the Constitution.

It should be noted that Beard's thesis has its critics. One historian, Forrest McDonald, wrote a whole book in which he set out "to subject Beard's thesis to the most careful scrutiny," and "to discover whether the details are compatible with the broad outlines he sketched" (in other words, whether his premises were correct and whether they supported his con-

---

[20]Charles A. Beard, *An Economic Interpretation of the United States* (New York: Mac-Millan, 1968), pp. 16–17. Originally published in 1913.

clusions). McDonald collected data on the delegations to the Philadelphia conventions that ratified the Constitution, and found no support for Beard's assumption that there was a division between propertied elements, on the one hand, and small farmers and debtors, on the other. He concluded that "Beard's thesis is entirely incompatible with the facts."[21]

It goes without saying that McDonald's study also has its critics, and historians still debate the validity of Beard's thesis. Such is the nature of the intellectual enterprise. For every argument there is almost certain to be a counterargument, and no sooner is a debate resolved than it is opened up again. This only underscores the importance of good writing and cogent argument. We must write with the knowledge that our arguments will have to withstand the scrutiny of critics.

As a rhetorical strategy, argument lends itself to a number of fallacies:

Faulty Generalization. This refers to instances where the conclusions are not adequately supported by the evidence, precisely what McDonald meant when he wrote that Beard's "details were found to be incompatible with the broad outlines he sketched."[22]

The Faulty Premise. Not a few social theorists have propounded erudite theories whose only flaw is that the facts that they purport to explain are untrue. Again, this is what McDonald meant when he claimed that Beard's "facts did not substantiate his assumptions."[23] Facts are like the cornerstone of a building: if seriously flawed, the entire edifice may collapse.

Begging the Question. This is also called *circular argument.* It refers to instances where something is assumed as a premise and then stated as a conclusion. For example, Beard would have been guilty of circular reasoning had he declared that the wealthy voted for the Constitution because it served their economic interests, if the only evidence he offered for his assumption that the Constitution served the economic interests of the wealthy was that they voted for it. To avoid circular reasoning, Beard had to present independent evidence showing that the Constitution served the interests of the wealthy and that this perception governed how they voted.

Evading the Issue. Wittingly or unwittingly, writers sometimes gloss over a flaw or gap in their argument by shifting the focus to a vaguely related but not completely relevant point. In Beard's case he makes much of the fact that women, slaves, and people who did not meet property qualifications were denied the franchise, and therefore excluded from the process of ratifying the Constitution. To be sure, these facts call into question the extent of the new nation's commitment to democratic principles. But they do not by themselves prove that the groups in question would not have voted for ratification if they had been empowered to do so. Similarly, to

[21]Forrest McDonald, *We the People* (Chicago: University of Chicago Press, 1958), p. 357.
[22]Ibid., p. 400.
[23]Ibid.

show, as Beard does, that the founding fathers were all men of considerable wealth evades the issue of whether their politics were governed by narrow self-interest, or whether they were not genuinely devoted to the democratic ideals enshrined in the Constitution.

Hopefully, it will be easier to avoid these pitfalls by being aware of them. This is why it is important to be self-conscious as a writer. To be cognizant of the rhetorical strategies in your writing will also help you to write with greater clarity and conviction.

SUGGESTIONS FOR WRITING AND THINKING

1. Take a subject area—adolescent culture, for example—and show how the eight rhetorical strategies discussed in this chapter might lead to useful questions for probing the subject. For example:

   Comparison-contrast: How does adolescent culture in this country compare to adolescent culture in Western Europe?

   Cause-effect: What effects does adolescent culture have on the relationship between parents and children?

   Continue with respect to the remaining six rhetorical strategies: narration, description, illustration, definition, classification, and argument. Repeat this exercise using another subject area of your choice.

2. The following passages are drawn from various studies, and delineate the main purpose or the overarching question that governs each study. For each, indicate the rhetorical strategy that is implied:

   In this paper, we attempt to describe the kind of idealism that characterizes the medical freshmen and to trace both the development of cynicism and the vicissitudes of that idealism in the course of the four years of medical training. [Howard S. Becker and Blanche Geer, "The Fate of Idealism in Medical School," *American Sociological Review*, 23 (1958), 50.]

   This essay is an attempt to interpret, from a sociological perspective, the effects of social class upon parent-child relationships. [Melvin L. Kohn, "Social Class and Parent-Child Relationships," *American Journal of Sociology*, 73 (January 1963), 471.]

   In this article, we offer a working definition of the garage sale, specifically how it can be distinguished from other sorts of informal sales, such as estate sales, tag sales or rummage sales. Next, we explain how we produced the ballpark figures of the number of garage sales and their revenues, and how the garage sale has been institutionalized, that is, how it has infiltrated the cultural mainstream. [Gretchen M. Herrmann and Stephen M. Soiffer, "For Fun and Profit: An Analysis of the American Garage Sale," *Urban Life*, 12 (January 1984), 397.]

   The main cause for our depressed industries is not foreign competition; nor are we becoming "a nation of hamburger stands." Our problem is slack demand

and an overvalued dollar. [Robert Z. Lawrence, "The Myth of U.S. Dein-dustrialization," *Challenge* (November-December 1983), 12.]

This paper attempts to specify some of the ways in which the modern family in the United States differs from its historical predecessor through a distinction between the public and private character of social institutions. [Barbara Laslett, "The Family as a Public and Private Institution: An Historical Perspective," in *The Family*, eds. Peter J. Stein, Judith Richman, and Natalie Hannon (Reading, Massachusetts: Addison-Wesley Publishing Company, 1977), p. 45.]

In summary, an attempt has been made to show that religious experiences, both diabolic and divine, can be analytically broken down into four general types and several further subtypes, on the basis of the configuration of relationships between the divine and human actor during any spiritual encounter. [Charles Y. Glock and Rodney Stark, *Religion and Science in Tension* (Chicago: Rand McNally, 1965), p. 64.]

This book tells the story of those east European Jews who, for several decades starting in the 1880s, undertook a massive migration to the United States. [Irving Howe, *World of Our Fathers* (New York: Harcourt Brace Jovanovich, 1976), p. xix.]

Current and emerging programs in bilingual-bicultural education represent a significant development in the evolution of the public school. . . . This chapter reports research on a bilingual-bicultural program in an elementary school with a high proportion of Mexican-American children. [Richard L. Warren, "Schooling, Biculturalism, and Ethnic Identity: A Case Study," in *Doing the Ethnography of Schooling*, ed. George Spindler (New York: Holt, Rinehart and Winston, 1982), p. 384.

Chapter 5
THE LOGICAL STRUCTURE OF SOCIAL SCIENCE WRITING

Not unlike a good story, good academic writing has a logical beginning, middle, and end. This is what gives shape or structure to an otherwise amorphous stream of words and ideas. In the social sciences this beginning, middle, and end tends to assume a more or less characteristic form. Generally speaking, the *logical beginning* consists of a statement of the research problem, or the questions or issues that are being addressed. The *logical middle* involves a marshalling of facts or data that pertain to the research problem. The *logical end* attempts a resolution of the original research problem, however tentative or incomplete it might be. This is also the place to assess the larger implications of the research for theory, future research, or social policy.

Our point is not that this model is or should be mechanically imposed on all social science writing. This would make for a deadly uniformity and stifle creative thought. Just as all stories should not begin with the stock phrase, "Once upon a time . . . ," it would be tedious, to say the least, if all social science papers began with the stock phrase, "The purpose of this paper is. . . ." Yet all writing has a purpose, whether or not it is stated explicitly, in bold type, or woven more subtly into a larger exposition. In the case of social science writing, there is typically an underlying structure centered around a search for answers to unresolved questions. Sometimes this structure is explicit; more often it is implicit. It will be of immense value to you, as students, to recognize this structure, both to sharpen your reading and comprehension of social science literature, and to help you write effectively when you are called upon to do so.

Thus, to say that all social science writing begins with questions, presents evidence, and reaches conclusions is not a narrow prescription on how to write a paper, but only a formula for calling attention to an underlying and often unstated logical structure. It may be helpful to think of this "structure" like that of a house, in the sense that every house has a foundation, a frame, and a roof, yet all houses do not look alike. By the same token, what is being proposed here is not a literary Levittown, but only an essential structure that will give shape and direction to social science writing, without restricting its content or hampering creative expression.

A LOGICAL BEGINNING: QUESTIONS

Virtually all social science writing is defined by questions put forward by the writer, typically at the beginning of the work. These questions are an indispensable first step in the writing process in that they govern the organization and flow of the paper. To be clear about the questions is to be headed resolutely down a path leading to a set of conclusions. On the other hand, to be muddled about the questions, or to lose sight of them, is like being cut adrift on an open sea, buffeted in every direction, never sure where you will end up. Thus, if there is a first principle in social science writing, it is to be clear about what questions are being addressed.

Consider this from the point of view of the reader. Nothing is more frustrating than to be lost in someone else's intellectual muddle. A paper that fails to define its purpose, that drifts from one topic to the next, that "does not seem to go anywhere," is certain to frustrate the reader. If that reader happens to be your instructor, he or she is likely to strike back with notations scrawled in the margin criticizing the paper as "poorly organized," "incoherent," "lacking clear focus," "discursive," "muddled," or the like. Most instructors have developed a formidable arsenal of terms that express their frustration at having to wade through papers that, in one way or another, are poorly conceived or disorganized.

From the student's standpoint, too, writing such a paper must be a frustrating experience. After all, if you are unclear yourself as to the purpose or direction of your paper, how do you get from one sentence or paragraph to the next? Finding yourself hopelessly stalled, you may tell yourself that you are suffering from "writer's block." If this happens, we would suggest that you brainstorm and freewrite until you are able to forge ahead. Once you have generated some ideas and are in the process of shaping them, you can resolve your block by thinking through the purpose and objectives of the study.

Questions, then, carefully formulated and clearly stated, are the key— or at least one key—to effective writing. Indeed, if one surveys major works in the various social science disciplines, more often than not there is *one* overarching question that defines the main purpose or objective of the study. There may well be numerous secondary or subordinate questions, but these are typically subsumed under that single larger question that frames the study.

Sometimes, though by no means always, this overarching question is stated explicitly. For example, in Winthrop Jordan's history, *White Over Black*, the very first words that the reader encounters in the preface are as follows:

> This study attempts to answer a simple question: What were the attitudes of white men toward Negroes during the first two centuries of European and African settlement in what became the United States of America?[1]

This "simple question" is the prelude to a 600-page book based on pro-digious research. Indeed, one prominent reviewer of *White Over Black* extolled Jordan for having "tackled one of the most abstruse, subtle, tangled, controversial and certainly one of the most important problems of American history."[2] It is worth repeating that this ambitious undertaking sprung from "one simple question." Nor did the fact that Jordan shaped his study around "one simple question" prevent him from carrying it out, as his reviewer said, "with imagination and insight."

In short, simple questions do not presuppose simple answers. What they do achieve is *clarity of purpose*. Let us return to the social science literature for two other examples of how leading writers go about formulating the overarching questions for their research and writing.

The psychologist Stanley Milgram sought to understand why people obey authority, even when this involves transgressing the normal rules of conduct, and inflicting great harm on others. At the outset of his article, he alludes to the biblical story in which Abraham is commanded by God to kill his son, and notes that in war, too, people are commanded to destroy the enemy. Milgram designed a series of psychological experiments that would allow him to probe this general phenomenon, and he framed his study as follows:

> In the more limited form possible in laboratory research, the question becomes: if an experimenter tells a subject to hurt another person, under what conditions will the subject go along with this instruction, and under what conditions will he refuse to obey?[3]

Having thus delineated the overarching question of his study, Milgram has set the stage for a systematic presentation of his findings.

As suggested earlier, the paradigmatic questions that govern research differ from discipline to discipline. As a psychologist, Milgram was con-cerned primarily with the psychological factors that explain obedience to authority. On the other hand, Emile Durkheim studied a phenomenon—suicide—that is usually regarded as a psychological phenomenon, but he

---

[1]Winthrop Jordan, *White Over Black* (Baltimore: Penguin Books, 1969), p. vii.

[2]C. Vann Woodward, *New York Times Book Review*, March 31, 1968, p. 6.

[3]Stanley Milgram, "Some Conditions of Obedience and Disobedience to Authority," *Human Relations*, 18, no. 1 (1965), 57.

studied it from a sociological perspective. Indeed, his book *Suicide* marks the beginning of modern sociology. The question behind Durkheim's study was not why this or that individual commits suicide; this, he conceded, was the province of psychology. Durkheim was struck by the fact that every society had a characteristic *rate* of suicide that hardly varied from one year to the next. He also observed that the suicide rate was higher for some groups than for others: for example, among Protestants as compared to Catholics, and among the unmarried as compared to the married. Durkheim called this "the social suicide rate," and the overarching purpose of his study was to understand why it is higher for some groups than for others.[4]

Our purpose in citing these studies has been to demonstrate how questions, and the pursuit of answers, govern research and writing in the social sciences. If the first step is the formulation of research *questions*, the next step is the collection and presentation of *evidence*.

A LOGICAL MIDDLE: EVIDENCE

Who dunnit? This is the question that informs all Agatha Christie novels. As the novel unfolds, Hercule Poirot, her fictitious detective, relentlessly pursues every clue and collects shreds of evidence until they form a pattern that points, unmistakably, to the culprit and hence resolves the mystery.

The mission of social science, one might say, is to unravel the mysteries of the social world, and social scientists are engaged in a kind of detective work that involves the marshalling of evidence leading to a resolution of the original research question. The kind of evidence, and the ways in which it is collected, takes many forms. Social scientists have at their disposal a number of different research strategies and tools. Which strategy and which tools are applied in any particular instance depends on the questions that are being addressed.

To return to our earlier examples, the stated purpose of Winthrop Jordan's study—his "simple question"—concerned the nature of racism during the first two centuries that Europeans and Africans were together on American soil. How does a historian go about reconstructing social patterns that existed in the distant past? In Jordan's case, he used reports by travellers, personal diaries, private letters, newspapers, and early histories, as well as legislation and other kinds of official documents. From these varied sources Jordan sought to piece together the process of domination and oppression of "white over black."

If Stanley Milgram were a historian, he might have studied obedience and disobedience to authority within a specific historical context—for example, by conducting a comparative study of draftees and draft resisters

---

[4]Emile Durkheim, *Suicide* (Glencoe, Illinois: The Free Press, 1951).

during the Vietnam war. But Milgram is an experimental psychologist, and consistent with his training, he designed a series of experiments in which subjects were duped into believing that they were participating in a learning experiment, and were told to administer a memory test to a "learner" who was strapped into an "electric chair." The subject was instructed by the experimenter to administer electric shocks to the learner whenever he gave a wrong answer. Of course, the learner was a confederate in the experiment, and he played his role to the hilt—grunting and moaning and writhing with pain as the subjects dutifully turned up the voltage when instructed to do so. In the extreme position, labeled "Danger: Severe Shock," the learner demanded to be let out of the experiment, while the experimenter dispassionately instructed the subject to treat the absence of an answer as equivalent to a wrong answer, and to follow the usual shock procedure. In this way the experiment allowed Milgram to examine the process whereby people exhibit "blind obedience" to authority.

If Durkheim had been a psychologist, he might have sought to determine the psychological makeup of suicide victims, for example, by analyzing their suicide notes or by interviewing family members. Given his interest in the social suicide rate, however, Durkheim collected a mass of statistical data on the social characteristics of suicide victims. Were they more likely to be male or female? Old or young? Married or unmarried? Urban or rural? Protestant or Catholic or Jewish? From these empirical data Durkheim sought to identify the factors that groups with high or low suicide rates have in common.

As these examples suggest, there is a close logical connection between the questions that are posited and the evidence that is collected. This is worth stressing because students often err either by asking questions that cannot be answered with available evidence, or by collecting evidence that is not directly related to the stated objectives of their study.

A LOGICAL END: ANSWERS

A paper without a conclusion is like a story without an end, or even more disconcerting, a joke without a punch line. Yet a common flaw of student papers is that they reach no conclusion. To be sure, they come to an end, but all too abruptly, without forewarning or logical preparation. Readers of such papers—your instructors—are left in a state of intellectual suspension as they read along and suddenly realize that they have come to the end of the paper. Once again, they retaliate with notations such as "lacks closure," "stops in midair," or an incredulous "Is this the end of your paper?"

When a paper lacks a conclusion, this is not necessarily because the student has run out of time, or energy, or even material. Rather, the problem may go back to the very conception of the paper. A student who has not formulated a clear topic, but is merely writing diffusely about a subject, will be hard pressed to find a graceful or logical way to end the paper. On the other hand, the student who begins with a clear statement of purpose, and who carefully formulates the questions that control the inquiry, will be compelled by the paper's internal logic to bring it to clear resolution.

Generally speaking, the conclusion ought to provide the best possible answer to the original questions on the basis of the evidence that has been marshalled in the body of the paper. However, the conclusion should be more than a summation. That is, it should go beyond the specific findings, and analyze some of the implications of these findings, whether for theory, research, or public policy.

Say, for example, that you did a study of the 1988 presidential election, with an eye to exploring voting patterns. The body of the paper might involve a detailed analysis of election returns, focusing on the social characteristics of areas where each candidate ran strong. Having thus waded through the data, the time is ripe to step back and to reassess the original question in light of what has been learned. What, in a nutshell, explains the election outcome? What overall conclusion is warranted by the evidence? Different implications of the findings might be explored. For example:

> On the level of theory, what does the election reveal about the political values of the American people? The nature of electoral politics? The future of liberalism and conservatism?

> On the level of research, are there any questions that are unresolved or suggested by the findings or analysis in the body of the paper? Insofar as the purpose of research is to push back the frontier of knowledge, it is certainly appropriate that a study end by taking stock of both what has been learned and what questions remain.

> On the level of social policy, does the research have any implications concerning political strategy in future elections? The public financing of elections? The need to reform the electoral system?

These are the kinds of "larger questions" that might be explored in a concluding section of a paper on a presidential election. Obviously, the specific content that goes into a conclusion depends on the subject matter and the interests of the author. Our main point is that, as a matter of form, a good conclusion provides a sense of resolution to the original research question. However, it not only summarizes the main findings established in the body of the paper but also engages in some speculation or analysis about the implications or relevance of these findings for larger concerns.

Let us illustrate the operation of this principle by alluding again to the three studies discussed earlier in this chapter.

As a historical chronicle of racism in seventeenth- and eighteenth-century America, *White Over Black* does not come to a conclusion that can easily be encapsulated in a few sentences. The objective of Jordan's study was to provide a detailed account of the origins and development of racism on American soil. Its main thrust is to demonstrate how a nation that fought for its own freedom from colonial domination and that declared that "all men are created equal," could at the same time exclude blacks from its national covenant and justify slavery. Even those who opposed slavery rejected the idea of racial equality, and in his final chapter Jordan describes the campaign that developed among antislavery forces to "colonize" blacks to Africa or the Caribbean.

In the case of Milgram's study of obedience to authority, the conclusion was developed around one significant finding. Over half of Milgram's subjects were fully obedient to the experimenter's commands and delivered the maximum "shock." Milgram concluded that this finding had dire implications for the future. As he wrote:

> The results, as seen and felt in the laboratory, are to this author disturbing. They raise the possibility that human nature, or—more specifically—the kind of character produced in American democratic society, cannot be counted on to insulate its citizens from brutality and inhumane treatment at the direction of malevolent authority. . . . If in this study an anonymous experimenter could successfully command adults to subdue a fifty-year-old man, and force on him painful electric shocks against his protests, one can only wonder what government, with its vastly greater authority and prestige, can command of its subjects.[5]

Durkheim's evidence indicated that certain groups—for example, Catholics, rural dwellers, and married people—had relatively low rates of suicide. What did these groups have in common that might account for their relative immunity to suicide? The key factor, according to Durkheim, is that all three groups are marked by a relatively high degree of social integration. That is, the ties between the individual and the group tend to be strong. Compared to Protestantism, which stresses free will and individual responsibility, Catholicism is a more dogmatic and highly structured religion that defines a less ambiguous relationship between individual and church. Compared to the anonymity of urban life, rural dwellers tend to have more stable and enduring ties with family, neighbors, and community. Compared to those who live alone, married people are more likely to have kinship ties that give them a sense of purpose and responsibility to others. Durkheim postulated that people with strong social bonds are protected from feelings of isolation and despair that, in times of personal crisis, might otherwise lead them to suicide. Does this finding mean that too much freedom is a bad thing? This is the issue that Durkheim ponders in the closing pages of his book.

Perhaps the one abiding lesson in this chapter is that if you are clear about your questions, your research and writing will be guided by your search for answers. The content—that is, your purpose and argument—will motivate and direct your prose. If you concentrate on *what* you wish to say, you will have less trouble deciding *how* to say it.

[5]Milgram, "Some Conditions of Obedience and Disobedience to Authority," p. 75.

ORGANIZATION

The schema of questions-evidence-answers corresponds to certain general principles for organizing papers. Specifically, there is a title and an introduction leading into the main body of the paper, which builds to a conclusion. Finally, there is a list of sources, usually at the end of the paper. Let us comment briefly on each of these organizational features.

Title

All too often, students hand in papers without titles. Sometimes this may be a mere oversight. Usually it is a first sign of trouble, indicating that the paper lacks clear definition or focus. In this book we lay down very few unbending rules, but one is: Never hand in a paper without an appropriate title. The next question, of course, is, What makes a title "appropriate?"

An appropriate title is one that encapsulates the main thrust of the paper. It should be straightforward and concise. Social scientists usually avoid titles that use figurative language or that evoke images. Note the titles of the sample essays in Chapters 6 to 9 of this book:

"Teacher Expectations for the Disadvantaged"

"The Hustler"

"Emerging Sex-Role Attitudes, Expectations, and Strains Among College Women"

"Send Me Some of the Children's Hair"

These titles are straightforward, if not bland, with the exception of the last one which comes from Herbert Gutman's history of the black family. Perhaps reflecting their humanist traditions, historians are more likely than other social scientists to use evocative titles. In this instance, the title comes from a personal letter written by a slave to his wife, and is used to epitomize the desperate longing that slaves felt when they were separated from their children.

One further point. An appropriate title should be faithful to the contents of the paper. Do not promise more than you deliver.

Introduction

The introduction should provide a clear statement of the problem that your paper addresses. Directly or indirectly, it should make the purpose clear. It should also include sufficient background material without overwhelming or distracting the reader with information that is tangential to the main thrust of the paper.

The introduction often includes a concise review of the previous literature on the topic. This should not be done ritualistically, however. The purpose of this review is to define your paper within the context of previous research or thought, and to set the stage for your own investigation. For students who do not yet have sufficient mastery of a subject area, this "review of the literature" might be limited to whatever related works you are familiar with and that stimulated your interest in the topic.

The introductory section should also define the limits of your study. Be explicit about what aspects of the subject you are treating and what aspects are "beyond the scope" of your paper. Identify and define key terms that are central to your paper, and provide appropriate examples or illustrations.

Body of the Paper

The midsection of your paper is the exposition of the subject under study. If you have done original research, this would be the place to systematically report your findings. If you are writing about research that others have done, you will still need to marshall together relevant facts or ideas. Many student papers compare more than one work on a selected topic with an eye toward developing a point of view. In this case the synthesis of related sources constitutes the main body of the paper.

Conclusion

A conclusion should evolve logically out of the prior sections of the paper. Even if you choose to have a separate heading labeled "Conclusions," it should not seem as if it were "tacked on" to the paper. As we cautioned in Chapter 2, do not depart from your focus or inject topics that constitute a whole new departure from the main body of the paper. You may, however, offer solutions to a problem or assess future trends, as long as this is a logical extension of the foregoing analysis.

While you should be careful not to raise new topics, you must also avoid merely repeating yourself. The conclusion affords an opportunity to step back and to reflect on the full import of whatever findings or observations were presented in the body of the paper. It should "stretch" the analysis presented in the body of the paper, but not to the point where the logical connection is broken.

Sources

As we commented in Chapter 3, the accurate and appropriate use of source materials is essential to scientific or referential discourse. These references must be made accessible to the reader. A detailed discussion of how to incorporate source material into the body of your paper is presented in Chapter 12.

SUGGESTIONS FOR WRITING AND THINKING

1. At the end of Chapters 6 to 9 we provide annotated lists of studies in various social science disciplines. Read one of these articles, and ana-

lyze its structure in terms of the questions-evidence-answers schema. In a single paragraph, discuss the questions that govern the research; in a second paragraph, sum up the evidence; in a third paragraph, state the major conclusion.

Part II

THE FORMS OF SOCIAL RESEARCH

Chapter 6

THE EXPERIMENT

INTRODUCTION

For the most part, social scientists are obliged to accept the world as they find it. The unique feature of the experiment is that social scientists actually manipulate the environment in order to test certain theories or assumptions. Just as the natural scientist conducts an experiment, say, to see what happens when an atom is split into smaller particles, the social scientist deliberately alters a social setting to see how human behavior is affected.

In the classical model of an experiment, the researcher begins with two groups that are initially identical in every respect. One of these, *the experimental group*, is then subjected to a "stimulus" by the researcher, while the second group, *the control group*, is not altered. The stimulus is then presumed to be the cause of whatever differences show up between the two groups at a later point in time.

For example, a number of experimental studies have been conducted in order to identify the conditions under which people will offer assistance to someone in need. One such experiment was called "Lady in Distress: A Flat Tire Study." The researchers concocted the following situation: A car with a flat tire was placed conspicuously on a street in a residential section of Los Angeles. In one instance (the control group) a woman stood helplessly by the car, which had a fully inflated tire leaning against it. In the other instance (the experimental group), the car was raised by a jack, and the woman stood by while a man changed the tire. The purpose of the experiment was to gauge whether helping behavior increased through the observation of other people being helpful. As it turned out, more people stopped when the woman was being helped by someone else than when she was stranded by herself. The authors concluded that the perception of someone else's altruistic behavior tends to elicit the same response on the part of the observer.[1]

Experiments are used more often in psychology than in the other social sciences. The reason is that psychologists are often preoccupied with problems that involve how individuals react to stimuli that can be produced or simulated in a laboratory under experimental conditions. For example, in Milgram's study of obedience to authority, discussed in Chapter 5, the researchers artificially contrived a situation where subjects were directed by some authority to inflict punishment on others, and their behavior could be observed and measured.

This is an example of a laboratory experiment. Other experiments occur "in the field," such as the Lady in Distress study described above. The sample essay in this chapter is also a field experiment, except that the experiment was carried out in a natural setting—an elementary school—rather than one contrived by the experimenter. In the experiment, two Harvard researchers wanted to test whether some students do poorly in school because their teachers have such low expectations of them that they neglect the children or underestimate their abilities. In other words, their hypothesis was that poor academic performance is the result of a self-fulfilling prophecy on the part of teachers who expect certain students—especially those of minority or lower-class backgrounds—to do poorly.[2]

The experiment was conducted in an elementary school in an economically and racially mixed neighborhood in San Francisco. At the beginning of the experiment, students were scored on a standard intelligence test. Teachers were then duped into believing that certain students were "potential spurters." In actuality, these students were chosen at random and were no different from the other students. The purpose of the experiment was to test whether students designated as "potential spurters" actually performed better because teachers had high expectations of them. The following is an excerpt from Rosenthal and Jacobson's study, as reported in *Scientific American*.

---

[1]James H. Bryan and Mary Ann Test, "Models and Helping: Naturalistic Studies in Aiding Behavior," *Journal of Personality and Social Psychology*, 6 (August 1967), 400–407.

[2]Robert Rosenthal and Lenore F. Jacobson, "Teacher Expectations for the Disadvantaged," *Scientific American*, 218 (April 1968), 19–23.

Teacher Expectations for the Disadvantaged*

Robert Rosenthal and Lenore F. Jacobson

It is widely believed that poor children lag in school because they are members of a disadvantaged group. Experiments in a school suggest that they may also do so because that is what their teachers expect.

[1] One of the central problems of American society lies in the fact that certain children suffer a handicap in their education which then persists throughout life. The "disadvantaged" child is a Negro American, a Mexican American, a Puerto Rican or any other child who lives in conditions of poverty. He is a lower-class child who performs poorly in an educational system that is staffed almost entirely by middle-class teachers.

[2] The reason usually given for the poor performance of the disadvantaged child is simply that the child is a member of a disadvantaged group. There may well be another reason. It is that the child does poorly in school because that is what is expected of him. In other words, his shortcomings may originate not in his different ethnic, cultural, and economic background but in his teachers' response to that background.

[3] If there is any substance to this hypothesis, educators are confronted with some major questions. Have these children, who account for most of the academic failures in the U.S., shaped the expectations that their teachers have for them? Have the schools failed the children by anticipating their poor performance and thus in effect teaching them to fail? Are the massive public programs of educational assistance to such children reinforcing the assumption that they are likely to fail? Would the children do appreciably better if their teachers could be induced to expect more of them?

[4] We have explored the effect of teacher expectations with experiments in which teachers were led to believe at the beginning of a school year that certain of their pupils could be expected to show considerable academic improvement during the year. The teachers thought the predictions were based on tests that had been administered to the student body toward the end of the preceding school year. In actuality the children designated as potential "spurters" had been chosen at random and not on the basis of testing. Nonetheless, intelligence tests given after the experiment had been in progress for several months indicated that on the whole the randomly chosen children had improved more than the rest.

[5] The central concept behind our investigation was that of the "self-fulfilling prophecy." The essence of this concept is that one person's prediction of another person's behavior somehow comes to be realized. The prediction may, of course, be realized only in the per-

*Reprinted with permission from Robert Rosenthal and Lenore F. Jacobson, "Teacher Expectations for the Disadvantaged." Copyright © 1968 by Scientific American, Inc. All rights reserved.

ception of the predictor. It is also possible, however, that the predictor's expectation is communicated to the other person, perhaps in quite subtle and unintended ways, and so has an influence on his actual behavior.

[6] An experimenter cannot be sure that he is dealing with a self-fulfilling prophecy until he has taken steps to make certain that a prediction is not based on behavior that has already been observed. If schoolchildren who perform poorly are those expected by their teachers to perform poorly, one cannot say in the normal school situation whether the teacher's expectation was the cause of the performance or whether she simply made an accurate prognosis based on her knowledge of past performance by the particular children involved. To test for the existence of self-fulfilling prophecy the experimenter must establish conditions in which an expectation is uncontaminated by the past behavior of the subject whose performance is being predicted.

[7] It is easy to establish such conditions in the psychological laboratory by presenting an experimenter with a group of laboratory animals and telling him what kind of behavior he can expect from them. One of us (Rosenthal) has carried out a number of experiments along this line using rats that were said to be either bright or dull. In one experiment 12 students in psychology were each given five laboratory rats of the same strain. Six of the students were told that their rats had been bred for brightness in running a maze; the other six students were told that their rats could be expected for genetic reasons to be poor at

running a maze. The assignment given the students was to teach the rats to run the maze.

[8] From the outset the rats believed to have the higher potential proved to be the better performers. The rats thought to be dull made poor progress and sometimes would not even budge from the starting position in the maze. A questionnaire given after the experiment showed that the students with the allegedly brighter rats ranked their subjects as brighter, more pleasant and more likable than did the students who had the allegedly duller rats. Asked about their methods of dealing with the rats, the students with the "bright" group turned out to have been friendlier, more enthusiastic and less talkative with the animals than the students with the "dull" group had been. The students with the "bright" rats also said they handled their animals more, as well as more gently, than the students expecting poor performances did.

[9] Our task was to establish similar conditions in a classroom situation. We wanted to create expectations that were based only on what teachers had been told, so that we could preclude the possibility of judgments based on previous observations of the children involved. It was with this objective that we set up our experiment in what we shall call Oak School, an elementary school in the South San Francisco Unified School District. To avoid the dangers of letting it be thought that some children could be expected to perform poorly we established only the expectation that certain pupils might show superior performance. Our experiments had the financial support of the National Science Foundation

and the cooperation of Paul Nielsen, the superintendent of the school district.

[10] Oak School is in an established and somewhat run-down section of a middle-sized city. The school draws some students from middle-class families but more from lower-class families. Included in the latter category are children from families receiving welfare payments, from low-income families and from Mexican-American families. The school has six grades, each organized into three classes—one for children performing at above-average levels of scholastic achievement, one for average children and one for those who are below average. There is also a kindergarten.

[11] At the beginning of the experiment in 1964 we told the teachers that further validation was needed for a new kind of test designed to predict academic blooming or intellectual gain in children. In actuality we used the Flanagan Tests of General Ability, a standard intelligence test that was fairly new and therefore unfamiliar to the teachers. It consists of two relatively independent subtests, one focusing more on verbal ability and the other more on reasoning ability. An example of a verbal item in the version of the test designed for children in kindergarten and first grade presents drawings of an article of clothing, a flower, an envelope, an apple and a glass of water; the children are asked to mark with a crayon "the thing that you can eat." In the reasoning subtest a typical item consists of drawings of five abstractions, such as four squares and a circle; the pupils are asked to cross out the one that differs from the others.

[12] We had special covers printed for the test; they bore the high-sounding title "Test of Inflected Acquisition." The teachers were told that the testing was part of an undertaking being carried out by investigators from Harvard University and that the test would be given several times in the future. The tests were to be sent to Harvard for scoring and for addition to the data being compiled for validation. In May, 1964, the teachers administered the test to all the children then in kindergarten and grades one through five. The children in sixth grade were not tested because they would be in junior high school the next year.

[13] Before Oak School opened the following September about 20 percent of the children were designated as potential academic spurters. There were about five such children in each classroom. The manner of conveying their names to the teachers was deliberately made rather casual: the subject was brought up at the end of the first staff meeting with the remark, "By the way, in case you're interested in who did what in those tests we're doing for Harvard. . . ."

[14] The names of the "spurters" had been chosen by means of a table of random numbers. The experimental treatment of the children involved nothing more than giving their names to their new teachers as children who could be expected to show unusual intellectual gains in the year ahead. The difference, then, between these children and the undesignated children who constituted a control group was entirely in the minds of the teachers.

[15] All the children were given the same test again four months after school had started, at the end of that school year and finally in May of the

following year. As the children progressed through the grades they were given tests of the appropriate level. The tests were designed for three grade levels: kindergarten and first grade, second and third grades and fourth through sixth grades.

[16] The results indicated strongly that children from whom teachers expected greater intellectual gains showed such gains. The gains, however, were not uniform across the grades. The tests given at the end of the first year showed the largest gains among children in the first and second grades. In the second year the greatest gains were among the children who had been in the fifth grade when the "spurters" were designated and who by the time of the final test were completing sixth grade.

[17] At the end of the academic year 1964–1965 the teachers were asked to describe the classroom behavior of their pupils. The children from whom intellectual growth was expected were described as having a better chance of being successful in later life and as being happier, more curious and more interesting than the other children. There was also a tendency for the designated children to be seen as more appealing, better adjusted and more affectionate, and as less in need of social approval. In short, the children for whom intellectual growth was expected became more alive and autonomous intellectually, or at least were so perceived by their teachers. These findings were particularly striking among the children in the first grade.

[18] An interesting contrast became apparent when teachers were asked to rate the undesignated children. Many of these children had also gained in I.Q. during the year. The more they gained, the less favorably they were rated.

[19] From these results it seems evident that when children who are expected to gain intellectually do gain, they may be benefited in other ways. As "personalities" they go up in the estimation of their teachers. The opposite is true of children who gain intellectually when improvement is not expected of them. They are looked on as showing undesirable behavior. It would seem that there are hazards in unpredicted intellectual growth.

[20] A closer examination revealed that the most unfavorable ratings were given to the children in low-ability classrooms who gained the most intellectually. When these "slow track" children were in the control group, where little intellectual gain was expected of them, they were rated more unfavorably by their teachers if they did show gains in I.Q. The more they gained, the more unfavorably they were rated. Even when the slow-track children were in the experimental group, where greater intellectual gains were expected of them, they were not rated as favorably with respect to their control-group peers as were the children of the high track and the medium track. Evidently it is likely to be difficult for a slow-track child, even if his I.Q. is rising, to be seen by his teacher as well adjusted and as a potentially successful student.

[21] How is one to account for the fact that the children who were expected to gain did gain? The first answer that comes to mind is that the teachers must have spent more time with them than with the children of whom nothing was said. This hypothesis seems to be wrong,

judging not only from some questions we asked the teachers about the time they spent with their pupils but also from the fact that in a given classroom the more the "spurters" gained in I.Q., the more the other children gained.

[22] Another bit of evidence that the hypothesis is wrong appears in the pattern of the test results. If teachers had talked to the designated children more, which would be the most likely way of investing more time in work with them, one might expect to see the largest gains in verbal intelligence. In actuality the largest gains were in reasoning intelligence.

[23] It would seem that the explanation we are seeking lies in a subtler feature of the interaction of the teacher and her pupils. Her tone of voice, facial expression, touch and posture may be the means by which—probably quite unwittingly—she communicates her expectations to the pupils. Such communication might help the child by changing his conception of himself, his anticipation of his own behavior, his motivation or his cognitive skills. This is an area in which further research is clearly needed.

[24] Why was the effect of teacher expectations most pronounced in the lower grades? It is difficult to be sure, but several hypotheses can be advanced. Younger children may be easier to change than older ones are. They are likely to have less well-established reputations in the school. It may be that they are more sensitive to the processes by which teachers communicate their expectations to pupils.

[25] It is also difficult to be certain why the older children showed the best performance in the follow-up year. Perhaps the younger children, who by then had different teachers, needed continued contact with the teachers who had influenced them in order to maintain their improved performance. The older children, who were harder to influence at first, may have been better able to maintain an improved performance autonomously once they had achieved it.

[26] In considering our results, particularly the substantial gains shown by the children in the control group, one must take into account the possibility that what is called the Hawthorne effect might have been involved. The name comes from the Western Electric Company's Hawthorne Works in Chicago. In the 1920's the plant was the scene of an intensive series of experiments designed to determine what effect various changes in working conditions would have on the performance of female workers. Some of the experiments, for example, involved changes in lighting. It soon became evident that the significant thing was not whether the worker had more or less light but merely that she was the subject of attention. Any changes that involved her, and even actions that she only thought were changes, were likely to improve her performance.

[27] In the Oak School experiment the fact that university researchers, supported by Federal funds, were interested in the school may have led to a general improvement of morale and effort on the part of the teachers. In any case, the possibility of a Hawthorne effect cannot be ruled out either in this experiment or in other studies of educational practices. Whenever a new educational practice is undertaken in a school, it cannot be demonstrated to have an

intrinsic effect unless it shows some excess of gain over what Hawthorne effects alone would yield. In our case a Hawthorne effect might account for the gains shown by the children in the control group, but it would not account for the greater gains made by the children in the experimental group.

[28] Our results suggest that yet another base line must be introduced when the intrinsic value of an educational innovation is being assessed. The question will be whether the venture is more effective (and cheaper) than the simple expedient of trying to change the expectations of the teacher. Most educational innovations will be found to cost more in both time and money than inducing teachers to expect more of "disadvantaged" children.

[29] For almost three years the nation's schools have had access to substantial Federal funds under the Elementary and Secondary Education Act, which President Johnson signed in April, 1965. Title I of the act is particularly directed at disadvantaged children. Most of the programs devised for using Title I funds focus on overcoming educational handicaps by acting on the child—through remedial instruction, cultural enrichment and the like. The premise seems to be that the deficiencies are all in the child and in the environment from which he comes.

[30] Our experiment rested on the premise that at least some of the deficiencies—and therefore at least some of the remedies—might be in the schools, and particularly in the attitudes of teachers toward disadvantaged children. In our experiment nothing was done directly for the child. There was no crash program to improve his reading ability, no extra time for tutoring, no program of trips to museums and art galleries. The only people affected directly were the teachers; the effect on the children was indirect.

[31] It is interesting to note that one "total push" program of the kind devised under Title I led in three years to a 10-point gain in I.Q. by 38 percent of the children and a 20-point gain by 12 percent. The gains were dramatic, but they did not even match the ones achieved by the control-group children in the first and second grades of Oak School. They were far smaller than the gains made by the children in our experimental group.

[32] Perhaps, then, more attention in educational research should be focused on the teacher. If it could be learned how she is able to bring about dramatic improvement in the performance of her pupils without formal changes in her methods of teaching, other teachers could be taught to do the same. If further research showed that it is possible to find teachers whose untrained educational style does for their pupils what our teachers did for the special children, the prospect would arise that a combination of sophisticated selection of teachers and suitable training of teachers would give all children a boost toward getting as much as they possibly can out of their schooling.

CRITICAL ANALYSIS: CONTENT

Let us now analyze this sample essay in terms of the schema outlined in Chapter 5. What were the major *questions* that governed the study? What *evidence* was brought to bear on these questions? And what *conclusions* were finally reached? In other words, let us observe the "logical structure of social science writing" in practice. (To repeat, even though the schema of questions-evidence-conclusions can be detected in virtually all social science writing, it is not applied in rote fashion and does not result in a dull uniformity. That it takes varied and subtle forms will become apparent from the four sample essays in Chapters 6 to 9 of this book.)

Questions

The authors waste no time in raising the main issue of their study. In the first paragraph they allude to the commonplace notion that minority children do poorly in school because they are culturally "disadvantaged." In the second paragraph they suggest an alternative explanation: that the problems of minority children may stem from the fact that teachers have low expectations of them. In a nutshell, this is the supposition or hypothesis that the authors wish to test, and that provides the background and rationale for their study. By the third paragraph the authors are prepared to elaborate on the central question and its implications for social policy:

> If there is any substance to this hypothesis, educators are confronted with some major questions. Have these children, who account for most of the academic failures in the U.S., shaped the expectations that teachers have for them? Have the schools failed the children by anticipating their poor performance and thus in effect teaching them to fail? Are the massive public programs of educational assistance to such children reinforcing the assumption that they are likely to fail? Would the children do appreciably better if their teachers could be induced to expect more of them?

These questions not only form the agenda for the research but they imply a format for organizing the remainder of the research report as well.

Evidence

Having thus established the rationale and purpose of the study, the authors have set the stage to discuss their research procedures and to present their findings. First, they tell us why Oak School was chosen, how teachers were duped into believing that certain students were "potential spurters," and how students were periodically retested in order to measure any change that could be attributed to teacher expectations. The specific findings are reported in detail. However, there is one major finding—that teacher expectations are in fact associated with student performance—that is highlighted in the text and repeated at several intervals:

The results indicated strongly that children from whom teachers expected greater intellectual gains showed such gains. [paragraph 16]

The children from whom intellectual growth was expected were described as having a better chance of being successful in later life and as being happier, more curious and more interesting than the other children. [paragraph 17]

In short, the children for whom intellectual growth was expected became more alive and autonomous intellectually, or at least were so perceived by their teachers. These findings were particularly striking among the children in the first grade. [paragraph 17]

Answers

In science, as in life, resolving one question often raises numerous others. The finding that students designated as potential spurters did in fact perform better resolved the empirical question, but raised a more fundamental issue: "How is one to account for the fact that the children who were expected to gain did gain?" [paragraph 21]. After discounting two possible interpretations, the authors come to the conclusion that the key factor has to do with the communication between teacher and student: "Her tone of voice, facial expression, touch and posture may be the means by which—probably quite unwittingly—she communicated her expectations to the pupils" [paragraph 23]. However, the authors indicate that this is a tentative conclusion, since they do not have the necessary data to substantiate it more fully.

In Chapter 5 we noted that the conclusion often goes beyond the specific issue under analysis, and assesses the larger implications of the study. In this case, Rosenthal and Jacobson weigh the policy implications of their findings. Instead of focusing educational reform on the children and the presumed disadvantages in their background, they argue, ". . . some of the deficiencies—and therefore at least some of the remedies—might be in the schools, and particularly in the attitudes of teachers toward disadvantaged children" [paragraph 30]. Conceding that their findings are suggestive but inconclusive, the authors urge future researchers to focus on the teacher, and in the closing paragraph, they suggest some directions that this research could take.

CRITICAL ANALYSIS: COMPOSITION

In rhetorical terms, "Teacher Expectations for the Disadvantaged" is organized around a cause-effect analysis of a problem. Rosenthal and Jacobson are looking for a cause of the educational problems of disadvantaged children. The question that governs their study is not *whether* but *why* these problems exist, and their experiment is designed to test their hypothesis that teacher expectations are one cause of student failure.

The Introduction (paragraphs 1 to 5)

The first paragraph of the essay fulfills the main requirements of a good introduction: It states the research problem, establishes its significance, and arouses our interest as readers. Note how the authors' choice of words conveys a sense of the importance of their research, beginning with the very first sentence: "One of the central problems of American society lies in the fact that certain children suffer a handicap in their education which then persists throughout life." This is provocative language. It engages the reader, and suggests that the problem is not only worthy of academic study, but warrants the concern of all civic-minded people.

The problems that disadvantaged children have in school are defined in the context of two possible explanations. The first, which reflects the conventional wisdom, is that the background of disadvantaged children deprives them of values and skills needed to excel in school. But, Rosenthal and Jacobson suggest, "there may well be another reason." With this transitional sentence, they put forward an alternative explanation which is stated as a hypothesis:

> It is that the child does poorly in school because that is what is expected of him. In other words, his shortcomings may originate not in his different ethnic, cultural, and economic background but in his teachers' response to that background. [paragraph 2]

This hypothesis functions as a thesis statement for the entire essay. It is the central idea that is repeated at appropriate junctures in the essay, and that controls the direction and the content of the writing. All of the data that is subsequently introduced is done so in order to test the validity of this thesis.

Paragraphs 1 to 5 comprise the full introduction to the essay. After elaborating on the thesis statement in the second and third paragraphs, the authors use paragraph 4 to provide a capsule summary of the experiment and its major findings, which bear out their hypothesis. Paragraph 5 then functions as a transition to the main body of the paper by identifying the key concept behind the investigation: the self-fulfilling prophecy.

The Body Paragraphs (paragraphs 6 to 20)

For the most part the body of the paper consists of a step-by-step account of the experiment, followed by a detailed presentation of the findings. Thus, much of this section is descriptive and relies on careful reporting. Note the attention to detail:

> Oak School is in an established and somewhat run-down section of a middle-sized city. [paragraph 10]

> We had special covers printed for the test; they bore the high-sounding title "Test of Inflected Acquisition." [paragraph 12]

> The manner of conveying their names to the teachers was deliberately made rather casual: the subject was brought up at the end of the first staff meeting

with the remark, "By the way, in case you're interested in who did what in those tests we're doing for Harvard. . . ." [paragraph 13]

In paragraphs 16 to 20 the authors present the results, beginning with the transitional phrase, "The results indicated strongly that. . . ." These results, however, do not constitute the conclusion. Rather, they comprise the material on which the conclusion is based. As a bridge to the concluding section Rosenthal and Jacobson pose a question that calls for an interpretation of the data: "How is one to account for the fact that the children who were expected to gain did gain?" [paragraph 21].

The Conclusion (paragraphs 21 to 32)

In addressing the question of why the "potential spurters" actually did better, Rosenthal and Jacobson first weigh the possibility that teachers spent more time with these students. The interpretation, however, is not supported by the data, and is readily dismissed. Why then discuss it at all? Rosenthal and Jacobson use it as a "straw man"—that is, an idea that is proposed in order to be knocked down, thus eliminating one possible interpretation and making their own appear more credible. At this point Rosenthal and Jacobson advance their own interpretation; namely, that through subtle cues teachers communicate their expectations to students. These expectations are then internalized, and influence how children perform in school.

Unfortunately, Rosenthal and Jacobson have no direct evidence to support this interpretation, since they have not observed the interaction between teachers and students. Indeed, this is one of the weaknesses of their study. Note how the authors deal with this problem in terms of their writing. First of all, they are somewhat tentative in stating their conclusion: "*It would seem that the explanation we are seeking* lies in a subtler feature of the interaction of the teacher and her pupils" [paragraph 23, italics added]. Secondly, in the closing paragraphs of the article the authors argue that there is a need for "further research," and indicate the directions this should take. Finally, they discuss the implications of their research assuming that they are ultimately proved correct. *If* future research bears them out, they write, then funds for educational assistance should go toward the "sophisticated selection" and "suitable training" of teachers. (Note that this issue, which is taken up in the very last paragraph, is not introduced as a new topic that departs from the paper. Rather it is presented as an issue of broader significance that is a logical extension of the research findings.)

RHETORICAL STANCE: PERSUADING THE READER

As we stated in Chapter 4, the rhetorical stance is a manner of persuasion that involves the interaction of subject, audience, and voice. The writer's mastery of a subject is only a necessary first step. He or she must also develop a point of view about that subject, and communicate it effectively. Tone, sequence, and detail are all important elements in persuasive writing.

If we step back and look at "Teacher Expectations for the Disadvantaged" as a whole, we can see that Rosenthal and Jacobson have made their overarching purpose clear to their readers: They want to better understand why disadvantaged children fail in school. They have hypothesized a reason, conducted an experiment to test this hypothesis, and are prepared to defend their conclusions. The authors persuade their audience in the following ways:

1. They engage their readers by calling attention to a shared concern with a serious national problem: the education of disadvantaged children.
2. They elicit the trust of their readers by presenting an objective overview of the problem. By discussing the results of earlier learning experiments on rats, they demonstrate their knowledge of educational research and establish their authority to discuss the subject.
3. They convince their readers of the validity of their experiment by providing essential information about how they set up the experiment, and took precautions to prevent teachers from discovering its true purpose.
4. The authors strengthen their case by demonstrating that they have not jumped to a conclusion. In presenting their findings, the authors wrestle with conflicting interpretations, thus anticipating points that might be advanced by critics.
5. Finally, Rosenthal and Jacobson are very cautious in making their claims. They attempt to persuade their readers by finding a common ground from which to argue. They acknowledge the cause with which most people are familiar—the effect of social class and cultural influences—and instead of rejecting this explanation outright, they suggest that "there may well be" another explanation. They are careful to define teacher expectations as a "contributory cause"—that is, one cause among many. Note their language:

   > Our experiment rested on the premise that *at least some of the deficiencies—and therefore at least some of the remedies*—might be in the schools, and particularly in the attitudes of teachers toward disadvantaged children. [paragraph 30, italics added]

   This note of caution inspires confidence. Rosenthal and Jacobson are careful not to overstate their case. Rather, they make a balanced and reasonable appeal.

Language

The language of this essay is admirably clear and straightforward. It is neither overblown nor obscure. Although the original study was oriented to an audience of educational psychologists, this piece was published in a popular journal, *Scientific American*, and thus intended for a general but informed audience with some background or interest in science. The authors presuppose a basic understanding of the experimental model. However, in writing their essay, they had to make decisions about which terms needed to be defined. In some instances they assumed that their readers were familiar with specific terms or would understand them in context (for example, "hypothesis" [paragraph 3] and "control group" [paragraph 14]). In other instances they were careful to define their terms (for example, "self-fulfilling prophecy" [paragraph 5] and "the Hawthorne effect" [paragraph 26]).

Several other observations about language are worth noting:

> The authors use the first person plural (we) when describing the experiment, making their presentation of data seem more personal and less mechanistic.

> They use transitional phrases which function as markers of the direction of their discussion ("We have explained . . ."; "Our task was to . . ."; "The results indicated . . ."; "From these results it seems evident . . ."; "Our results suggest . . .").

> Through language, Rosenthal and Jacobson establish a tone that is serious, direct, and empathetic toward disadvantaged children. In one startling turn of phrase, they restate their thesis in a way that jolts the reader into confronting its full impact: "Have the *schools failed* the children by anticipating their poor performance and thus in effect *teaching them to fail?*" [paragraph 3, italics added]. This language is highly effective because it has inverted familiar words and meanings. Children have not simply failed; they have been taught to fail.

SUGGESTIONS FOR WRITING AND THINKING

1. This exercise is modeled after the "Lady in Distress" experiment described at the beginning of this chapter. This time *you* will be the person in distress, and the goal of the experiment will be to determine whether male or female bystanders are more likely to offer assistance.

    To carry out this experiment, it will be necessary to create a mock "distress situation." For example, you could drop a stack of books and school supplies in the corridor of your classroom building as unsuspecting subjects pass by. Repeat this twenty times, ten times when the bystander is male, and ten times when the bystander is female. The main observation is whether or not the bystander volunteers assistance. You might also want to record other aspects of verbal and nonverbal behavior. Do bystanders who offer assistance do so willingly or grudgingly? Do they express sympathy or remain silent? Do bystanders who refuse assistance pretend not to see what happened, or do they pretend they are too harried to stop?

    On the basis of these twenty trials, determine whether there are any systematic differences in the responses of male and female bystanders. By collating your results with other students in the class, you can increase your sample size and thus the reliability of your findings. In addition, you can determine whether results differ when the person in distress is male or female.

    Once the findings are established, you are ready to write up the results. Develop a context for presenting your research findings by discussing the purpose of the research, what you hope to learn, and why this is worth knowing. Like Rosenthal and Jacobson, describe the design of the research—where it was conducted, how you staged a mock distress situation, and so on. Finally, present your findings, and in a concluding section, discuss the implications of the research.

2. Read "The Experience of Living in Cities" by Stanley Milgram, published in *Science*, 167 (March 1970), 1461–68. This article reports the results of a series of experimental studies that attempt to determine how people in cities adapt to the overstimulation and stresses of urban life.

    Analyze the article in terms of the questions-evidence-conclusions schema. Then analyze the article in terms of its rhetorical strategy. Discuss how the concept of "overload" helps to tie together the disparate empirical findings. What is Milgram's thesis? Where is it stated? Is his argument altogether persuasive? Why or why not?

EXPERIMENTAL STUDIES ACROSS THE DISCIPLINES

Economics

MOFFITT, ROBERT, "The Negative Income Tax: Would It Discourage Work?" *Monthly Labor Review*, 104 (April 1981), 23–27. This article summarizes the results of four field experiments that sought to test whether government cash transfer payments to the poor, in the form of a negative income tax, would discourage work effort among recipients.

Political Science

COLOMBOTOS, JOHN, "Physicians and Medicare: A Before-After Study of the Effects of Legislation on Attitudes," *American Sociological Review*, 34 (June 1969), 314–18. When Medicare was first proposed, it was adamantly opposed by the organized medical profession. This study uses an experimental design to determine how individual physicians reacted in terms of their attitudes and behavior after the legislation was enacted.

Experimental Psychology

BRANSFORD, JOHN D., and MARCIA K. JOHNSON, "Contextual Prerequisites for Understanding: Some Investigations of Comprehension and Recall," *Journal of Verbal Learning and Verbal Behavior*, II (1972), 717–26. Experiments show that comprehension and memory are enhanced if a reader or listener is able to put the information into a relevant context.

Social Psychology

ROSENHAN, D. L., "On Being Sane in Insane Places," *Science*, 179 (January 1973), 250–58. Eight confederates in this experiment gained admission to psychiatric hospitals merely by complaining that they heard voices. Once labeled as schizophrenic, the pseudopatients had trouble overcoming this tag, proving that health care professionals have difficulty distinguishing the sane from the insane in psychiatric hospitals.

Chapter 7
OBSERVATION

INTRODUCTION

All social scientists are "observers" of human society, although observation takes very different forms depending on the research methods that are employed. Since firsthand observation is not possible, historians must rely on documents to "observe" the past. Sociologists typically focus on contemporary society, but often need to observe patterns—for example, shifts in political opinion—that may not be visible to the naked eye. By drawing a sample and conducting interviews, survey researchers collect fragments of information which are then pieced together, much like a jigsaw puzzle, in order to construct the larger picture.

Still another approach involves direct, firsthand observation of people in their natural surroundings. Here the challenge for researchers is to immerse themselves as much as possible in the life of the community or group under observation. They become "participants," which happens, as one writer puts it, "when the heart of the observer is made to beat as the heart of any other member of the group under observation, rather than as that of a detached emissary from some distant laboratory."[1] Ideally, the participant observer is both a "detached emissary" and an empathetic insider, and writing based on participant observation should reflect both perspectives.

Howard Becker, who helped to pioneer the use of participant observation in sociology, describes the method as follows:

> The observer places himself in the life of the community so that he can see, over a period of time, what people ordinarily do as they go about their daily round of activity. He records his observations as soon as possible after making

[1]John Madge, *The Tools of Social Science* (Garden City, New York: Anchor, 1953), p. 137.

them. He notes the kinds of people who interact with one another, the content and consequences of the interaction, and how it is talked about and evaluated by the participants and others after the event. He tries to record this material as completely as possible by means of detailed accounts of actions, maps of the location of people as they act, and of course, verbatim transcriptions of conversation.[2]

Unlike the experimenter, who deliberately manipulates a setting in order to test for results, participant observers usually try to be as unobtrusive as possible, sometimes concealing their identity altogether.

Although participant observation is used to greater or lesser extent in all of the social sciences, its origins are in anthropology where it is still the prevalent research method. Franz Boas, the founder of academic anthropology, spent more than forty years studying the native peoples of the Pacific Northwest. Ever since, cultural anthropologists have used participant observation to develop an anthropological record of preliterate peoples in every corner of the planet.

A celebrated example is Margaret Mead's *Coming of Age in Samoa*. After years of living among the native people of the Samoan Islands, Mead reported that adolescents in Samoa were spared the intense anxiety and emotional conflict associated with adolescence in modern western societies. This conclusion, however, has been challenged by more recent investigators who also have done field work in the Samoan Islands. Over against Mead's image of an island paradise, these observers portray a society with a great deal of strife, and they specifically reject Mead's contention that adolescence is free of anxiety and conflict.[3]

This controversy points up one of the pitfalls almost inherent in the participant-observation approach: subjectivity and selectivity on the part of the observer. The danger is that field workers will see "what they want to see," and will unconsciously filter out observations that are inconsistent with their expectations or bias. Before rejecting participant observation as hopelessly subjective, however, remember that this is a problem that applies to all social research. Even the historian must select out which facts and observations to include in the historical record. The only recourse is to strive for objectivity, to muster as much evidence as possible, and to be clear and persuasive in the presentation of research findings. If other researchers come up with different conclusions, as in the case of Margaret Mead, then the issue is debated in books and journals and at academic conferences.

---

[2]Howard Becker, "Observation: Case Studies," *International Encyclopedia of the Social Sciences*, 11 (New York: The Macmillan Co. and The Free Press, 1968), p. 233.

[3]Margaret Mead, *Coming of Age in Samoa* (New York: W. Morrow & Co., 1928). For a prominent critique of Mead's work, see Derek Freeman, *Margaret Mead and Samoa: The Making and Unmaking of an Anthropological Myth* (New York: Penguin, 1985). The controversy over Mead's work is itself the subject of a book by Lowell D. Holmes, *Quest for the Real Samoa* (South Hadley, Mass.: Bergin & Garvey Publishers, 1986).

Although participant observation was pioneered by anthropologists engaged in the study of preliterate societies, social scientists subsequently applied the method to contemporary societies as well. In the 1940s and 1950s sociologists at the University of Chicago came to regard the city as "a mosaic of small worlds" that provided fertile ground for research by participant observers. The works they published had such titles as *The Hobo*, *The Gold Coast and the Slum*, *The Ghetto*, and *The Taxi Dance-Hall*.[4] More recently, urban ethnographers have provided rich accounts of various ethnic communities and subcultures. Two prominent examples are Herbert Gans's *Urban Villagers*, which is a study of an Italian community on Boston's North End, and Elliot Liebow's *Tally's Corner*, which is a study of streetcorner life in a ghetto in Washington, D.C.[5] There also have been countless studies of groups that stand outside the respectable mainstream—for example, prostitutes, pimps, and criminals. Still other studies— most notably by Erving Goffman and his followers—have focused on the routine aspects of everyday life, exploring such subjects as how people walk through doors or distance themselves in conversation. Indeed, there is hardly any sphere of social life that is not potential material for the participant observer.

This last comment has special relevance to you, as students. In effect, you are uncertified participant observers by virtue of living in distinctive neighborhoods or having access to such locales as student cafeterias, streetcorner hangouts, discos, and the like. Remember to make use of your insider experience when formulating topics for research papers.

In contrast to quantitative studies that are encumbered with numerical data and statistics, studies based on participant observation lend themselves to a more imaginative and vivid prose style. The challenge for the writer is to recreate the setting under observation as graphically as possible, in order to capture its essential character and to convey this even to readers who may have never experienced it firsthand.

Consider, for example, the opening paragraph from the following article "Rappin' in the Black Ghetto":

> "Rapping," "shucking," "jiving," "running it down," "gripping," "copping a plea," "signifying" and "sounding" are all part of the black ghetto idiom and describe different kinds of talking. Each has its own distinguishing features of form, style, and function; each is influenced by, and influences, the speaker, setting, and audience; and each sheds light on the black perspective and the black condition—on those orienting values and attitudes that will cause a

---

[4]Nels Anderson, *The Hobo* (Chicago: University of Chicago Press, 1923); Harvey Zorbaugh, *The Gold Coast and the Slum* (Chicago: University of Chicago Press, 1929); Louis Wirth, *The Ghetto* (Chicago: University of Chicago Press, 1928); Paul G. Cressey, *The Taxi Dance-Hall* (Chicago: University of Chicago Press, 1936).

[5]Herbert Gans, *Urban Villagers* (New York: The Free Press, 1982); Elliot Liebow, *Tally's Corner* (Boston: Little, Brown, 1967).

speaker to speak or perform in his own way within the social context of the black community.[6]

The author, Thomas Kochman, is a sociolinguist, and his study was based on field work that he conducted with the help of students and informants. The purpose of Kochman's study was not only to describe the "black ghetto idiom," but also to analyze its social and psychological functions. His article is peppered with actual quotes that illustrate different kinds of talking, and the thrust of his analysis can be gauged from the concluding paragraph:

> In conclusion, by blending style and verbal power, through rapping, sounding and running it down, the black ghetto male establishes his personality; through shucking, gripping and copping a plea, he shows his respect for power; through jiving and signifying he stirs up excitement. With all of the above, he hopes to manipulate and control people and situations to give himself a winning edge.[7]

The sample essay for this chapter fits squarely in the tradition of studies that seek to penetrate one of the small, self-contained "worlds" that lie outside the purview and experience of the average person. It is an ethnographic study of the poolroom hustler. The investigator, Ned Polsky, was a true participant-observer in that billiard playing had been his chief recreation for many years. As he discloses to the reader: "I have frequented poolrooms for over 20 years, and at one poolroom game, three-cushion billiards, am considered a far better than average player. In recent years I have played an average of more than six hours per week in various New York poolrooms, and played as much in the poolrooms of Chicago for most of the eight years I lived there."[8] Polsky's other life was that of a doctoral student in the University of Chicago's Department of Sociology, where the field of urban ethnography had been pioneered. Polsky decided to make the poolroom hustler the subject of his dissertation. Clearly, he was in a unique position to describe the world of the hustler from an insider's point of view.

---

[6]Thomas Kochman, "Rappin' in the Black Ghetto," *Transaction*, 6 (February 1969), 26. For the original version on which the *Transaction* article was based, see "Toward an Ethnography of Black American Speech Behavior," in Thomas Kochman, *Rappin' and Stylin' Out* (Urbana: University of Illinois Press, 1972), pp. 241–64.

[7]Ibid., p. 34.

[8]Ned Polsky, *Hustlers, Beats, and Others* (Chicago: University of Chicago Press, 1985), p. 44.

The Hustler*

Ned Polsky

Such a man spends all his life playing every day for small stakes. Give him every morning the money that he may gain during the day, on condition that he does not play—you will make him unhappy. It will perhaps be said that what he seeks is the amusement of play, not gain. Let him play then for nothing; he will lose interest and be wearied.
—Blaise Pascal

They talk about me not being on the legitimate. Why, lady, nobody's on the legit when it comes down to cases; you know that.—Al Capone[1]

[1] The poolroom hustler makes his living by betting against his opponents in different types of pool or billiard games, and as part of the playing and betting process he engages in various deceitful practices. The terms "hustler" for such a person and "hustling" for his occupation have been in poolroom argot for decades, antedating their application to prostitutes. Usually the hustler plays with his own money, but often he makes use of a "backer." In the latter event the standard arrangement is that the backer, in return for assuming all risk of loss, receives half of the hustler's winnings.

[2] The hustler's offense in the eyes of many is not that he breaks misdemeanor laws against gambling (perhaps most Americans have done so at one time or another), but that he does so daily. Also—and again as a necessary and regular part of his daily work—he violates American norms concerning (a) what is morally correct behavior toward one's fellow man and (b) what is a proper and fitting occupation. For one or another of these related reasons the hustler is stigmatized by respectable outsiders. The most knowledgeable of such outsiders see the hustler not merely as a gambler but as one who violates an ethic of fair dealing; they regard him as a criminal or quasi-criminal not because he gambles but because he systematically "victimizes" people. Somewhat less knowledgeable outsiders put down the hustler simply because gambling is his trade. Still less knowledgeable outsiders (perhaps the majority) regard hustlers as persons who, whatever they may actually do, certainly do not hold down visibly respectable jobs; therefore this group also stigmatizes hustlers—"poolroom bums" is the classic phrase—and believes that society would be better off without them. Hustling, to the degree that it is known to the larger society at all, is classed with that large group of social problems composed of morally deviant occupations.

[3] However, in what follows I try to present hustlers and hustling on their own terms. The material below

*Reprinted with permission of the publisher and author from Ned Polsky, *Hustlers, Beats, and Others.* Copyright © 1985 by University of Chicago Press. All rights reserved.

[1]The Pascal quotation is from *Pensées,* V. Al Capone's remark is quoted in Paul Sann, *The Lawless Dècade* (New York: Crown Publishers, 1957), p. 214.

avoids a "social problems" focus; to some extent, I deliberately reverse that focus. Insofar as I treat of social problems, they are not the problems posed by the hustler but for him; not the difficulties he creates for others, but the difficulties that others create for him as he pursues his career.

[4] This approach "from within" has partly dictated the organization of my materials. Some sections below are built around conceptual categories derived less from sociologists than from hustlers, in the hope that this may help the reader to see hustling more nearly as hustlers see it. The disadvantage for the scientifically-minded reader is that the underlying sociological framework may be obscured. Therefore I wish to point out that this framework is basically that of Everett Hughes's approach to occupational sociology.

[5] I try mainly to answer three types of questions: *(a) The work situation.* How is the hustler's work structured? What skills are required of him? With whom does he interact on the job? What does he want from them, and how does he try to get it? How do they make it easy or hard for him? *(b) Careers.* Who becomes a hustler? How? What job risks or contingencies does the hustler face? When and how? What is the nature of colleagueship in hustling? What are the measures of success and failure in the career? In what ways does aging affect the hustler's job skills or ability to handle other career problems? What leads to retirement? *(c) The external world.* What is the place of the hustler's work situation and career in the larger society? What changes in the structure of that society affect his work situation or career?

PREVIOUS RESEARCH

[6] A bibliographic check reveals no decent research on poolroom hustling, sociological or otherwise. Apart from an occasional work of fiction in which hustling figures, there are merely a few impressionistic accounts in newspapers and popular magazines. With a couple of exceptions, each article is based on interviews with only one or two hustlers. No article analyzes hustling on any but the most superficial level or provides a well-rounded description. The fullest survey of the subject not only omits much that is vital, but contains numerous errors of fact and interpretation.[2]

[7] The desirability of a study of hustling first struck me upon hearing comments by people who saw the movie *The Hustler* (late 1961, re-released spring 1964). Audience members who are not poolroom habitués regard the movie as an

[2]Jack Olsen, "The Pool Hustlers," *Sports Illustrated*, Vol. 14 (March 20, 1961), pp. 71–77. Jack Richardson's "The Noblest Hustlers," [*Esquire*, Vol. IX (September, 1963), pp. 94, 96, 98] contains a few worthwhile observations, but it is sketchy, ill-balanced, and suffers much from editorial garbling, all of which makes it both confusing and misleading for the uninitiated. One article conveys quite well the lifestyle of a particular hustler: Dale Shaw, "Anatomy of a Pool Hustler," *Saga: The Magazine for Men*, Vol. 23 (November, 1961), pp. 52–55, 91–93. Useful historical data are in Edward John Vogeler's "The Passing of the Pool Shark," *American Mercury*, Vol. 8 (November, 1939), pp. 346–51. For hustling as viewed within the context of the history of pool in America, see Robert Coughlan's "Pool: Its Players and Its Sharks," *Life*, Vol. 31 (October 8, 1951), pp. 159 ff.; although Coughlan's account of the game's history contains errors and his specific consideration of hustling is brief (p. 166), the latter is accurate.

accurate portrait of the contemporary hustling "scene." The movie does indeed truly depict some social characteristics of pool and billiard hustlers and some basic techniques of hustling. But it neglects others of crucial importance. Moreover, the movie scarcely begins to take proper account of the social structure within which hustling techniques are used and which strongly affects their use. *The Hustler* is a reasonably good but highly selective reflection of the poolroom hustling scene as it existed not later than the mid-1930s. And as a guide to today's hustling scene—the terms on which it presents itself and on which the audience takes it—the movie is quite misleading.

METHOD AND SAMPLE

[8]   My study of poolroom hustling extended over eight months. It proceeded by a combination of: (a) direct observation of hustlers as they hustled; (b) informal talks, sometimes hours long, with hustlers; (c) participant observation—as hustler's opponent, as hustler's backer, and as hustler. Since methods (b) and (c) drew heavily on my personal involvement with the poolroom world, indeed are inseparable from it, I summarize aspects of that involvement below.

[9]   Billiard playing is my chief recreation. I have frequented poolrooms for over 20 years, and at one poolroom game, three-cushion billiards, am considered a far better than average player. In recent years I have played an average of more than six hours per week in various New York poolrooms, and played as much in the poolrooms of Chicago for most of the eight years I lived there. In the course of traveling I have played occasionally in the major rooms of other cities, such as the poolrooms on Market Street in San Francisco, West 25th Street in Cleveland, West Lexington in Baltimore, and the room on 4th and Main in Los Angeles.

[10]   My social background is different from that of the overwhelming majority of adult poolroom players. The latter are of lower-class origin. As with many American sports (e.g., baseball), pool and billiards are played by teenagers from all classes but only the players of lower-class background tend to continue far into adulthood. (And as far as poolroom games are concerned, even at the teenage level the lower class contributes a disproportionately large share of players.) But such differences—the fact that I went to college, do highbrow work, etc.—create no problems of acceptance. In most good-sized poolrooms the adult regulars usually include a few people like myself who are in the poolroom world but not of it. They are there because they like to play, and are readily accepted because they like to play.

[11]   The poolroom I play in most regularly is the principal "action room" in New York and perhaps in the country, the room in which heavy betting on games occurs most often; sometimes, particularly after 1:00 a.m., the hustlers in the room well outnumber the non-hustlers. Frequently I play hustlers for money (nearly always on a handicap basis) and occasionally I hustle some non-hustlers, undertaking the latter activity primarily to recoup losses on the former. I have been a backer for two hustlers.

[12]   I know six hustlers well, and during the eight months of the study I talked or played with over 50

more. . . . It seems safe to assume that the sample is at least representative of big-city hustlers. Also, it is probable that it includes the majority of part-time hustlers in New York, and certain that it includes a good majority of the full-time hustlers in New York.

THE HUSTLER'S METHODS OF DECEPTION

[13] The structure of a gambling game determines what methods of deception, if any, may be used in it. In many games (dice, cards, etc.) one can deceive one's opponent by various techniques of cheating. Pool and billiard games are so structured that this method is virtually impossible. (Once in a great while, against a particularly unalert opponent, one can surreptitiously add a point or two to one's score—but such opportunity is rare, usually involves risk of discovery that is judged to be too great, and seldom means the difference between winning and losing anyway; so no player counts on it.) One's every move and play is completely visible, easily watched by one's opponent and by spectators; nor is it possible to achieve anything via previous tampering with the equipment.

[14] However, one structural feature of pool or billiards readily lends itself to deceit: on each shot, the difference between success and failure is a matter of a small fraction of an inch. In pool or billiards it is peculiarly easy, even for the average player, to miss one's shot deliberately and still look good (unlike, say, nearly all card games, where if one does not play one's cards correctly this is soon apparent). On all shots except the easiest ones, it is impossible to tell if a player is deliberately not trying his best.

[15] The hustler exploits this fact so as to deceive his opponent as to his (the hustler's) true level of skill (true "speed"). It is so easily exploited that, when playing good opponents, usually the better hustlers even disdain it, pocket nearly every shot they have (intentionally miss only some very difficult shots), and rely chiefly on related but subtler techniques of failure beyond the remotest suspicion of most players. For example, such a hustler may strike his cue ball hard and with too much spin ("english"), so that the spin is transferred to the object ball and the object ball goes into the pocket but jumps out again; or he may scratch (losing a point and his turn), either by "accidentally" caroming his cue ball into a pocket or by hitting his cue ball hard and with too much top-spin so that it jumps off the table; or, most commonly, he pockets his shot but, by striking his cue ball just a wee bit too hard or too softly or with too much or too little english, he leaves himself "safe" (ends up with his cue ball out of position, so that he hasn't another shot). In such ways the hustler feigns less competence than he has.

[16] Hustling, then, involves not merely the ability to play well, but the use of a kind of "short con." Sometimes the hustler doesn't need to employ any con to get his opponent to the table, sometimes he does; but he always employs it in attempting to keep his opponent there.

[17] The best hustler is not necessarily the best player among the hustlers. He has to be a very good player, true, but beyond a certain point his playing ability is not nearly so important as his skill at various kinds of conning. Also, he has to possess personality traits that make him "rocklike," able to exploit fully

his various skills—playing, conning, others—in the face of assorted pressures and temptations not to exploit them fully.

JOB-RELATED SKILLS AND TRAITS

[18] Although the hallmarks of the good hustler are playing skill and the temperamental ability to consistently look poorer than he is, there are other skills and traits that aid him in hustling. Some are related to deceiving his opponent, some not.

[19] Chief of these is argumentative skill in arranging the terms of the match, the ability to "make a game." The prospective opponent, if he has seen the hustler play, may when approached claim that the hustler is too good for him or ask for too high a spot, i.e., one that is fair or even better. The hustler, like the salesman, is supposed to be familiar with standard objections and "propositions" for overcoming them.

[20] Another side of the ability to make a game reveals itself when the prospective opponent simply can't be argued out of demanding a spot that is unfair to the hustler, or can be convinced to play only if the hustler offers such a spot. At that point the hustler should of course refuse to play. There is often a temptation to do otherwise, not only because the hustler is proud of his skill but because action is his lifeblood (which is why he plays other hustlers when he can't find a hustle), and there may be no other action around. He must resist the temptation. In the good hustler's view, no matter how badly you want action, it is better not to play at all than to play when you are disadvantaged; otherwise you are just hustling yourself.

(But the hustler often will, albeit with much argument and the greatest reluctance, agree to give a fair spot if that's the only way he can get action.)

[21] The hustler, when faced, as he very often is, with an opponent who knows him as such, of course finds that his ability to make a game assumes greater importance than his ability to feign lack of skill. In such situations, indeed, his game-making ability is just as important as his actual playing ability.

[22] On the other hand, the hustler must have "heart" (courage). The *sine qua non* is that he is a good "money player," can play his best when heavy action is riding on the game (as many non-hustlers can't). Also, he is not supposed to let a bad break or distractions in the audience upset him. (He may pretend to get rattled on such occasions, but that's just part of his con.) Nor should the quality of his game deteriorate when, whether by miscalculation on his part or otherwise, he finds himself much further behind than he would like to be. Finally, if it is necessary to get action, he should not be afraid to tackle an opponent whom he knows to be just about as good as he is.

[23] A trait often working for the hustler is stamina. As a result of thousands of hours of play, all the right muscles are toughened up. He is used to playing many hours at a time, certainly much more used to it than the non-hustler is. This is valuable because sometimes, if the hustler works it right, he can make his opponent forget about quitting for such a "silly" reason as being tired, can extend their session through the night and into the next day. In such sessions it is most often in the last couple of hours, when the betting

per game is usually highest, that the hustler makes his biggest killing.

[24] Additional short-con techniques are sometimes used. One hustler, for example, entices opponents by the ancient device of pretending to be sloppy-drunk. Other techniques show more imagination. For example, a hustler preparing for a road trip mentioned to me that before leaving town he was going to buy a soldier's uniform: "I walk into a strange room in uniform and I've got it made. Everybody likes to grab a soldier."

[25] Finally, the hustler—the superior hustler at any rate—has enough flexibility and good sense to break the "rules" when the occasion demands it, will modify standard techniques when he encounters non-standard situations. An example: Once I entered a poolroom just as a hustler I know, X, was finishing a game with non-hustler Y. X beat Y soundly, by a higher margin than a hustler should beat anyone, and at that for only $3. Y went to the bathroom, whereupon I admonished X, "What's the matter with you? You know you're not allowed to win that big." X replied:

> Yeah, sure, but you see that mother-fucking S over there? [nodding discreetly in the direction of one of the spectators]. Well, about an hour ago when I came in he and Y were talking, and when S saw me he whispered something to Y. So I had a hunch he was giving him the wire [tipping him off] that I was pretty good. And then in his middle game it looked like Y was stalling a little [missing deliberately] to see what I would do, so then I was sure he got the wire on me. I had to beat him big so he'll think he knows my top speed. But naturally I didn't beat him as big as I *could* beat him. Now he'll come back cryin' for a spot and bigger action, and I'll nail him.

And he did nail him.

THE HUSTLER AS CON MAN

[26] As several parts of this study illustrate in detail, hustling demands a continuous and complicated concern with how one is seen by others. Attention to this matter is an ineluctably pervasive requirement of the hustler's trade, and is beset with risks and contradictions. The hustler has not only the concerns that one ordinarily has about being esteemed for one's skills, but develops, in addition to and partly in conflict with such concerns, a complex set of special needs or desires about how others should evaluate him, reactions to their evaluations, and behaviors designed to manipulate such evaluating.

[27] The hustler is a certain kind of con man. And conning, by definition, involves extraordinary manipulation of other people's impressions of reality and especially of one's self, creating "false impressions."[3] If one compares the hustler with the more usual sorts of con men described by David Maurer in *The Big Con,* part of the hustler's specialness is seen to lie in this: the structural contexts within which he operates—the game, the setting of the game within the poolroom, the setting of the poolroom within the larger social structure—are not only more predetermined but more constraining.

[3]Of course, conning is only a matter of degree, in that all of us are concerned in many ways to manipulate others' impressions of us, and so one can, if one wishes, take the view that every man is at bottom a con man. This form of "disenchantment of the world" is central to Herman Melville's *The Confidence Man* (one of the bitterest novels in all of American literature) and to the sociological writings of Erving Goffman. Its principal corollary is the view expressed by hustlers, by other career criminals, and by Thorstein Veblen, that all businessmen are thieves.

Structures do not "work for" the poolroom hustler to anywhere near the extent that they often do for other con men, and hence he must involve himself in more personal ways with active, continuous conning.

[28] The point is not simply that the hustler can't find an ideal structural context, but that much less than the ordinary con man is he able to bend a structure toward the ideal or create one *ab ovo* (come up with an analogue of the con man's "store"). That is, the hustler is far less able to be a "producer" or "director" of ideal social "scenes." To a much greater extent he must work in poor settings, and to a correspondingly greater extent he must depend on being a continuously self-aware "actor."[4]

[29] The hustler needs to be continually concerned about evaluation of him by other persons. But the nature and degree of his concern vary with the particular kind of "others" that these persons represent. The victim or prospective victim, the hustler's orientation toward whom we have discussed at several points, is only one kind of other.

---

[4]The kinds of structural problems faced today by the pool or billiard hustler are by no means all endemic. Some are the result of recent social change.

On the other hand, such change does not create structural problems for all types of hustling. Today the golf hustler, for example, finds that with precious little "acting" he can (a) get heavy action from non-hustlers, (b) lose the good majority of the 18 holes and still clean up, and at the same time (c) not be suspected as a hustler. The structure of the game of golf itself, the peculiar structurally predetermined variations in the betting relationship as one makes the round of the course ("presses," etc.), and the present setting of the game within the larger society—all these combine to create a situation that is tailor-made for hustling. But that is another story.

Obviously the hustler must take cognizance of at least two additional types of significant others: outsiders and colleagues. . . .

CONCLUSIONS

. . . Here I would like to point out certain other findings that seem to have no analogue in the literature of occupational sociology.

[30] *(1) The work situation.* We saw that the hustler must be not only a skilled player, but that he must be skilled at pretending *not* to have great playing skill. . . . As far as I know, this hustling reliance on competence at feigning incompetence is unique, and nowhere treated in the occupational literature. . . .

[31] *(2) Careers.* Certain occupational roles require youthfulness by definition (e.g., acting juvenile parts), and thus enforce unusually early retirement. In certain other occupations (airline pilots, for example) age-related career contingencies also force early retirement. It is common to cite competitive sports or games requiring high physical skills as examples of this type—but pool or billiard playing doesn't fit the pattern.

[32] *(3) The external world.* We saw that changes in American sporting life over the past three decades have severely damaged the hustler's work situation and career. These changes have reduced the number of places he can hustle in, the time-span in which he can stay unknown, the number of people he can hustle, and the average amount of money he can get from someone he hustles. Hustling is a dying trade.

[33] Whenever an occupational group faces a disappearance or

major decline of the market for its skills and a consequent inability to make ends meet, we conceptualize this situation as "technological unemployment." But this concept doesn't fit the situation of hustlers at all well. They suffer not from a shift in technology but from a shift in America's demographic structure, i.e., the decline of the bachelor subculture that populated poolrooms so heavily, and secondarily from a shift in fashion, i.e., the decline in the average amount of money bet on poolroom games. . . .

[34] A more general lesson of this essay is that sociology has unduly neglected the study of people who engage in sports or games for their livelihood. The sociological reason for this neglect is that sociology is compartmentalized into "fields" that tend to make such people, for all their visibility to the sociologist as citizen, invisible to him in his role as sociologist: such people are neglected by students of leisure because the latter are by definition concerned with sports involvement only in its impact on avocational life; and because sports involvement is for the very great majority of people strictly avocational, and those who earn a living at it constitute a minuscule fragment of the labor force, the study of the latter is neglected by occupational sociologists. Thus a largely unexplored area of social research consists of the people who work at what most of us play at.

CRITICAL ANALYSIS: CONTENT

Polsky's study is an example of *qualitative* (as opposed to *quantitative*) research. That is, it is based on observational techniques that are less structured than those employed in experiments or surveys, and the analysis is not based on the enumeration of "hard" data, but rather attempts to reconstruct a social setting, the world of the hustler. Nevertheless, it is striking how well the schema of questions-evidence-answers fits both the research and writing.

Questions

Stated in its broadest terms, the purpose of Polsky's study is to describe the world of the poolroom hustler to readers who probably never heard of a poolroom hustler, unless they happened to see Paul Newman's celebrated movie *The Hustler*. Furthermore, Polsky wants to describe it "from within," that is, from the vantage point of the participants themselves.

Is this approach different from that of a journalist or any other casual observer? Yes, in at least three respects. First of all, Polsky approaches his subject with greater discipline, making use of social science methods. Despite years of personal involvement in the world of poolroom hustling, he did not just write about it "off the top." On the contrary, once he decided to make this the focus of his dissertation, he went back into the field for over eight months, combining direct observation of hustlers, informal interviews, and finally participant observation in which he took on the role of the various actors—the hustler's opponent, the hustler's backer, and the hustler himself. This is a good example of how "controlled inquiry" differs from casual observation.

Secondly, as a social scientist Polsky must approach his subject with scientific objectivity. This does not mean that values play no role in his inquiry. On the contrary, the empathy that Polsky has for the poolroom hustler, and his own passion for billiards, are not only unavoidable, but actually useful if he is to present an insider's account. Objectivity in this instance involves a willingness to suspend moral judgment. As Polsky points out, the hustler tends to be stigmatized by "respectable outsiders" as morally deviant. Clearly, it is necessary to put aside this moral judgment if we are to understand hustlers and hustling in their own terms.

Third, Polsky adopts a more analytical stance toward his subject than one would expect from a journalist or a casual observer. He is preoccupied not only with the journalistic questions of "who, what, when, and where," but also with the more conceptual issue of how perceptions of reality are manipulated and exploited. Moreover, Polsky brings a body of theory and research to bear on his analysis of the poolroom hustler, making comparisons and exploring linkages to other work situations. Thus, in style and content this ethnographic study of the poolroom hustler is markedly different from what one would expect to find, say, in *Esquire* or *Playboy*.

Indeed, Polsky's overall approach is to treat hustling as any other occupation, and to ask the same kinds of questions that any occupational sociologist would ask. Thus, Polsky posits three sets of questions pertaining to (1) the work situation, (2) careers, and (3) the external world (see paragraph 5, which lists no fewer than fifteen questions under these three headings).

Evidence

In ethnographic studies the presentation of evidence usually involves a detailed description of the social setting under observation. The problem, from the standpoint of writing, is how to select and arrange this material in order to achieve a reconstruction of the social setting that is meaningful, accurate, and effective. Polsky organizes his presentation around several subheadings:

The Hustler's Methods of Deception
Job-Related Skills and Traits
The Hustler as Con Man

Each of these subheadings denotes a particular facet of the hustling scene. Like parts of a jigsaw puzzle, they combine to produce a graphic whole.

What emerges is a profile of an unusual occupation where appearances define reality, and skill consists of *not* looking as good as you really are. The hustler must be more than an accomplished player. In order to entice opponents he has to be able to deceive them as to his true level of skill—for example, by putting so much spin on the ball that it "jumps" out of the pocket, or by pocketing his shot in such a way that his cue ball is out-of-position for the next shot. In this and other ways, the hustler manipulates appearances to his ultimate advantage. Time and again, Polsky restates and reformulates the notion that the hustler's playing abilities are not nearly as important as his skill at conning, and that the real challenge for a hustler is to look poorer than he really is. Thus, much of the "evidence" that Polsky presents consists of documenting the various methods of deception that constitute the "stuff" of a good hustler.

Answers

Insofar as detailed description is the goal of ethnographic research, such studies do not always come to a tidy conclusion that goes beyond the ethnographic material itself. In the case of Polsky's study, the original questions—how the hustler's work is structured, what skills are required of him, and so on—are so specific that they are answered by the ethnographic detail in the body of the paper.

On the other hand, Polsky's essay is not completely descriptive. Consistent with his view of the hustler as a special kind of occupation, Polsky wishes to make a contribution to general occupational theory. He concludes that his findings "seem to have no analogue in the literature of occupational sociology," and conversely, that established principles of occupational sociology do not seem to apply to the hustler. Thus, Polsky not only succeeds in providing an insider's perspective of the "world" of the hustler, but uses this as a basis for reflecting on mainstream society as well.

CRITICAL ANALYSIS: COMPOSITION

Although "The Hustler" treats a subject far removed from the "ivory tower" of the university, its author, Ned Polsky, brings the trained eye of the sociologist to observe and analyze the world of the poolroom. He asks the questions: *What* is a hustler and *how* does hustling function as work? Polsky is ultimately concerned not simply with describing the hustler but in *defining* him in his work setting. Thus, the principle rhetorical mode for organizing this essay is *definition*, that is, an extended definition of the hustler as worker and hustling as an occupation.

At the outset of his essay Polsky uses the terms "hustler" and "hustling" as they are used in common parlance. He then proceeds to discuss the attributes that distinguish the hustler from the general class of con men. Eventually, he identifies the most essential quality of the hustler—that he must be the "self-aware 'actor'" in a situation where he manipulates the way others see him.

These defining attributes are verified by detailed observation. In this way Polsky builds his definition through observation and inference. He is not a totally objective observer, however. He is also a participant who describes his personal observations in the poolroom, recounts the testimony of hustlers he has known, and recalls his own experience as player and hustler.

The Introduction (paragraphs 1 to 5)

The essay is framed by two epigraphs or quotations: one by Al Capone, the notorious underworld gangster; the other by Blaise Pascal, the illustrious French philosopher. This startling juxtaposition in a sense mirrors Polsky's own straddling of two worlds: the ivory tower of academe and the "real world" of the poolroom. The specific content of these quotations also presages Polsky's own point of view: Hustling is more than "action." It is work, and like other kinds of work, skirts the edges of legitimacy.

In the introductory section Polsky begins to develop this perspective. The hustler's shadowy activities influence how others regard him, as well as how he regards himself and his "work." Paragraph 1 presents the simple definition: "The poolroom hustler makes his living by betting against his opponents in different types of pool or billiard games, and as part of the playing and betting process he engages in various deceitful practices."

The remainder of the introduction extends this definition by allowing readers to see the hustler from more than one vantage point. Thus, paragraph 2 presents the outsider's view of the hustler, which stigmatizes him to some extent, and influences his self-conception. Paragraph 3 then considers the insider's point of view, that is, how the hustler regards himself and the "difficulties that others create for him." Finally, paragraphs 4 and 5 introduce the sociologist's perspective, which sees hustling as having affinities with other occupations. Drawing on all these frameworks, with an unmistakable emphasis on the insider's point of view, Polsky generates research questions that will probe an aspect of the hustler that has not been considered: the hustler as worker in an admittedly unusual occupation.

The Body Paragraphs (paragraphs 6 to 29)

The body of the essay fills out the definition of hustler. However, Polsky does not plunge into a description of the hustler's world. First he reviews the previous research (which is quite sparse) on this topic. Then he outlines his own research strategy, disclosing how he came to select his "sample." In effect, we follow him step by step from the library to the poolroom.

Finally, we encounter the hustler. Polsky gives us a detailed description of the hustler's "methods of deception," carefully placing his observations of the hustler's moves in the context of the game and its setting. For example, the structure of pool and billiard games makes certain techniques of cheating almost impossible, since "one's every move and play is completely visible, easily watched by one's opponent and by spectators" [paragraph 13]. Polsky then goes on to observe and catalogue the artifices that *are* possible within this game: the plays and "cons" that the hustler uses to deceive an opponent as to his "true speed."

These specific observations of hustling lead to a number of inferences about the nature of the hustler. In other words, Polsky moves from the concrete to the abstract. For example, after describing how the hustler operates, Polsky infers the "job-related skills and traits" needed to perform as a successful hustler: playing skill, argumentative skill, courage, patience, flexibility, and stamina.

Under another subheading, "The Hustler as Con Man," Polsky identifies *one essential characteristic* that distinguishes the hustler from other con men. His "con" depends upon his being a "continuing self-aware actor" in a more "constraining" and "predetermined" setting than those in which other con men operate. Since the hustler cannot manipulate the situation, he has to manipulate the way that he is seen by others.

The Conclusion (paragraphs 30 to 34)

As Polsky brings his essay to a conclusion, he leaves the poolhall and adopts the persona of the sociologist. He analyzes the hustler's work in terms of "general occupational theory," and organizes this discussion around the three categories that he proposed at the outset of the study: the work situation, careers, and the external world.

In his final paragraph Polsky places his subject in an even larger framework: the implications for sociology in general. He comments on the blindness of his profession to groups who "work at what most of us play at," and implies a need to break out of established categories.

RHETORICAL STANCE: PERSUADING THE READER

The author's primary means of persuasion is to bring his readers into the hustler's world. From a rhetorical standpoint, this is achieved primarily through Polsky's use of the first-person, "I." This is effective because it establishes a tone of immediacy (he is there, we are there). Polsky distances himself from those scornful outsiders, instead presenting himself as one who accepts the hustler on his own terms.

However, Polsky is also the scholar who persuades us by citing other authorities, and by being systematic in framing the research problem and presenting the findings. First he establishes his purpose—to view hustling as an occupation. Then he observes the hustler at work. And finally he infers what the hustler "is" by what he does and how he does it. Note that the inferences or conclusions follow the actual observations. Through systematic analysis and attention to detail, Polsky establishes himself as a credible observer, and is able to present a complex analysis without overwhelming the reader.

Language

Like his point of view, Polsky's language reflects the academician/hustler. Polsky skillfully weaves the argot, the almost secret vocabulary of the hustler, into his categories of "methods and traits." Words, such as "speed," "english," and "short con" punctuate the complicated descriptions of how the hustler deceives his opponents. Phrases such as the ability to "make a game" or simply have the "heart" to play it are highly effective because we can almost hear the hustler's banter.

In the end, however, the author returns to the language of the sociologist as he concludes with references to "ideal social scenes." And note his frequent allusions to hustling as an occupation (for example, paragraph 2: ". . . as a necessary and regular part of his daily work"; paragraph 5: "How is the hustler's work structured?"; paragraph 19: "The hustler, like the salesman . . ."). We stand back and try to understand the hustler, not by removing him from the poolroom, but by contrasting him with other kinds of con men. The sociologist's understanding of groups at work provides a larger perspective of the hustler at work. The sociologist's vocabulary, kept to a minimum, provides additional categories with which to analyze and thereby understand the hustler.

SUGGESTIONS FOR WRITING AND THINKING

1. This exercise is modeled after Polsky's participant-observation study of the poolroom hustler. Instead of a poolroom, choose some other locale or hangout, preferably one that you know firsthand. Examples are: a video parlor, a disco, a streetcorner hangout, a ball park, or a student cafeteria. You can proceed in either of two ways:
   a. Assume that you are describing this setting to someone who knows it only superficially. Your objective should be to provide a rich and detailed ethnographic description based on direct observation and interviews with participants. Specific details should be selected and organized to support some overall statement or interpretation that functions as a thesis statement. (For example, the local video parlor provides a harmless outlet for pent-up frustration and aggression. Or, to take the opposite tack, the video parlor is a refuge for alienated adolescents.)
   b. Like Polsky, focus on a particular "actor" in a social setting (for example, a coach, a campus leader, or a charismatic person at a disco or hangout). Define his or her role within that context and the charac-

teristics that account for "success." Again, organize your essay around some overall statement or interpretation that functions as a thesis statement.

2. Read "The Fate of Idealism in Medical School" by Howard Becker and Blanche Geer, published in the *American Sociological Review*, vol. 23 (February 1958), pp. 50–56.

Analyze the article in terms of the questions-evidence-conclusions schema. Then analyze it in terms of its rhetorical strategy. What thesis emerges about the fate of idealism in medical school? How do the authors trace the process whereby students modify their ideals during their student career? How is this reflected in the organization of the paper?

OBSERVATIONAL STUDIES ACROSS THE DISCIPLINES

Anthropology

GMELCH, GEORGE, "Baseball Magic," *Trans-action*, 8, no. 8 (June 1971), 39–41, 54. The author applies Malinowski's theory that magic flourishes in unpredictable situations, and describes the rituals, taboos, and fetishes that pervade baseball in the field, on the mound, and in the batter's box.

Economics

TOBIN, JAMES, "The Economy of China: A Tourist's View," *Challenge*, 16, no. 1 (March/April 1973), 20–31. The author, a leading economist, was one of the first American scientists to travel to the People's Republic of China after the American-Chinese rapprochement in the early 1970s. This is his account of his travels.

Political Science

BORGOS, SETH, "The ACORN Squatters' Campaign," *Social Policy*, 15, no. 1 (Summer 1984), 17–26. In 1982 a small army of 200 people, led by a cadre of political organizers, launched a squatters' campaign to lay claim to abandoned houses in a poor Philadelphia neighborhood. This is an eyewitness account by one of the leaders.

Psychology

COLES, ROBERT, "The Moral Life of Children," *Educational Leadership*, 43, no. 4 (December 1985/January 1986), 19–25. Robert Coles, a prominent child psychiatrist, explores the moral life of children, based on observation of high school students in New Hampshire, Illinois, and Georgia.

Sociology

THOMPSON, WILLIAM E., "Hanging Tongues: A Sociological Encounter with the Assembly Line," *Qualitative Sociology*, 6 (Fall 1983), 215–37. On the basis of nine weeks as a participant observer on an assembly line in a slaughter division of a large beef processing plant, the author analyzes how the workers coped with the danger, strain, and monotony of the assembly line, as well as the dehumanizing aspects of their jobs.

Chapter 8
THE INTERVIEW

INTRODUCTION

Among the various research tools available to the social scientist, the interview is undoubtedly the one most often used in social research. In an interview the researcher, or a trained assistant, goes out and questions subjects in order to elicit information. Needless to say, there is great variation in terms of who gets interviewed, how they are interviewed, and for what purpose.

Generally speaking, interviewees (people selected for interviews) fall into two categories: influentials and ordinary people who belong to some group or population that is being studied. The first group—influentials—includes people in positions of status or authority, such as government officials, politicians, clergy, journalists, and other decision makers and opinion leaders. As a discipline political science takes special interest in such groups, and countless studies of influentials have been conducted using interviews as the primary source of data.

One such study sought to find out how leaders of different kinds stand on the issue of equality. Conducted by two political scientists, Sidney Verba and Gary Orren, the study was published under the title *Equality in America: The View from the Top.* The reason for studying leaders, according to the authors, is that "their views influence both the political establishment and the public at large."[1] Nine different types of leaders were interrogated in order to measure the extent to which they supported various government programs designed to reduce the gap between the haves and the have-nots. The researchers found large differences among different kinds of leaders. Support for these programs was relatively low among Republican, farm, and

[1]Sidney Verba and Gary R. Orren, *Equality in America: The View from the Top* (Cambridge: Harvard University Press, 1985), p. 53.

business leaders, and relatively high among Democrats, blacks, feminists, and intellectuals. Even among the more liberal groups, however, only a minority endorsed the idea that government should put a top limit on income. Thus, through the interview Verba and Orren were able to document "the view from the top" in precise detail.

Most studies based on interviews, however, use ordinary people as interviewees. Social scientists often need to know what "people" think on any number of topics, ranging from their favorite television program to their views on nuclear disarmament. In the study of influentials cited above, Verba and Orren also sampled the general public so that they could contrast the views of leaders with the public at large. Indeed, studies of the mass public are so common that they have virtually become a hallmark of modern social science.

Whether interviews are conducted with influentials or with ordinary people, researchers have to consider whether interviewees are altogether truthful, and whether their professed beliefs correspond to how they behave in actual situations. On the other hand, researchers have developed techniques to minimize dissembling on the part of interviewees. It is surprising how much people are willing to reveal about themselves, even on very personal matters. Whatever its limitations, the interview is still the best available tool for getting people to talk about themselves.

The need to know what people think has given rise to a whole field of *survey research*. The main feature of a survey is that it is based on a *sample* of a given population. The rationale for sampling is obvious. Since it is usually impossible or too costly to interview all members of a given population, we draw a sample that is a representative cross-section of that population. Representativeness is assured by selecting subjects according to some random procedure. For example, we could obtain a random sample of students at your college by taking every tenth name from the student directory. If the sample is truly representative, it allows the researcher to generalize findings based on the sample to the larger population from which the sample was drawn. Social scientists have perfected sampling techniques to the point that it is possible to predict the outcome of a national election with a high degree of accuracy based on samples of only 2,000 cases.

Many surveys, including most opinion polls, are based on *personal interviews*, conducted face-to-face or by telephone. Because the costs of personal interviews run very high, however, many surveys rely instead on *self-administered questionnaires*. In effect, subjects "interview" themselves by filling out the questionnaire and returning it to the researcher.

The form that questions take is also subject to variation. Most interviews and questionnaires are highly "structured," that is, subjects are offered a set of predetermined answer categories and forced to choose the one that best fits them. For example, a study of religious commitment among students might ask, "On the whole, how religious are you? Would you say very religious, fairly religious, or not too religious?" Studies that rely on structured questions are often criticized for pigeon-holing how people think. As an alternative, less restrictive, open-ended questions are sometimes used that allow subjects to answer in their own words. Thus, one might ask: "On the whole, how religious would you say you are?" This latter technique no doubt produces more varied, interesting, and authentic responses. The disadvantage of open-ended questions, however, is that they do not lend themselves to systematic analysis since responses cannot be easily compared to one another.

There is another genre of studies that employ less structured interviewing techniques, called *depth interviewing*. The point of these studies is *not* to classify and aggregate responses, but as the term suggests, to probe "in depth." Again, either influentials or ordinary people may serve as subjects.

For example, in his study *A Government of Strangers*, Hugh Heclo wanted to learn more about the relations between elected officials and appointed government bureaucrats. He conducted 200 interviews over a four-year period with present and past government executives. Heclo describes his sample as "an unassembled seminar with approximately 200 interviewees as the teachers and me as the student."[2] His modesty is somewhat misleading, however. After all, Heclo did not simply turn on his tape recorder, transcribe the interviews, and publish them as a book. Quite the contrary, he had to know what questions to ask. Then he had to develop a framework for analyzing the interview material. In fact, his book advances a general interpretation of the relation between elected officials and appointed government bureaucrats, and he uses quotations from his subjects only very selectively, to illustrate or document his analysis.

Ordinary people are also used as subjects for depth interviews. Compared to the highly structured questions used in surveys, depth interviews have the advantage of probing beyond the superficial responses elicited by such questions. Especially in psychological studies, depth interviews are useful for exploring the deeper feelings or motives underlying surface attitudes and behavior.

For example, the authors of *The Authoritarian Personality*, published in 1950, combined survey techniques and depth interviewing in order to explore the psychological roots of anti-Semitism. Surveys were used to tap the beliefs and attitudes that people have about Jews and other groups. Then in-depth interviews were used to probe "the deeper layers of the subject's personality."[3] Excerpts from two such interviews follow. The first

[2]Hugh Heclo, *A Government of Strangers* (Washington: The Brookings Institution, 1977), p. 1.

[3]T. W. Adorno and others, *The Authoritarian Personality* (New York: John Wiley & Sons, Inc., 1964), p. 17.

is with Mack, who typifies someone high on prejudice; the second with Larry, who is low on prejudice. The interviewer's questions are in parentheses.[4]

MACK: A MAN HIGH ON PREJUDICE

This subject is a twenty-four-year-old college freshman who intends to study law and hopes eventually to become a corporation lawyer or a criminal lawyer. His grades are B − on the average. His brief sojourn in the Army was terminated by a medical discharge. He is a Methodist, as was his mother, but he does not attend services and says that religion is not important to him. His political party affiliation is, like his father's, Democratic. The subject is of Irish extraction and was born in San Francisco. Both of his parents were born in the United States.

> "My mother comes from an Irish-English-German background. I think of myself as Irish—perhaps because my father is definitely so, and proud of it. . . . I never met an Irishman I didn't like." (What about groups of people you dislike?) "Principally those I don't understand very well. Austrians, the Japanese I never cared for; Filipinos—I don't know—I'd just as soon leave them as have them. Up home there were Austrians and Poles, though I find the Polish people interesting. I have a little dislike for Jewish people. I don't think they are as courteous or as interested in humanity as they ought to be. And I resent that, though I have had few dealings with them. They accent the clannish and the material. It may be my imagination but it seems to me you can see their eyes light up when you hand them a coin. I avoid the Jewish clothiers because they have second-rate stuff. I have to be careful about how I dress. I mean, I buy things so seldom I have to be careful I get good things." (Can you tell that a person is a Jew?) "Sometimes, usually only after I get their ideas." (You mean there are certain ideas which characterize the Jews?) "Yes, to stick together, no matter what; to always be in a group; to have Jewish sororities and Jewish organizations. If a Jew fails in his business, he's helped to get started again. Their attention is directed very greatly toward wealth. Girls at the Jewish sorority house all have fur coats, expensive but no taste. Almost a superiority idea. I resent any show of superiority in people, and I try to keep it down myself. I like to talk with working people." (Do you think they would mingle more if they felt there was no prejudice against them?) "If they would mingle more, there would be more willingness to break down the barriers on the part of other people. Of course, they have always been downtrodden, but that's no reason for resentment."

LARRY: A MAN LOW ON PREJUDICE

This subject is a twenty-eight-year-old college sophomore, a student of business administration, with a B − average. He is of "American" extraction and was born in Chicago. His father owns a café and bar as well as his own

[4]Ibid., pp. 32–39.

home and some other real estate. Like his parents, the subject is a Methodist, though he seldom attends church. He is a Republican, again like his parents.

(What do you think about the minority problem in this country?) "I can say that I haven't any prejudices; I try not to." (Negroes?) "They should be given social equality, any job they are qualified for; should be able to live in any neighborhood, and so on. When I was young, I may have had prejudices, but since the war I've been reading about the whole world . . . I believe in life, liberty, and the pursuit of happiness for all . . . Racial and economic questions are at the root of the war. I don't believe in the suppression of anyone. I think the Japs are taken off the coast for undemocratic reasons. It's just that a lot of people wanted their farms and businesses. There was no democratic reason for it. The segregation of one nationality just leads to more segregation, and it gets worse. The discrimination toward Negroes is because they aren't understood and because they are physically different. Towards Jews it's because of their business ability—the fear that they'll take over business control of the country. There should be education in Negro history, for instance, the part Negroes have played in the development of the country; and education in the history of other minorities, too. How the Jews came to be persecuted, and why some of them are successful."

The researchers do not just present these case studies, but go on to analyze them in terms of broader issues. Here is a brief excerpt:

Mack rejects a variety of ethnic groups. And Larry, for his part is opposed to all such "prejudice." The first question for research, then, would be: Is it generally true that a person who rejects one minority group tends to reject all or most of them? Or, is it to be found more frequently that there is a tendency to have a special group against which most of the individual's hostility is directed? . . . Is the tendency, found in Mack but not in Larry, to make a rigid distinction between the ingroup and the outgroup, common in the population at large? Are Mack's ways of thinking about groups—rigid categories, always placing blame on the outgroup, and so forth—typical of ethnocentric individuals?[5]

These case studies point up both the advantages and limitations of depth interviewing. On the one hand, Mack and Larry are living examples of individuals who are high and low on prejudice. The reader sees them as whole people, and gets a sense of how their attitudes toward minorities reflect broader personality trends. On the other hand, we do not know to what extent Mack and Larry are typical or representative of the population at large. Indeed, this is why the authors of The Authoritarian Personality used in-depth interviews as a basis for generating ideas and questions that were then pursued through a general population survey.

Because surveys are so prevalent in the social sciences, we have chosen one for the sample essay in this chapter. The population under

[5]Ibid., p. 45.

study is the student body at Douglass College, a branch of Rutgers, the State University of New Jersey, that admits only women. The researcher, Ann Parelius, wanted to gauge the extent to which the new generation of college women have changed their "sex-role expectations"—that is, their conceptions of the appropriate roles of men and women with respect to family and career. In order to measure change, Parelius drew two samples, one in 1969, the other in 1973. Subjects were selected at random, and the research instrument was a self-administered questionnaire. When reading the results of this study, ask yourself how the women at your college would compare to the women at Douglass College in 1973.

Emerging Sex-Role Attitudes, Expectations, and Strains Among College Women*

Ann P. Parelius

Questionnaire data are used to assess the attitudes of female college students toward various dimensions of their adult sex roles, their perceptions of men's attitudes toward women's roles, the degree to which these attitudes and perceptions have changed between 1969 and 1973, and the possibility that strains are arising with these changes. A marked shift toward feminism was found in the women's attitudes, but little change occurred in their perception of men as relatively conservative. Strains may be developing as more women adopt attitudes which they believe men reject.

[1] In spite of general agreement that sex-role attitudes and expectations are changing, little is actually known about the specific dimensions, extent, or consequences of this change. A perusal of the sex-role literature suggests several themes. First, sex-role behavior, as measured by women's participation in the workforce, has changed radically over the last few decades. Second, although some sex-role attitudes have apparently shifted, others, such as those toward women working while their children are still young, have remained remarkably stable (Mason and Bumpass, 1973). Third, many women have experienced considerable anxiety as they have been caught between conflicting normative definitions of appropriate sex-role behavior (Horner,

*Reprinted by permission of the author and the National Council on Family Relations from Ann P. Parelius, "Emerging Sex-Role Attitudes, Expectations, and Strains Among College Women," Journal of Marriage and the Family, 37 (February 1975), 146–53.

1969). Fourth, at least part of this anxiety has been traced to the relatively persistent belief that men want only "extremely nurturant and traditional" females (Steinmann and Fox, 1969; and Rapoport et al., 1970).

[2] The sex-role literature from which these themes are drawn is limited in several respects, however. Most of the currently available studies were done too early to tap the influence of the Women's Liberation Movement. Few studies have documented change with longitudinal data, and much of the research has focused on populations least likely to evidence changes in sex-role orientations (Millman, 1971). Consequently, both the extent to which sex-role expectations are changing and the degree to which such changes are generating strain may be grossly underestimated.

THE PRESENT STUDY

[3] This study assesses women's attitudes toward various dimensions of their adult sex roles, their perceptions of men's attitudes toward women's roles, the degree to which these attitudes and perceptions have changed over the last four years, and the possibility that strains are arising with these changes. The subjects were students attending Douglass College, a state-supported women's college in New Jersey. As a women's college, Douglass was especially sensitive to the Women's Liberation Movement, offering numerous courses and activities related to women's issues. These students, exposed to the Movement while still relatively free to experiment with new life-styles and identities, should reflect generously

the impact of changing sex-role attitudes and perceptions.[1]

The Sample

[4] Two independent random samples of the entire student body were selected, one in 1969, and another in 1973. The first sample consisted of 175 women; 147 (84 percent) returned completed questionnaires. The second sample consisted of 250 women; 200 (80 percent) returned completed questionnaires.

The Instrument

[5] The instrument consisted of a Likert-type questionnaire. The items were short "descriptions of various women," each expressing either a "feminist" or a "traditional" orientation toward sex-role behavior. Traditional orientations suggest that a woman's primary purpose is to marry, bear children, and spend most of her time in the home doing housework and childrearing tasks. Feminist orientations stress equality between the sexes, encouraging women to develop talents and pursue careers. Within marriage, feminist orientations give both partners an equal share of financial and domestic responsibilities.

[6] Each subject read the descriptions and indicated whether or not she was "just like" the women described in each. The women then went over the same items and indicated whether or not men would "want to marry a woman" like the one described. The answer to each question was given on a five-point scale with "yes" and "no" marking the extremes. Examples of the descriptions can be seen in Table 1.

[1]We will not be able to attribute attitudinal change specifically to exposure to the Women's Liberation Movement. We are merely arguing that this particular sample is likely to be in the forefront of those evolving new gender-role expectations.

Table 1.   Percent Giving Feminist Responses and Percent Believing that Men Would Want
to Marry a Feminist, 1969 and 1973

Descriptive Item	Feminist Responses		Belief that Men Would Want to Marry a Feminist	
	1969	1973	1969	1973
Work and Finances	%	%	%	%
Believes that a wife's career is of equal importance to her husband's.	49	81	20	31
Believes that both spouses should contribute equally to the financial support of the family.	37	65	27	45
Intends to work all her adult life.	29	60	15	32
Division of Labor in the Home Does not expect to do all the household tasks herself.*	56	83	18	24
Expects her husband to help with the housework.	47	77	14	28
Expects her husband to do 50% of all household and childrearing tasks.	17	43	10	10
Marital and Maternal Role Supremacy Does not think the most important thing for a woman is to be a good wife and mother.*	31	62	8	9
Would marry only if it did not interfere with her career.	10	22	8	13
Would forego children if they would interfere with her career.	17	28	7	8
	(N = 147)	(N = 200)	(N = 147)	(N = 200)

*These questions were actually phrased in the affirmative; a negative answer was considered to be a feminist response.

Analysis

[7] The nine items selected for analysis covered three central issues: (1) women's work patterns and financial responsibilities, (2) the division of labor in the home, and (3) the importance of marital and maternal roles relative to other goals a woman might have. For purposes of analysis, the responses in the two boxes at either end of each scale were combined. The responses were then classified as either "feminist" or "traditional." A response was defined as "feminist" if the subject indicated that she was "just like" the woman in a "feminist" description or "not like" the woman in a "traditional" description. All other responses were defined as "traditional." The perceptual data were treated in a similar manner. Subjects who indicated that men "would want to marry" a woman "just like" the one in a feminist description or that men "would not" want to marry a woman "just like" the one in a traditional description were regarded as perceiving men as accepting of feminism. All other subjects were regarded as perceiving men to be rejecting of feminism.

FINDINGS

Sex-Role Orientations, 1969 and 1973

[8] The first two columns of Table 1 indicate the sex-role orientations of the two samples. Looking first at the women of 1969, it is evident that on all but three items, only a minority gave feminist responses. On the remaining items, believing that "a wife's career is of equal importance to her husband's," not expecting to "do all household tasks alone," and expecting husband's "help with the housework," approximately half of the sample gave feminist responses. The women were especially conservative on the two items involving a choice between occupational success and the traditional roles of wife and mother. Only 17 percent "would forego children" for the sake of occupational success, and only 10 percent "would marry only if it did not interfere" with their careers. The item suggesting a fifty-fifty division of labor also evoked only 17 percent in feminist responses.

[9] Turning to the women of 1973, we see that the percentages giving feminist responses increased by approximately 30 points on seven of the nine items. The two items positing a choice between occupational success and familial roles showed much smaller shifts, only about 10 percentage points each.

[10] These data suggest that a substantial shift toward feminism occurred between 1969 and 1973. The 1973 sample was more strongly oriented toward occupational activity and more supportive of equal rights and duties for both sexes than the 1969 sample. Only a minority of either sample would forego marriage or motherhood in order to maximize occupational success, but a much greater percentage of the 1973 sample denied that marriage and motherhood were a woman's most important goals. The 1973 women also took their economic responsibilities more seriously and expected help if not absolute equality in the division of labor in the home.

Perception of Male Attitudes, 1969 and 1973

[11] Turning to the last two columns of Table 1 and looking first at the 1969 sample, it is clear that few women believed that men wanted to marry feminists. This was particularly true when questions of marital and maternal role supremacy were involved. Fewer than 10 percent of the women believed that men would want to marry women who expressed feminist views on any of the three items relevant to this issue. Men were perceived as most willing to accept feminism in the area of work and finances, especially when it involved a wife contributing equally to the financial support of the family. On this item, 27 percent of the women believed that men would want to marry women with feminist perspectives.

[12] Turning to 1973, we find that few major changes occurred in the women's perception of men's attitudes. Only four items showed a shift of 10 percentage points or more, with the 1973 sample perceiving men to be more ready to marry feminists in all four cases. The greatest and most consistent change occurred in the area of work and finances, where all three items shifted towards greater perceived acceptance of feminism.

[13] These data suggest that the women in both samples tended to view men as basically traditional in

their sex-role orientations. Men were perceived as most likely to accept feminism when it involved women sharing the financial responsibilities normally shouldered by the man alone. Men were seen as less accepting of feminism when it involved recognizing their wives' careers as of equal importance to their own, accepting a wife's working all her adult life, or assuming household responsibilities. Men were seen as most conservative on issues of marital and maternal role supremacy, where women's occupational interests might challenge their primary commitment to home and family.

[14] Comparing the women's own sex-role orientations to their perception of men, it is clear that in both samples women were much more likely to express feminist perspectives than they were to believe that men wanted women with these perspectives. This tendency is particularly strong in the 1973 sample. Thus, many of the women sampled probably had attitudes which they believed men would reject in a potential spouse. . . .

SUMMARY AND CONCLUSIONS

[15] A comparison of the two samples indicated that sizeable shifts toward feminism occurred between 1969 and 1973. These shifts appeared among women who were attending college during this period as well as among those who were just entering as freshmen. Attitudes toward work, financial responsibilities, and the division of labor in the home showed the greatest amount of change. By 1973, a majority of those sampled believed

that their careers were of equal importance to their husbands' and that they should share equally in the financial support of their families. They also expected to work all of their adult lives and to have substantial help from their husbands with household chores. Attitudes toward the importance of marital and maternal roles changed also, but to a lesser degree. Although the majority of women in the 1973 sample denied that "the most important thing for a woman is to be a good wife and mother," few would sacrifice marriage or motherhood for occupational success. The far-reaching changes observed in the women's attitudes and expectations were not accompanied by equal shifts in their perceptions of men's willingness to marry feminist women. . . .

[16] The combined effect of the shifts in the women's own attitudes and the relative stability of their perception of men was to increase the proportion of women holding views which they did not believe men would accept in a wife. Since most of these women were still interested in marriage and motherhood, many were probably experiencing considerable anxiety about their futures.

[17] These findings suggest several conclusions about emerging trends in sex-role definitions. First, it is clear that these definitions are shifting rapidly, at least among some segments of our population. Young women, such as those studied here, are rejecting the economic dependence and unalleviated household responsibilities of the traditional wife-mother role. Yet, these women remain basically positive about both marriage and motherhood. They reject neither men nor children. Their

goals imply a restructuring of the family, but not its dissolution.

[18] We do not yet know the extent to which new sex-role definitions are being accepted by various segments of American society nor the various forms in which these new definitions can be found. Research is needed on individuals at all stages of the life cycle, on both sexes, and all racial and ethnic groups. But in addition, research is needed on the behavioral consequences of changing sex-role orientations. Attitudes are not necessarily expressed in behavior (Teevan, 1972) and attitudinal shifts which occur on campus sometimes revert to previous patterns once students leave the college environment. This is especially true when attitudes are not widely supported by individuals' reference groups and peers. It is possible, therefore, that these women will leave college to live relatively traditional lives.

[19] It is more likely, however, that these women will lead lives that differ from the traditional pattern. First, behavior has already begun to change. The median age at first marriage is rising, the birth rate is declining and women are pressing for equality. Second, there is considerable social support available now for women who are adopting feminist perspectives. Women's centers, communes, consciousness-raising groups, literature, and organizations extoll the virtues of feminist lifestyles and provide some of the structure within which these lifestyles might be realized. With such support, attitude shifts which occur at college can become remarkably stable (Newcomb, 1967). Third, women seem ready to maintain feminist attitudes in spite of perceived male rejection of these attitudes.

[20] Research is needed in order to determine what proportions of American women are in fact experiencing strain and anxiety as sex-role definitions change. What is the effect of such strains on other dimensions of women's lives? If many women wish to marry in spite of having attitudes which they believe men reject, how do they expect to resolve this dilemma? Will young women increasingly put off marriage, waiting for a man who they regard as "exceptional" to appear? Will young women become increasingly hesitant to commit themselves to marriage at all? And what about men? Research is desperately needed on male sex-role attitudes and expectations. If male attitudes are changing in the same direction and as rapidly as those of females, new patterns of family life will surely emerge. This would take time, of course, and will be delayed if women stereotype men as more conservative than they actually are. If male attitudes are remaining rigidly traditional, or if they are lagging substantially behind female attitudes, however, increased marital instability and strain between the sexes may result. In the long run, though, this strain will dissipate. Research (cf. Axelson, 1963, and Meier, 1972) has already shown that the husbands of working wives and the sons of working mothers are more positive toward sexual equality than are the spouses and children of traditional women. In time, with increasing numbers of wives and mothers entering the workforce, most men and women will stand together as spouses and parents, but also as equals.

REFERENCES

Axelson, Leland
  1963   "The marital adjustment and role definitions of husbands of working and nonworking wives." *Journal of Marriage and the Family*, 25 (2):189–195.

Festinger, Leon
  1957   *The Theory of Cognitive Dissonance*. New York: Harper and Row.

Horner, Matina
  1969   "Fail: bright women." *Psychology Today*, 3 (6):36–41.

Mason, Karen Oppenheim and Larry L. Bumpass
  1973   "Women's sex-role attitudes in the United States, 1970." Revision of a paper presented at the annual meetings of the American Sociological Association (August, 1973).

Meier, Harold C.
  1972   "Mother-centeredness and college youths' attitudes toward social equality for women: some empirical findings." *Journal of Marriage and the Family*, 34 (1): 115–121.

Millman, Marcia
  1971   "Observations on sex-role research." *Journal of Marriage and the Family*, 33 (4): 772–776.

Newcomb, Theodore M. et al.
  1967   *Persistence and Change: Bennington College and its Students After Twenty-Five Years*. New York: Wiley.

Rapaport, Alan F., David Payne, and Anne Steinmann
  1970   "Perceptual differences between married and single college women for the concepts of self, ideal woman, and man's ideal women." *Journal of Marriage and the Family*, 32 (3): 441–442.

Steinmann, Anne and David J. Fox
  1969   "Specific areas of agreement and conflict in women's self-perception and their perception of men's ideal woman in two South American communities and an urban community in the United States." *Journal of Marriage and the Family*, 31 (2):281–289.

Teevan, James J., Jr.
  1972   "Reference groups and premarital sexual behavior." *Journal of Marriage and the Family*, 34 (2):283–291.

CRITICAL ANALYSIS: CONTENT

Parelius frames her study against the background of the conventional wisdom with respect to the women's liberation movement. She concedes that there is "general agreement" that sex-role attitudes and expectations are changing, but as a social scientist she wants to scrutinize these changes more closely, and to reach a clearer and more precise understanding of the nature, extent, and consequences of these changes.

Questions

After a review of the social science literature on changing sex roles, Parelius offers a clear statement of purpose for her own study:

This study assesses women's attitudes toward various dimensions of their adult sex roles, their perceptions of men's attitudes toward women's roles, the degree to which these attitudes and perceptions have changed over the last four years, and the possibility that strains are arising with these changes. [paragraph 3]

Implicitly, this statement of purpose contains a series of questions:

1. How does the present generation of college women view adult sex roles?
2. How do they perceive men's attitudes toward "the new woman"?
3. To what extent have these attitudes and perceptions changed over the last four years?
4. Are the changes in women's self-definitions producing "strains" in their relations with men?

Evidence

Parelius attempts to answer these questions through a survey of women at Douglass College. To measure change she sent questionnaires to a representative sample of women in 1969 and then repeated this in 1973. In her analysis she compares responses on a series of questions pertaining to women's role. The survey produced two basic findings:

1. The percentage of women giving "feminist responses" to questions regarding gender, family, and work increased dramatically between 1969 and 1973. For example, in 1969 only 49 percent of the women said that a wife's career is of equal importance to her husband's, but by 1973 the figure had increased to 81 percent. All nine items showed similar increases in feminist sentiment.

2. On the other hand, perceptions of male attitudes had hardly changed between 1969 and 1973. For example, in both years less than 10 percent of the women thought men would want to marry a woman who did not think the most important thing for a woman is to be a good wife and mother. Yet the percentage of women who rejected this traditional definition of women's role doubled from 31 to 62 percent. Thus, even as women became more feminist they continued to believe that men would not want to marry women with their feminist orientations. Put another way, increasing numbers of women hold views that they do not believe men would accept in a wife.

Answers

Parelius is struck by the fact that "women seem ready to maintain feminist attitudes in spite of perceived male rejection of these attitudes" [paragraph 19]. Since these women typically also want to get married, they are left with a high degree of "role strain." Having carried the analysis to this crucial point, Parelius raises a number of questions that go an interpretive step beyond the actual findings. What, she asks, are the behavioral consequences of changing attitudes? Once these students leave college, will they revert to traditional sex roles, especially as they confront the prospect or reality of marriage? Parelius speculates that it is becoming easier to maintain feminist attitudes since marriage and childbearing are occurring later, and there are more institutional supports for feminist attitudes than there used to be. Still, she argues, role strain is a topic on which research is badly needed. How widespread is role strain? What effect does it have? Will some women avoid marriage, or be unable to find husbands? And what about men? Are attitudes changing? If not, can we expect increased marital instability? Parelius brings her paper to closure with this cluster of questions. In the final two sentences, she offers a tentative answer, speculating that role strain may diminish over time since it has been shown that the husband and sons of working women tend to be more positive toward sexual equality.

CRITICAL ANALYSIS: COMPOSITION

As already indicated, Parelius's article on sex-role attitudes of college women focuses on *change*, specifically a change that she believes has been influenced by the women's liberation movement and the increased participation of women in the workplace. Any study that looks for change has comparison-contrast built into its design. "What it was like before" is compared to "What it is like now." This comparison-contrast approach, then, becomes the principal rhetorical mode.

The Introduction (paragraphs 1 to 3)

Like other writers we have cited, Parelius begins by presenting a common or popular assumption: that sex-role attitudes are changing. In this case, however, she does not take issue with the conventional wisdom. Rather, she argues that there is a need to collect "hard data," not to prove that sex-role attitudes are changing, but to gauge the extent and consequences of this change. Note that her statement of purpose is contained in her very first sentence.

Consistent with the conventions of much academic writing, the first two paragraphs allude to previous research. In her review of the literature, Parelius identifies several themes that will be central to her own study. Paragraph 2 then indicates some ways in which previous studies have been inadequate, thus establishing another rationale for her study.

Paragraph 3 is the transition paragraph that introduces and describes the study. Here she outlines four facets of the research problem that will govern the presentation of the evidence in the body of her paper: (1) attitudes toward sex-roles; (2) perceptions of men's attitudes toward sex-roles; (3) changes in these attitudes over four years; (4) possible strains arising with these changes.

The Body Paragraphs (paragraphs 4 to 14)

The body paragraphs of this article present the details of the survey under a series of headings and subheadings:

"The Sample" (the population surveyed)
"The Instrument" (the questionnaire)
"Findings" (observations based on the responses)
"Summary and Conclusions" (an overall statement about the findings)

The heading "Findings" has two subheadings which not only organize the presentation but also highlight the key comparisons:

"Sex-Role Orientations, 1969 and 1973" (changes in what women think)
"Perception of Male Attitudes, 1969 and 1973" (changes in what women believe men think)

To make matters more complicated, these two changes are then analyzed in relation to each other. To deal with this complexity, a tight organizational format is needed.

Below is a paragraph outline of the "Findings" section. Note that (1) the two subheadings are parallel in construction, and (2) each paragraph begins with a general statement or topic sentence that unifies the various facts and observations within the paragraph.

I. Sex-Role Orientations, 1969 and 1973
   A. Attitudes of women toward sex roles in 1969
      1. General statement: "Looking first at the women of 1969, it is evident that . . . only a minority gave feminist responses."
      2. Specific observations substantiating general statement
   B. Attitudes of women toward sex roles in 1973
      1. General statement: "Turning to the women of 1973, we see that the percentages giving feminist responses increased . . ."
      2. Specific observations substantiating general statement
   C. General statement comparing the two samples: "These data suggest that a substantial shift toward feminism occurred between 1969 and 1973."

II. Perception of Male Attitudes, 1969 and 1973
   A. Women's perception of male attitudes in 1969: ". . . looking first at the 1969 sample, it is clear that few women believed that men wanted to marry feminists."
   B. Women's perceptions of male attitudes in 1973: "Turning to 1973, we find that few major changes occurred in the women's perception of men's attitudes."
   C. General statement comparing the two samples: "These data suggest that the women in both samples tended to view men as basically traditional. . . ."

III: Summary Statement and Inference: Comparing Women's Sex-Role Orientations to their Perceptions of Men ("Thus many of the women sampled [in 1973] probably had attitudes which they believed men would reject in a potential spouse.")

The method for organizing the final comparison is whole-subject by whole-subject rather than point by point. In other words, women's attitudes on the whole are compared to women's perceptions of men's attitudes on the whole.

Note that paragraph 14 functions as a transition and begins to compare the two subsections. It concludes with a general but pointed observation that is then further developed in the conclusion: ". . . many of the women sampled probably had attitudes which they believed men would reject in a potential spouse."

The final heading is "Summary and Conclusions." To be precise, the first two paragraphs (15 and 16) constitute a summary, while the next four paragraphs (17 to 20) constitute the conclusion. Note the transitional sentence: "These findings suggest several conclusions."

The Conclusion (paragraphs 17 to 20)

The conclusion goes beyond a restatement of the findings. Parelius is clearly interested in looking at the overall picture. Sex-role definitions are shifting rapidly in some segments of the population. However, the values that young women reject are qualified by the values they continue to hold. This general observation leads to an equally broad inference about what these values mean for the family as an institution: "Their goals imply a restructuring of the family, but not its dissolution" [paragraph 17].

In the remainder of the conclusion, Parelius explores the implications of her findings for the family and for American society as a whole. Like much scholarly writing, this article ends with some suggestions for further research.

RHETORICAL STANCE: PERSUADING THE READER

Clarity is a goal for all writing, one not easily achieved when writing is based on quantitative research. All too often the data are ambiguous, confusing, and even contradictory. The challenge for the researcher-writer is to sift through the data, discerning patterns that are clear and consistent, and as a next step, to organize this material into a cogent argument. Like Parelius, you will need to begin with the "raw data," making connections between categories and forming generalizations out of these connections.

For example, Parelius often deals with clusters of items at a time (as in paragraph 12: "Turning to 1973, we find that few major changes occurred in the women's perception of men's attitudes. Only four items showed a shift . . ."). Her aim is always to locate trends that will help to answer the primary research question: How are women's sex-role expectations changing, and are such changes generating strain?

Organization

A simple device for achieving clarity is the use of headings and subheadings—the social scientist's trademark. The headings divide the discussion into discrete sections that function as signposts for the reader. Under the major heading "Findings," for example, the subheadings highlight the two categories that are to be compared and contrasted. This visual distinction is useful in helping the reader to grasp the difference between categories.

Another device for clarifying the data in terms of the argument is a clear hierarchy of ideas. In this case Parelius moves from specific observations of patterns in the responses to general inferences about what these patterns might mean, always in terms of the research question and hypothesis. Note the increasing generalization as we move through the essay:

> Comparisons between 1969 and 1973 indicate a substantial shift toward feminist conceptions of sex-roles.
>
> There is no comparable shift, however, in women's perceptions of men's sex-role orientations.
>
> As a result, many of the women embrace roles which they believe men would reject in a potential spouse.
>
> Since most of these women are still interested in marriage and motherhood, presumably many are experiencing intense anxiety about their futures.
>
> Since women increasingly want equality as well as marriage and motherhood, this may lead to a restructuring of the family.

Each of these statements grows out of the previous one, leading to the conclusion that changes in sex-role attitudes among women are producing anxiety in women, as well as strain between the sexes.

In rhetorical terms this is an example of cause-effect analysis. The causal factor is that women have different attitudes than they believe men have. The effect is role strain.

Language

This article was written for a professional journal and conforms to the conventions of academic writing: an abstract precedes the article; distinct sections describe the research design, sum up the findings, and argue the conclusions; appropriate tables present the raw data. Yet the actual writing is relatively free of jargon. Given the intended audience (professional social scientists), Parelius cannot be faulted for assuming familiarity with such terms as "sex roles," "division of labor," and "longitudinal data." However, she is careful to define the two terms that are at the heart of her study: "traditional" and "feminist":

> Traditional orientations suggest that a woman's primary purpose is to marry, bear children, and spend most of her time in the home doing housework and childrearing tasks. Feminist orientations stress equality between the sexes, encouraging women to develop talents and pursue careers. Within marriage, feminist orientations give both partners an equal share of financial and domestic responsibilities. [paragraph 5]

Precisely because "traditional" and "feminist" are popular terms and subject to many meanings, Parelius did well to define exactly how they would be employed within the context of her study.

As we suggested earlier, quantitative studies do not lend themselves to a rich and imaginative prose style. The paramount goal is clarity. In this case Parelius is skillful at communicating her findings to her audience within the scientific community.

SUGGESTIONS FOR WRITING AND THINKING

1. Conduct in-depth interviews with two female students, one of whom might be described as a "feminist," the other as "traditional" with respect to women's role. On the basis of the issues raised in Parelius's article, explore their sex-role attitudes. You might also explore the experiences and emotions that accompany these attitudes.

    When writing up your interviews, first develop a context or framework for presenting your interview material. For example, like Parelius, you might discuss recent changes in the prevailing definition regarding women's role. Then state the rationale for doing in-depth interviews. That is, indicate why these are worth doing and what you hope to learn. In the introduction to your paper, you should either present a hypothesis or suggest the major finding that emerges from the interviews. In other words, you need a clear thesis statement that organizes the presentation. Finally, introduce your subjects and present your findings.

    This last step—the presentation of findings—can be executed in at least two different ways. Like the interviews with Mack and Larry in this chapter, you might simply present an edited version of the interview. By "edited version," we mean that you should improve the readability of the interview—for example, by deleting unnecessary repetition, unfruitful digressions, or answers that run on too long. Once you have presented the interviews themselves, develop your analysis of the results, leading to one or more conclusions.

    As an alternative to an edited transcription, develop one or more themes that are suggested by the interview, and that focus on areas of similarity or difference between your two subjects. For example, you could focus on the sexual division of labor in the household. Do your subjects think that women should be responsible for most of the household tasks? How would they deal with an uncompromising male? Weave relevant quotations from your interviews into the text, in order to highlight, illustrate, and document the particular forms that "feminist" and "traditional" attitudes take, as represented by your two subjects.

2. This exercise involves a survey of sex-role attitudes among women at your college. The questionnaire should consist of the ten items in Table 1 of Parelius's study. These can be framed as questions. (For example: Do you think that a wife's career is of equal importance to her hus-

band's?) To simplify matters, do not ask interviewees about their perceptions of men.

If this exercise is conducted as a class project, then each student should interview ten undergraduate women. At the next class, collate the results. That is, tally up the number of students who gave "feminist" responses to each question, and compute the percentage. Now create a table modeled after the one in Parelius's article, showing the percentages who gave a feminist response to each question in Parelius's 1969 sample, her 1973 sample, and your current sample. The table should be constructed as follows:

	Feminist Responses		
	Douglass		My College
Sex-Role Attitudes	1969	1973	Today
A wife's career is as important as her husband's	49%	81%	
Both spouses should contribute equally to the financial support of the family	37	65	
Etc.			

Now you are ready to "write up the results." In doing so, you should first develop a context for your study. For example, you could argue a need to update Parelius's findings, since they are somewhat dated. Or you might say that you wish to contrast the level of feminist sentiment at your college with what Parelius found at Douglass College in 1973. (What is your initial hunch—that your college will be even more feminist than Douglass College or less so? Why?)

Present your findings as they relate to the questions raised at the outset of your study. Discuss areas of similarity and difference between Parelius's findings and your own. Do you think that differences exist because women at your college are different from those that attended Douglass College? Or do you think that differences exist because times have changed? Bring your paper to a logical conclusion.

3. This exercise is identical to the previous one, except that males at your college will be interviewed instead of females. In some cases you will have to reword the question. (For example: Do *you* expect to do 50 percent of all household and childrearing tasks?) Questions 3, 8, and 9 should either be deleted or rephrased. After you have tallied the results and constructed a table modeled after the one in Parelius's article, develop your analysis of the findings.

4. Read "What Professors Think about Student Protest and Manners, Morals, Politics and Chaos on the Campus," by Seymour Martin Lipset and Everett Carl Ladd, Jr., published in *Psychology Today*, 4 (November 1970), pp. 49ff. The article is based on surveys of faculty and student

opinion that were conducted in 1969 at the height of the student activism on the nation's campuses.

Analyze the article in terms of the questions-evidence-answers schema. Then analyze the article in terms of its rhetorical strategy. What is the authors' thesis regarding faculty opinion and student activism? How do the authors organize the presentation of their findings? Is the article persuasive?

INTERVIEW STUDIES ACROSS THE DISCIPLINES

Anthropology

ZAVELLA, PATRICIA, "Abnormal Intimacy: The Varying Work Networks of Chicana Cannery Workers," *Feminist Studies*, 11 (Fall 1983), 541–47. On the basis of in-depth interviews with Chicana women employed in canneries in Santa Clara Valley, California, the author explores the nature of work networks and how they operate within women's private lives.

Economics

HORVATH, FRANCIS W., "Work At Home: New Findings From the Current Population Survey," *Monthly Labor Review*, 109 (November 1986), 31–35. The article summarizes the results of a recent government survey that found that more than 8 million Americans worked at home in 1985. The most common category was services, ranging from consulting to child care.

History

STAHL WEINBERG, SYDNEY, "The World of Our Mothers: Family, Work, and Education in the Lives of Jewish Immigrant Women," *Frontiers*, VII, no. 1 (1983), 71–79. This article is based on oral histories with forty immigrant Jewish women who arrived in this country between 1901 and 1924. The focus of the interviews was on family, work, and education, and the role that each played in the adjustment to life in America.

Political Science

LANE, ROBERT E., "The Fear of Equality," *American Political Science Review*, 53 (1959), 35–51. On the basis of interviews with working-class men in New Haven, the author explores how people who themselves have low status rationalize inequality, and actually fear a more egalitarian society.

Psychology

BART, PAULINE B., "Mother Portnoy's Complaints," *Trans-action*, 8 (November-December 1970), 69–74. The author conducted intensive interviews with twenty clinically depressed middle-aged women in psychiatric hospitals. A common pattern was that these women adhered to an exaggerated version of "supermother," and as their children reached maturity, had great trouble dealing with maternal role loss.

Sociology

HIRSCHI, TRAVIS, and RODNEY STARK, "Hellfire and Delinquency," *Social Problems*, 17 (Fall 1969), 202–13. On the basis of a survey of over 4000 junior- and senior-high school students in a California community, the authors found that religious devotion, including fears of "hellfire and damnation," seemed to have little effect as a deterrent to delinquency.

Selections taken from:
Writing Research Papers in the Social Sciences
by James D. Lester and James D. Lester, Jr.

1 Writing from Research

A t some point you will write a fully developed research report based on your investigations and reading. This text gives complete coverage of the process of report writing in the social sciences and the techniques for meeting the demands of form and style. Here are examples of such reports:

- A report based on interviews with minimum wage workers.
- A field report on a speed reading unit in a fifth-grade class to test reading comprehension.
- An observation of student drivers on campus parking lots, with a subsequent report.

These papers require investigation followed by a report on the nature of the project, the methods employed, the results of the study, and the implications to be drawn from the findings. Papers similar to these will appear on your assignment syllabus during your first two years of college, and the writing assignments will increase in frequency in upper-division courses. This text lessens the pressure by showing you how to conduct research in the field, in the library, and on the Internet. It also demonstrates the correct methods for designing the paper and documenting your reports.

Keep in mind that social science research is used in different ways, in different amounts, and for different purposes as instructors make demands on your talents of investigation into social issues and your ability to write reports. This text therefore introduces research as an engaging, sometimes exciting pursuit on several fronts—the lab, the field, the library, the Internet, the control group in a classroom, and so forth.

1a Why Do Research?

Instructors ask you to report on your investigations for several reasons:

Research teaches methods of discovery. It asks you to discover what you know about a topic and what others can teach you. Beyond reading articles and books, writing in the social sciences usually requires you to observe and experiment. The process tests your curiosity as you probe a complex subject to confirm a hypothesis, which is a theory requiring testing to prove its validity. For example, the hypothesis "A child's toy is determined by television

1

commercials" requires an investigation of the literature as well as a survey of parents, your observation of children at a toy store, or your interview with a set of children (see pages 4–5 for more information about writing a hypothesis). You will learn to make a claim, research it carefully, and synthesize your ideas and discoveries with the knowledge and opinions of others.

Research teaches investigative skills. Your success will depend on your negotiating various sources of information taken from reference books in the library and computer databases to an observation of schoolchildren and interviews with their teachers. As you conduct research by observation, interviews, surveys, and laboratory experiments, you will gain experience in additional methods of investigation.

Research teaches critical thinking. As you examine the evidence on your subject, you will learn to discriminate between useful information and unfounded opinion, and between ill-conceived experiments and reliable evidence. Some sources, such as those on the Internet, may provide timely, reliable material, but they may also entice you with worthless and undocumented opinions.

Research teaches logic. Like a judge in the courtroom, you must make perceptive judgments about the issues surrounding a specific topic. Your discussion at the end of the report will be based on your findings and the insights you can offer. Your readers will rely on your logical response to your reading, observation, interviews, and testing.

Research teaches the basic ingredients of argument. You will be asked to discuss the implications of your findings. You should, in most cases, advance a hypothesis and then prove or disprove it. For example, if you argue that "nonverbal communication can reveal personality traits to an experienced psychologist," you will learn to anticipate

> Note: For help with making a claim and establishing a hypothesis, see 1d, pages 3–4.

challenges to your hypothesis and defend it with your evidence.

1b   Learning to Write Citations for Your Sources

Research reports in the social sciences must follow certain conventions to give uniformity to articles written by millions of scholars; in like manner, the rules must govern your written assignments in psychology, sociology, education, political science, social work, and similar fields.

Governed by guidelines from the *American Psychological Association,* this format employs the *name and year system,* which asks you to provide the last name of your source followed immediately by the year, set within parentheses. Page numbers should be added if the citation includes a quotation.

Roberts (2004) found significant variations in timed responses by participants.

Details of the source are presented in a references list at the end of the paper. A reference entry looks like this:

Roberts, R. C. (2004). Timed responses of fifth graders to flash cards.

Education News, 15, 14–19.

This system is explained fully in later chapters.

1c Learning the Variations in Form and Content

You may choose among three types of articles, or your instructor will specify one of these:

- The theoretical article.
- The report of empirical study.
- The review article.

Theoretical Article

The theoretical article draws on existing research to examine a theory. This type of paper is the one you will most likely write as a freshman or soph-

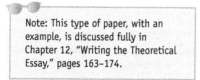

Note: This type of paper, with an example, is discussed fully in Chapter 12, "Writing the Theoretical Essay," pages 163–174.

omore. You will trace the development of a theory, compare theories, or discuss the controversy surrounding a theory. Your analysis will examine the literature to arrive at the current thinking on topics such as autism, criminal behavior, dys-

functional families, and learning disorders. The theoretical article generally accomplishes four aims:

1. Identifies a problem or theory that has historical implications in the scientific community.
2. Traces the development and history of the theory.
3. Provides a systematic analysis of articles that explore the problem.
4. Arrives at a judgment and discussion of the prevailing theory.

Report of an Empirical Study

When you conduct field research and perform laboratory testing, you must report the details of your original research. The empirical report accomplishes four purposes:

1. Introduces the problem or hypothesis investigated and explains the purpose of the work.

2. Describes the method used to conduct the research, including the design, procedures, tools, subjects, and so forth.

> Note: This type of paper, with an example, is discussed fully in Chapter 13, "Writing the Report of Empirical Research," pages 175–190.

3. Reports the results and the basic findings with tables and charts as necessary.

4. Discusses, interprets, and explores the implications of the findings.

Review Article

You may be required to write a critical evaluation of a published article, an entire book, or a set of articles on a common topic. The purpose of the review is to examine the state of current research to determine whether additional work is in order. A review article accomplishes four goals:

1. Defines the problem to clarify the issue or hypothesis.
2. Summarizes the article or book under review.

> Note: This type of paper, with an example, is discussed fully in Chapter 14, "Writing the Review of Literature," pages 191–200.

3. Analyzes the state of research to discover strengths and possible weaknesses or inconsistencies.

4. Recommends additional research that might grow logically from the work under review.

1d   Understanding the Scientific Terminology

Assignments in education, psychology, political science, and the other social sciences will usually require *analysis, definition, comparison,* or a search for *precedents* leading to a *proposal.* Your questions, theories, and hypotheses will motivate your work. Your experiments and testing will usually require a discussion of the *implications* of your findings. Therefore, you should understand the terms buried in the assignment, as explained here.

Theory and Hypothesis

Many scientific investigations begin with a theoretical question. This question is then stated as an assumption that serves as the hypothesis for the research project. The hypothesis is a prediction based on data that directs the research being done. Hence, a hypothesis is a prediction. It is the researcher's supposition or idea about the possible connection or relationship between variables.

Theoretical Question: Do students who live on campus have higher GPAs?
Hypothesis: Students who live on campus have higher GPAs.

This hypothesis is the researcher's idea and calls for research to prove or disprove the statement. In short, a hypothesis is a prediction about the outcome of the study. Briefly, a good research hypothesis has certain elements you can understand:

- It is a brief, clear declarative sentence.
- It often answers a question you are curious about.
- It usually offers an expected relationship, as shown above with students and their grade point averages.
- It implies that the statement can be tested for positive or negative results.

The driving force in social science writing is this system of assumptions that require research to prove or disprove various theories. Section 2e shows you how to frame a working theory or hypothesis and clarifies the differences in the basic forms.

Evaluation

To write a review article, you must evaluate the work in question with clear criteria of judgment. You then explain how the subject meets or fails to meet these criteria. For example, you may face one of these assignments:

- Evaluate the credibility of ACT scores in forecasting academic success.
- Evaluate a distance learning program for home-schooled children.
- Evaluate online therapy for persons with depression.
- Discuss the merits of medication for children with Attention Deficit Hyperactive Disorder (ADHD).

In many ways, every research paper is an evaluation. These few examples just scratch the surface of millions of topics.

Interpretation

To interpret, you must usually answer, "What does it mean?" You may be asked to examine a point of law, offer implications on test results, or interpret variations in scores. Questions often point toward interpretation:

What is Asperger's Syndrome?
What are the implications of anxiety in children?
What do these statistics on children and television violence tell us?
Can you explain your readings on dyslexia to others?

One student, writing about student success, found herself asking interpretive questions: Does joining a Greek letter organization increase the probability that a student will graduate? Does participation in a weekly study group improve student academic achievement in that course?

Definition

An extended definition shows that your subject fits into a selected and well-defined category. Note these examples:

Topic: Computers and Internet Addiction
You will need to define *addictive behavior* at the computer and discuss it from a psychological perspective.

Topic: Peer Pressure
You will need to define such terms as *school anxiety, self-esteem, personal responsibility*, and similar issues relevant to adolescents and teens.

Topic: Plagiarism as Criminal Misdemeanor
You will need to define the term *criminal misdemeanor* and prove that plagiarism fits the definition.

Topic: Political Theory
You will need to define such concepts as *the state, nationalism, political geography, nation building, consent of the governed,* and similar topics.

These examples demonstrate how vague and elusive our language can be. We know what *peer pressure* is in general, but your essay calls for a careful analysis of the terms *anxiety* and *self-esteem*.

A good definition usually includes three elements: the subject *(plagiarism)*; the class to which the subject belongs *(thievery)*; and its difference from others in this class *(theft of another's intellectual property)*. The argument might center on the legal term *misdemeanor,* which is a criminal act less serious than a felony.

Proposal

This type of argument says to the reader, "We should do something." It often has practical applications, as in these examples:

- We should examine and revise the reading curriculum for students in grades K–5 to reflect the influence of television, video games, and the Internet.
- We should cancel all drug testing of athletes because it presumes guilt and demeans the innocent.
- If mental health is important, access to mental health services by children in schools should be increased rather than decreased.

As shown by these examples, the proposal argument calls for action—a change in a program, a change in the law, or an alteration of accepted procedures. The writer must advance the proposal as the paper's hypothesis and must support it with reasons and evidence.

The proposal has three elements:

1. It should convince readers that a problem exists and is serious enough to merit action.

2. It must explain the consequences to convince the reader the proposal has urgency as well as validity.
3. It must address opposing positions on the issue.

Causal Argument

Unlike proposals that predict consequences, causal arguments show that a condition exists because of specific circumstances—that is, something has caused or created this situation, and we need to know why.

For example, one student asked this question: "Why do numerous students, like me, who otherwise score well on the ACT test, score poorly in the math section of the test and, consequently, enroll in developmental courses that offer no college credit?" This question produced a causal hypothesis (see page 18 for more details): The math section of the ACT examination imposes bias against otherwise bright students. The idea merited the student's investigation, so he gathered evidence from surveys, critical reading, and accumulated test results. Ultimately, he wrote passages on bias in the testing program and inadequate instruction in grade school and high school. He discovered specifics about the testing program.

Comparison and Analogy

A scientific argument often compares two subjects to discover differences, make a point, or defend a position. Investigating the behavior of rats in response to a stimulus is a standard assignment for psychology students. In educational research, students might compare a control group of fifth-graders with an experimental group. The stimulus is usually expressed in a hypothesis: "Overcrowding disrupts and destroys social harmony," or "A speed-reading component for fifth-graders will improve reading comprehension."

An analogy is a figurative comparison that allows the writer to draw parallels. For example, one student compared online matchmaking to the practice of prearranged marriages. When families arrange a marriage, they cautiously seek a good match in matters of nationality, economics, political alliances, and so forth. In comparison, argued this student, couples on the Internet seek a good match on similar grounds.

Precedence

Precedence refers to conventions or customs, usually established in the past. In judicial decisions, it is a standard established by previous cases, a *legal precedent*. If your subject is "performance assessment," you will be faced with the conflict between old testing methods and new theories and methods for evaluating student performance. For example, the SAT examination is well entrenched as a testing vehicle; it has precedence. Replacing it with a different measure would require careful research.

Implications

If you conduct any kind of test or observation, you will probably make field notes in a research journal and tabulate your results at regular intervals. At some point, you will be expected to explain your findings, arrive at conclusions, and discuss the implications of your scientific inquiry. Lab reports are elementary forms of this task. What did you discover, and what does it prove?

For example, in her paper "Arranged Marriages: The Revival Is Online," one student explored both the social and the psychological implications of online infidelity, the damage to self-esteem, and new demands on psychotherapy.

1e Establishing a Schedule

The steps for research are fundamental. You will do well to follow them, even to the point of setting deadlines on the calendar for each step. You may wish to write dates when deadlines should be met.

Topic. Your topic, which usually requires the approval of the instructor, should address a problem, issue, or question. It may offer a theoretical question and present the hypothesis as the subject of research. See Chapter 2 for details.

Research. Reading articles and books will establish a basis for your research. Conducting field research and laboratory testing will provide the necessary evidence for reaching conclusions. See Chapters 3, 4, and 5 for details.

Organization. Instructors require different types of plans. For some, your research journal will indicate the direction of your work. Others might ask for a formal outline. In either case, see Chapter 6 for details about basic organizational models.

Writing. Write plenty of notes, keep accurate lab records, and collect photocopied and downloaded articles, all of which you should carefully label. Some notes will be summaries, others will call for carefully drawn quotations from the sources, and some will be personal responses. Chapters 9 and 10 discuss matters of scientific writing in detail.

Format. Proper manuscript design places your paper within the required conventions of the name and year system used in the social sciences. Chapters 11 and 12 provide the guidelines for in-text citations and the entries for the references page.

Revision and proofreading. At the end of the project, you should be conscientious about examining the manuscript and making all necessary corrections. With the aid of computers, you can check spelling and aspects of style. Appendix A offers tips on revision and editing.

Submitting the manuscript. Like all writers, at some point you must "publish" the paper, or release it to the audience, which might be your instructor, your classmates, or perhaps a larger group. Plan carefully to meet this final deadline. You may publish the paper in a variety of ways—on paper, on a disk, on a CD-ROM, or on your own Web site. Chapter 15 discusses methods for producing electronic projects.

2 Discovering Your Topic

This chapter explores six important steps for investigation of a topic in the social sciences:

- Relating your experiences to scholarly problems and academic disciplines.
- Speculating about a subject by using idea-generating techniques.
- Focusing the subject by consulting with others.
- Exploring the literature.
- Framing a working hypothesis.
- Drafting your research proposal.

Instructors usually assign research topics in the social sciences, but they sometimes allow students to select their own. In either case, your topic will call for a scholarly perspective, and you must follow the six steps listed above in pursuit of a paper worthy of submission.

2a Relating Personal Experience to Scholarly Problems

To clarify what we mean, let's examine how one student launched her project.

Valerie Nesbitt-Hall was assigned by her sociology instructor to research some aspect of the Internet that affects human behavior. Nesbitt-Hall began searching the literature and found a magazine cartoon of a young woman sitting at her computer while saying to a young man, "Sorry—I only have relationships over the Internet. I'm cybersexual." Although she laughed, Valerie knew she had discovered a topic to investigate with a question and a possible answer that would require her research:

Does online romance affect human behavior?

Human behavior is affected by online romance and matchmaking.

Personal interest often provides the groundwork for interesting research projects. For example, the topic "The Sufferings of Native Americans" could be improved to "Urban Sprawl in Morton County: The Bulldozing of Indian Burial

10

Grounds." The topic "Computer Games" could be refined to "Learned Dexterity with Video and Computer Games." This latter topic would require a definition of *learned dexterity* and an analysis of how video games promote it.

Remember, your instructor will expect discipline-specific topics such as these:

Education:	The Visually Impaired: Options for Classroom Participation
Political Science:	Conservative Republicans and the Religious Right
Sociology:	Parents Who Lie to Their Children
Psychology:	Identifying Grade-School Children with Dyslexia

You conduct the research by making inquiries into the issues, identifying variables, and examining data to solve a problem. When your topic addresses serious issues, you have a reason to:

- Examine with intellectual curiosity the evidence found in professional or peer-reviewed articles at the library and on the Internet.
- Conduct observations in the field and experiments in the laboratory.
- Share your investigation of the issues with the reader.

Write a meaningful conclusion that discusses the implications of the study rather than merely summarizes it. Consider using one of the following techniques:

1. Combine personal interests with an aspect of academic studies:

Personal interest:	My Grandmother
Academic subject:	Psychology
Possible topics:	"The Effects of Board Games on Memory Recovery in Stroke Patients"
	"The Effect of Regular Soap Opera Viewing on Mood in Nursing Home Patients"
	"Alzheimer's Disease: Effects on Grandchildren"

2. Consider social issues that affect you and your family:

Personal interest:	Elementary education of a child
Academic subjects:	Sociology and Education
Social issue:	The behavior of children in school
Possible topics:	"Attention Deficit Hyperactivity Disorder in the Elementary Classroom"
	"Should Schoolchildren Take Medicine to Treat Hyperactivity?"

3. Let your cultural background prompt you toward detailed research into your roots, traditional culture, and social background:

Ethnic background:	Native American
Academic subject:	Social work
Personal interest:	Survival of the tribes

You can also reach for good subjects by answering a question:

Is eating in the cafeteria or buying groceries a better budgeting tool?
Purchasing and cooking food has advantages over eating at the cafeteria.
Does joining a Greek letter organization increase the probability that a
student will graduate?
Participation in sororities and fraternities improve a student's chances
of graduation.
Does participation in a weekly study group improve student academic
achievement in a course?
Study groups that meet nightly or weekly improve a student's academic
achievement.

Granted, each statement answers the question, but investigation, research, and the production of proof are necessary to substantiate it. These elements are explored in depth here and in other chapters.

2b   Speculating about a Subject by Using Idea-Generating Techniques

At some point you will need to contemplate the issues and generate ideas worthy of investigation. Ideas can be generated in the following ways:

Free Writing

To free write, focus on a topic and write whatever comes to mind. Do not worry about grammar, style, or penmanship, but keep writing nonstop for a page or so to develop phrases, comparisons, personal anecdotes, and specific thoughts that help focus issues of concern. Below, a student writes on violence for a political science project:

The savagery of the recent hazing incident at Glenbrook North High
School demonstrates that humans, both men and women, love a good fight.
People want power over others, even in infancy. Just look at how siblings
fight. And I read one time that twins inside the womb actually fight for
supremacy, and one fetus might even devour or absorb the other one.
Weird, but I guess it's true. And we fight vicariously, too, watching boxing
and wrestling, cheering at fights during a hockey game, and on and on. So
personally, I think human beings have always been blood thirsty and power
hungry. The French philosopher Rousseau might claim a "noble savage"
once existed, but personally I think we've always hated each other.

This free writing sets the path for this writer's investigation into the role of war in human history. He has found a topic for exploration.

Listing Key Words

Keep a list of fundamental terms you see in your readings. These can help focus the direction of your research. James Johnston built this list of terms:

prehistoric wars	early weapons	noble savages
remains of early victims	early massacres	slaves
sacrificial victims	human nature	power
limited resources	religious sacrifices	honor

These key words can help in writing the rough outline, as explained below.

Outlining Key Words

Writing a rough outline early in the research project might help you see if the topic has enough substance for the length required. At this point, try to recognize the hierarchy of major and minor issues.

```
Prehistoric wars
     Evidence of early brutality
          Mutilated skeletons
     Evidence of early weapons
          Clubs, bows, slings, maces, and so on
          Walled fortresses for defense
     Speculations on reasons for war
          Resources
          Slaves
          Revenge
          Religion
     Human nature and war
          Quest for power
          Biological urge to conquer
```

This initial ranking of ideas grew in length and depth during Johnston's research (see pages 166–174 for his paper).

Clustering

Another method for discovering the hierarchy of your primary topics and subtopics is to cluster ideas around a central subject. The cluster of related topics can generate a multitude of interconnected ideas. Here's an example by James Johnston:

Narrowing by Comparison

Comparison limits a discussion to specific differences. Any two works, any two persons, any two groups may serve as the basis for a comparative study. One writer expressed a comparison in this way:

> Ultimately, the key questions about the cause of war, whether ancient or current, centers on one's choice between biology and culture. On the one side, society as a whole wants to preserve its culture, in peace if possible. Yet the biological history of men and women suggests that we love a good fight.

That comparative choice could become the capstone of the student's conclusion.

Asking Questions

Stretch your imagination with questions.

1. General questions examine terminology, issues, causes, and other matters. For example, having read a section of Henry Thoreau's essay "Civil Disobedience" for a sociology class, one writer asked:

   > What is "civil disobedience"?
   >
   > Is dissent legal? Is it moral? Is it patriotic?
   >
   > Is dissent a liberal activity? Is it conservative?
   >
   > Should the government encourage or stifle dissent?
   >
   > Is passive resistance effective?

Answering these questions pointed the student to a central issue or argument:

Civil Disobedience: Shaping Our Nation by Confronting Unjust Laws

2. Rhetorical questions are based on the various modes of writing. One student in a sociology class framed these questions about state-sanctioned gambling and its effect on the social fabric of the state:

Comparison:	How does a state lottery compare with horse racing?
Definition:	What is a lottery in legal terms? in social terms? in religious terms?
Cause/Effect:	What are the consequences of a state lottery on funding for education, highways, prisons, and social programs?
Process:	How are winnings distributed? Does money pass from the rich to the poor or from the poor to the rich?
Classification:	What types of lotteries exist, and which are available in this state?
Evaluation:	What is the value of a lottery to the average citizen? What are the disadvantages?

3. Academic disciplines across the curriculum provide questions:

Psychology:	What is the effect of gambling on the mental attitude of the college athlete who knows huge sums hang in the balance on his or her performance?
Sociology:	What compulsion in human nature prompts people to gamble on athletic competitions?
Education:	What percentage of the lottery money actually goes into education?

4. Explore the basic elements of a subject with journalistic questions: Who? What? Where? When? Why? and How? For example:

Who?	Athletes
What?	Illegal drugs
When?	During off-season training and also on game day
Where?	Training rooms and elsewhere
Why?	To enhance performance
How?	Through pills and injections

The questions can prompt a writer to examine team pressure as a cause for drug usage by athletes.

2c   Focusing the Subject by Consulting with Others

Interviews

You may need to consult with your instructor, published experts, and other people with experience. Ask for ideas and reactions to your subject. For

---

CHECKLIST

Exploring Ideas with Others

- Consult with your instructor.
- Discuss your topic with three or four classmates.
- Listen to the concerns of others.
- Conduct a formal interview (see pages 26–28).
- Join a discussion group.
- Take careful notes.
- Adjust your research accordingly.

---

example, Valerie Nesbitt-Hall knew a couple who married after initially meeting in a chat room on the Internet. She requested an interview and got it (see pages 26–28 for the interview and pages 179–185 for her use of the interview in the finished paper). The techniques for interviewing are discussed in greater detail in Section 3a, pages 26–32.

Discussion Groups

What are other people saying about your subject? A discussion group of your peers can provide valuable insight into potential issues, problems, and sources. With a round-table discussion, you can ask questions to focus your work. You might also be challenged to focus on key issues you have overlooked. You might use the computer to share ideas and messages with other scholars interested in your subject. Somebody may answer a question or point to an interesting aspect that had not occurred to you.

With discussion groups, you have choices:

- A round-table discussion group at a study room in the library or dormitory.
- Classroom e-mail groups that participate in online discussions.
- Online courses that feature a discussion room for forums that require student participation.
- MUD and MOO discussion groups, or multi-user domains that work over the Internet rather than via e-mail.
- Online chatting with one or more participants in real time, even with audio and video, in some cases.

For example, your instructor may set up an informal classroom discussion list and expect you to participate by e-mail with her and your fellow students. You can also find many discussion groups on the Internet, but the manner in which you use them is vital to your academic success. Rather than chat, solicit ideas and get responses to your questions about your research.

CHECKLIST

Narrowing a General Subject to a Scholarly Topic

Unlike a general subject, a scholarly topic should:

- Examine one narrowed issue, as in Valerie Nesbitt-Hall's focus on Internet matching services as a way to arrange a date and even a marriage.
- Address knowledgeable readers and carry them to another plateau of knowledge.
- Have a serious purpose that demands analysis of the issues, argues from a position, and explains complex details.
- Investigate the subject by reviewing the literature, examining data, conducting empirical research, surveys, and interviews, and directly observing or collecting data in the field.
- Meet the expectations of the instructor and conform to the course requirements.

2d Exploring the Literature

Electronic databases now provide excellent, up-to-date information on most scholarly topics. Some can be found on the Internet, but many of the best databases are accessed through your library. Books on your topic can be identified by means of the library's electronic book catalog. Here are three suggestions:

1. Go to the reliable databases available through your library, such as Info-Trac (general), PsychLIT (psychology), PUBMED (health), ERIC (education), PAIS (political science), and others. These are monitored sites filtered by editorial boards and peer review. You can reach them from remote locations at home or the dorm room by connecting electronically to your library. See Chapter 4 for details on ways to access library resources.
2. Look for articles on the Internet that first appeared in a printed version. In many cases, the original print version was examined by an editorial board.
3. Look for Internet articles with reputable sponsors, especially universities, museums, or professional organizations. Chapter 3 discusses the pros and cons of Internet searching. You can also look at the Web site accompanying this book (http://www.ablongman.com/lester) for tips and examples on evaluating Internet sources.

Topic selection goes beyond choosing a general category such as "single mothers." It includes finding a research-provoking issue or question such as "The foster parent program seems to have replaced the orphanage system.

Has it been effective?" Then frame a subject you wish to explore—for example, "The foster parent program has failed the children just as the orphanage system of another age failed the children." Take a stand, make a claim, and begin your investigation to provide credence for your position.

2e Framing a Working Theory or Hypothesis

The hypothesis is an assumption that requires a review of the literature, careful testing in the lab, and/or a review of existing or new data to support its validity. You should expand your topic into a scholarly proposal to support and defend in your paper. However, be sure to consult with your instructor concerning the scope of your project. Here are several types of claims. Keep in mind that they go by different names and have different applications in specific disciplines.

The Variable Hypothesis:

Children with autism display various cognitive strengths and weaknesses.

The researcher must provide evidence to show that children with autism can concentrate for long periods of time; excel in music, math, mechanics, and science; display long-term memory; be creative; and demonstrate many other positive traits. Some variables are dependent only on the independent variable.

The Conditional Hypothesis:

Behaviors of self-abuse, such as overeating, head banging, self-mutilation, bulimia, and anorexia, can be reduced by counseling, monitoring, diet therapy, and medication.

Certain conditions must be met. The control will depend on the patient's ability to respond adequately to the tasks to prove the hypothesis valid. Examining one item—for example, bulimia—should suffice for an undergraduate study. Note: A study of this type may require field research that involves one or more human subjects.

The Statistical Hypothesis:

Class size has no effect on the number of laboratory experiments designed and demonstrated in class.

This type of examination is also known as a *null hypothesis.* The null hypothesis states that there is no difference between two conditions beyond chance differences. If a statistically significant difference is found, the null hypothesis is rejected.

The Causal Hypothesis:

A child's choice of toy is determined by television commercials.

In psychology, the search is for a relationship. How does one thing affect another? Thus, a causal hypothesis assumes the mutual occurrence of two factors and asserts that one is responsible for the other. The student who is a parent could conduct observational research to support or oppose the supposition. A review of the literature would certainly serve the writer.

In effect, your work will include an examination of the prevailing literature as well as some type of field research, such as a survey of an elementary classroom or a survey of senior citizens at a retirement community. Everything is subject to examination, even the number of times you blink while reading this text.

A theory can be a prevailing idea or the conventional wisdom that exists in the academic community, yet it too is subject to review and analysis. For example, the SAT and ACT examinations, theoretically, are effective measuring tools for predicting student success in college. The relationship is now undergoing careful scrutiny that suggests the subjective theory is flawed by objective evidence. In another case, subjective theories for treating adolescent substance abuse vary greatly from state to state and agency to agency because of objective evidence. Here is one student's subjective theory that requires objective evidence:

Chat rooms and online matching services are like prearranged marriages of the past. They enable people to meet only after a prearranged engagement by e-mail.

The writer will defend this subjective theory by citing evidence from interviews and the literature.

You might develop an argument with a *because* clause, as based on your reading:

Hyperactive children need medication because ADHD is a medical disorder, not a behavioral problem.

The subjective theory that children benefit from medication is supported by evidence in the literature, which argues for a medical solution rather than behavioral modification. This writer must defend the theory by citing evidence and addressing any unstated assumptions—for example, that medication alone will solve the problem.

Sometimes the theory will serve as the hypothesis for a paper:

Discrimination against young women in the classroom, known as "shortchanging," harms the women academically, socially, and psychologically.

Here the student will probably cite literature on shortchanging.

2f   Drafting a Research Proposal

A research proposal in APA style comes in two forms:

1. A short paragraph to describe the project for yourself and to inform your instructor of your project, or
2. A formal, multi-page report that provides background information, your rationale for conducting the study, a review of the literature, your methods, and the possible implications of the work.

In addition to the examples here, you can find a fully developed research proposal on pages 21–23.

The Short Proposal

A short proposal identifies four essential ingredients of your work:

- The specific topic
- The purpose of the paper (explain, analyze, argue)
- The intended audience (general or specialized)
- Your stance as the writer (informer or advocate)
- The preliminary theory or hypothesis

For example, here is Valerie Nesbitt-Hall 's short initial proposal:

This study will examine computer matchmaking as a viable alternative to traditional methods for initiating a friendship. The Internet provides an opportunity for people to meet, chat, reveal themselves at their own pace, and find, perhaps, a friend, lover, or even a spouse. Thus, computer matchmaking has social and psychological implications that can be explored in the literature of both psychologists and sociologists. In many ways, computer matchmaking is similar to the arranged marriages of past generations. Such arrangements are now considered old-fashioned or a product of foreign culture, but consider this hypothesis: The Internet, especially its online dating services and chat rooms, has brought arranged marriages into the twenty-first century. People are able to meet in a remote manner without immediate intimacy. Those persons who maintain an anonymous distance until a true romance blossoms are anticipating, in essence, a carefully arranged date that might become a marriage. This study will therefore examine the social and psychological implications for those persons seeking a match in cyberspace.

This writer has identified the basic nature of her project and can now search for evidence in the literature.

The Long Proposal

Some instructors may assign the long proposal, which includes some or all of the following elements:

1. A *cover page* with the title of the project, your name, and the person or agency to which you are submitting the proposal:

Arranged Marriage 1

Running Head: ARRANGED MARRIAGES: THE REVIVAL IS ONLINE

Arranged Marriages: The Revival Is Online

Valerie Nesbitt-Hall

Austin Peay State University

2. A preliminary *abstract* in 50 to 100 words.

Arranged Marriages 2

Abstract

Arranged marriages are considered old-fashioned or a product of some foreign cultures, but consider that the Internet, especially its online dating services and chat rooms, has brought arranged marriages into the twenty-first century. The Internet provides an opportunity for people to meet, chat, reveal themselves at their own pace, and find, perhaps, a friend, lover, or even a spouse. Thus, computer matchmaking has social and psychological implications that have been explored by psychologists and sociologists. The social implications affect the roles of both men and women in the workplace and in marital relations. The psychological implications involve online infidelity, cybersexual addiction, and damage to self-esteem; yet those dangers are balanced against success stories. Those persons who maintain an anonymous distance until a true romance blossoms are anticipating, in essence, a carefully arranged date that might become a marriage.

3. A *purpose statement* with the *rationale* for your project. In essence, this is your identification of the audience that your work will address, and the role you will play as investigator and advocate.

> This project was suggested by Dr. Lee Ling to fulfill the writing project for English 2100 and also to serve the University Committee on Computers, which has launched a project on student Internet awareness. This paper, if approved, would become part of the committee's Student Booklet on Internet Protocol.

4. A *statement of qualification* that explains your experience and perhaps the special qualities you bring to the project. Nesbitt-Hall included this comment in her proposal:

> I bring first-hand experience to this study. I have explored the Internet like many other students. I joined a service, entered my profile, and began looking at photographs and profiles. It was exciting at first, but then I became bored; it seemed that everything and everybody blended into a fog of indifference. Then, when some jerk sent a vulgar message, I withdrew my profile and username. I'll just remain old-fashioned and start my dates with a soda at the student center.

If you have no experience with the subject, you can omit the statement of qualification.

5. A *review of the literature,* which will survey the articles and books you examined in your preliminary work.

> Limited research is being done in the area of online romance. My search of the literature produced a surprisingly short list of journal articles. Maheu (1999) discussed methods of helping clients, even to the point of counseling in cyberspace itself, which would establish professional relationships online. Schneider and Weiss (2001) described it but offered little interpersonal insight. Cooper (2002) has published an excellent collection of articles in his guidebook for clinicians, and he has argued that online dating has the potential to lower the nation's divorce rate. Kass (2003) identified the "distanced nearness" of a chat room that encourages self-revelation while maintaining personal boundaries" (cited in Rasdan, 2003, p. 71). Epstein (2003) argued that many arranged marriages, by parents or by cyberspace, have produced enduring love because of rational deliberation performed before moments of passionate impulse. In addition,

Schneider and Weiss (2001) have listed some of the advantages to online romance: It links people who are miles apart; impressions are made by words, not looks; there is time to contemplate a message; there is time to compose a well-written response; and messages can be reviewed and revised before transmission (p. 66).

6. A *description of your research methods* is usually part of your proposal, which includes the design of the *materials* you will need, your *timetable,* and, where applicable, your *budget.* These elements are required in a proposal but omitted in the research paper. Consult with your instructor concerning the scope of your project. Here is Nesbitt-Hall's description:

This paper will examine online dating as a forum for arranged dates and arranged marriages. The Method section will explore the methods used by Match.com and other dating services as a testing board for people with similar interests to form communication lines that might last one minute or one year. The Subjects section will examine the people who participate, from the modest person to one who is aggressive, and from high-profile people like Rush Limbaugh to those with low profiles and quiet lifestyles. The Procedures section will examine the process so common to the services: to bring two compatible people together on the Web. There they can e-mail each other, participate in instant messaging (IM) chats, send attachments of favorite songs or personal photographs, and, eventually, exchange real names, phone numbers, and addresses. The various services provide not only lists of available people but also personality tests, detailed profiles of subjects, and even nightclubs with calling cards for patrons to share with others whom they find interesting. The Results section will explore online romance as productive for some people, as a haven for the lurking voyeur, and as potential disaster for the gullible and careless. The Case Study will provide a success story for online dating. The Discussion section will explore the social and psychological implications for men and women, especially those addicted to cyberspace.

CHECKLIST

Explaining Your Purpose in the Research Proposal

- Explain and define the topic. Use *explanation* to review and itemize factual data.
- Analyze the specific issues or variables. Use *analysis* to classify parts of the subject and to investigate each in depth.
- Persuade the reader with the weight of the evidence. Use *persuasion* to question the general attitudes about a problem and then to affirm new theories, advance a solution, recommend a course of action, or—in the least—invite the reader into an intellectual dialogue.

YOUR RESEARCH PROJECT

1. Ask questions about a possible subject, using the list on pages 14–15, and write answers that might serve as your hypothesis. Submit your list and answers to your instructor.

2. Look around your campus or community for subjects. Talk with your classmates and even your instructor about campus issues. Focus on your hometown community in search of a problem or social concern such as drug abuse, school busing, overcrowded classrooms, or road rage. If you are a parent, consider issues related to children, such as safe, adequate childcare. After you have a subject of interest, apply the techniques described on pages 12–15, such as clustering, free writing, or listing key words. Submit your topic, narrowed to a specific problem or hypothesis, to your instructor.

3. To determine if sufficient sources are available and to narrow the subject even further, visit the Internet, investigate the library's databases (e.g., InfoTrac), and dip into the electronic book catalog at your library. Keep printouts of interesting articles or book titles. Submit a copy of one article to your instructor.

4. Write a brief research proposal and submit it to your instructor (see pages 19–20).

3 Gathering Data by Field Research and Laboratory Testing

R esearch in the social sciences is often empirical, which means the researcher gathers data in practical and pragmatic ways to test a hypothesis. Let us consider the following hypothesis:

Overpopulation causes stress, which results in abnormal behavior.

That seems to be a reasonable proposition, but the scientific community wants supportive data and considers it a statistical hypothesis (see page 18). Data can be collected in a laboratory or in the field. For example, in the laboratory, the scientific researcher often uses rats. A control group of 12 rats might be placed in one cage and left without stimulus during the test period. An experimental group of 12 rats, placed in a cage, is stimulated. Each day, 12 additional rats are added to the cage and observed day after day for changes in behavior. This experiment continues until the rats react in negative or hostile ways, attacking each other for a number of reasons—food, space, or sex, to name three. Meanwhile, the control group lives in relative peace and harmony. The eventual report will describe the design of the study, chart the results, and discuss the implications of the findings.

The same hypothesis could be tested by field research, which means going outside the laboratory. For example, the researcher could observe classroom students with a control group and an experimental group. The latter is stimulated by overpopulation, the results are tabulated, and the findings are reported. Thirty-five students in a classroom, compared with fifteen, may result in stress for many of the crowded students, affecting their grades and their overall classroom behaviors.

Such reports have great value for educators who might reduce class size, for corporate managers who use cubicles to give employees their own space, and for traffic engineers who attempt to spread out the flow of automobiles.

In like manner, you will be called on to conduct research. You might find yourself observing student behavior at a parking lot or surveying a selected group with a questionnaire. This type of research is not beyond the realm of first-year and second-year students, and you should consider it an important element of your educational development.

Evidence for your study should come from reputable sources. Broad references to issues in society might include how the topic has been viewed on a television talk show or in weekly magazines; however, this type of information is not a source worth citing in a research project. Additionally, personal communication is not worthy of reference in an empirical study.

Beyond the library, source information can be found in a variety of places. Therefore, converse with people in person, by letter, or via e-mail. If time permits, conduct interviews or use a questionnaire. Watch television specials, visit the courthouse archives, and conduct research by observation under the guidance of an instructor (see page 39). Build a table, graph, or chart with the evidence collected, and make it part of your study. Maintain all of your field notes, interview transcripts, survey data, and so forth because your instructor may ask to see them or you may wish to place them in an appendix at the end of your paper.

Strict guidelines exist for the design of scientific reports in APA style, so you should follow the appropriate model as described on pages 3–8. For example, the report of empirical research requires four parts:

1. Introduction of the problem with the hypothesis
2. Your methods, tools, and subjects
3. The results of the study
4. A discussion of the implications

In addition, you should be objective while conducting the research. All writers get deeply involved in their subject, but they must couple that involvement with the skill of detachment. What are the facts? What conclusions do they support? Conduct the research, document the results, and then discuss their implications.

For example, student Gena Messersmith (see her letter on page 29) had strong personal feelings about her daughter's condition as she researched Attention Deficit Hyperactivity Disorder; hence, Messersmith forced herself to remain objective. As a safeguard, allow your instructor to review your methods and apparatus before launching the study.

3a   Investigating Local Sources

Interviewing Knowledgeable People

Talk to people who have experience with your subject. Personal interviews can elicit valuable in-depth information. They provide information few others have. Look to organizations for experienced persons. For example, if writing on the history of the local school system, you might contact the county historian, a senior citizen's organization, or a retired teacher or two. If convenient, post a notice soliciting help:

I am writing a study on the history of the local school system in 1950s. Wanted: People who have knowledge of the schools during that decade.

Try establishing e-mail conferences with knowledgeable people. Another way to accomplish this task is to request information from a discussion group. Try using the discussion board if you are in an online class. For accuracy, save files or record the discussions and interviews with a tape recorder (with written permission of the person interviewed, of course). Information worthy of documentation should come from credible sources, but for sociology and some other disciplines it might be necessary to include information from an interview, e-mail, or other personal correspondence. Do not include personal correspondence as an entry on your References page (see pages 75–76 for details).

Through research and personal interviews with M. S. Thornbright, the county historian, the precise location of various schools was identified. Schools were segregated at this time, and differences in facilities and locations were noted. The reality of equal but separate schools at the time of the Brown vs. Board of Education decision in 1954 is reflected in the history of this community.

Be prepared for the interview. Know your interviewee's professional background and have a set of pertinent questions, with follow-ups. Keep the interview focused on the principal issue. Subjects may wander to tangential ideas, so always bring them back to the central subject with an appropriate question. Maintain an ethical demeanor that honors with accuracy the statements of the subject. See also guidelines in the Checklist on page 32.

Student Valerie Nesbitt-Hall researched the role of computer matching services and chat rooms in promoting online romance. Because she knew two people who had met online and eventually married, she decided to request an interview—online, of course. These were her questions and, in brief form, the responses of the subjects—Steven of Scotland and Jennifer of the United States. (See Nesbitt-Hall's paper on pages 178–185):

1. When did you first meet online?
   Answer: *September of 1996.*
2. What prompted you to try an online matching service?
   Answer: *We didn't really try online matching services. We chatted in a chat room, became friends there, and met in person later.*
3. Who initiated the first contact?
   Answer: *Stephen initiated the first online chat.*

4. How long into the relationship did you correspond by e-mail before one of you gave an address and/or phone number? Who did it first, Steve or Jennifer?

   Answer: *We chatted and corresponded by e-mail for nine months before Jennifer shared her phone number.*

5. How long into the relationship did you go before sharing photographs?

   Answer: *At nine months we began to share written correspondence and photographs.*

6. Who initiated the first meeting in person? Where did you meet? How long were you into the relationship before you met in person?

   Answer: *Stephen first requested the meeting, and Jennifer flew from the States to Glasgow, Scotland. This was about a year into the relationship.*

7. How much time elapsed between your first online discovery of each other and your marriage?

   Answer: *One and a half years after our first chat, we were married.*

8. Did you feel that online romance enabled you to prearrange things and protect your privacy before meeting in person?

   Answer: *Yes. We were cautious and at times reluctant to continue, but we kept coming back to each other, online, until we knew the other well enough to trust in the relationship. Once we got offline into what we might call real-time dating, the love blossomed quickly.*

9. When you finally met in person, did you feel that you really knew the other person spiritually? emotionally? intellectually?

   Answer: *Yes.*

10. Not to put you on the spot, but do you feel as a couple that the relationship has been excellent to this point?

    Answer: *Yes, super.*

11. Has the difference in nationalities been a problem?

    Answer: *Yes, but only in relation to sorting out immigration matters. Also, Jennifer's parents were concerned that she was going to another country to see someone she had never met.*

> Note: To see how this interview was used in the student's paper, see pages 184–185.

12. Finally, would you recommend online matching services or chat rooms to others who are seeking mates?

    Answer: *Yes, in the right circumstances. We were lucky; others might not be.*

Writing Letters and Corresponding by E-Mail

Correspondence provides a written record for research. As you would in an interview, ask pointed questions so correspondents will respond directly to your central issues. Tell the person who you are, what you are attempting to do, and why you have chosen to write this particular person or set of persons. If germane, explain why you have chosen this topic and what qualifies you to write about it.

Gena Messersmith
12 Morningside Road
Clarksville, TN 37040

Ms. Rachel G. Warren, Principal
Glenview Elementary School
Clarksville, TN 37040

Dear Ms. Warren:

I am a college student conducting research into methods for handling hyperactive children in the public school setting. I am surveying each elementary school principal in Montgomery County. I have contacted the central office also, but I wished to have perspectives from those of you on the front lines. I have a child with ADHD, so I have a personal as well as a scholarly reason for this research. I could ask specific questions on policy, but I have gotten that from the central office. What I would like from you is a brief paragraph that describes your policy and procedure when one of your teachers reports a child with hyperactive behavior. In particular, do you endorse the use of medication for managing that child's behavior? Names will be confidential, for an assigned code will be used for each subject to ensure confidentiality and anonymity.

I have enclosed a self-addressed, stamped envelope for your convenience. You may e-mail me at messersmithg@apsu.edu.

Sincerely,

Gena Messersmith

This letter makes a fairly specific request for a minimum amount of information. It does not require an expansive reply. From the response, a generalization or specific example can be used, but the data should not be cited as a reference.

Basic policies were gathered from local elementary school principals. A common procedure is the principal counsels first with the school nurse and second with the parents. Seventy percent of the principals polled encouraged the use of medication. Some noted reasons for encouraging medication included its calming effect upon the child, the resulting benefits to the learning atmosphere of the classroom, and so on.

Note: If Messersmith decided to build a table or graph from the principals' replies, she would need to document the survey as shown on page 30.

Reading Personal Papers

Search out letters, diaries, manuscripts, family histories, and other personal materials that might contribute to your study. The city library may house private collections, and the city librarian can usually help you contact the county historian and other private citizens who have important documents. Obviously, handling private papers must be done with the utmost decorum and care. Again, provide an in-text citation to the source:

> R. C. Joplin (2003) shared with me her grandfather's notebooks, unpublished, which contained numerous references to the old Dunbar High School along with several photographs. Several drawings by Joseph Joplin, not to scale, provided clues to life at a segregated school.

Note: Every reference or source needs a bibliography note except for personal communications.

> Joplin, J. (1924). *Notes on my life.* Unpublished manuscript.

Attending Lectures and Public Addresses

Watch bulletin boards and the newspaper for a featured speaker who might visit your campus. When you attend, take careful notes and, if you can, request a copy of the lecture or speech. Remember, too, that many lectures, reproduced on video, are available in the library or in departmental files. Provide an in-text citation to the source and make a bibliography entry on the reference page. The in-text citation might read like this:

> One psychologist reminded attorneys that the most prevalent reaction of children who are physically and sexually abused is a retreat into silence, a withdrawal so deep that memory can be erased (Lockerby, 2004).

The reference entry would look like this:

> Lockerby, R. W. (2004, January). *Sounds of silence from abused children.* Paper presented to the meeting of the Sumner County Bar Association, Gallatin, TN.

Investigating Government Documents

Documents are available at four levels of government: city, county, state, and federal. As a constituent, you are entitled to examine many kinds of records on file at various agencies. If your topic demands it, you may contact the mayor's office, attend and take notes at a city council assembly, or search out printed documents.

Local government

Visit the courthouse or county clerk's office for facts on elections, marriages, births, and deaths. These archives include wills, tax rolls, military assignments,

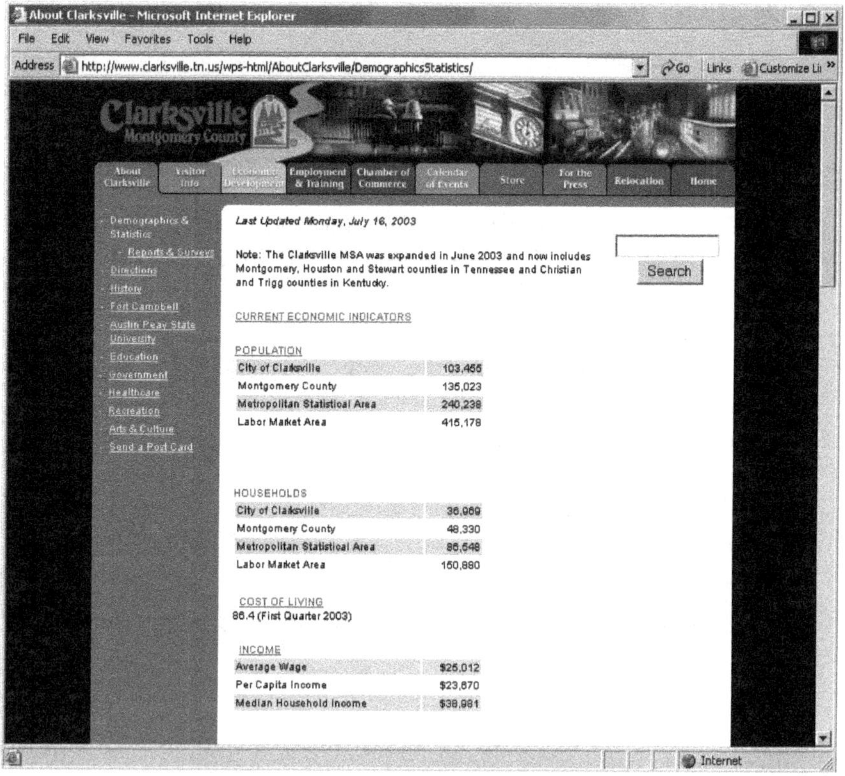

FIGURE 3.1 Population and Demographics: Clarksville/Montgomery County, Tennessee

deeds to property, and much more. Therefore, a trip to the local courthouse can be rewarding, helping you trace the social history of the land and its people. Figure 3.1 shows the type of information readily available to a student conducting research on a city's population and demographics.

State government

Telephone a state office that relates to your research, such as Consumer Affairs (general information), the Public Service Commission (which regulates public utilities such as the telephone company), or the Department of Human Services (which administers social and welfare services). The agencies may vary by name in your state. Remember, too, that the state's archival storehouse makes its records available for public review.

Federal government

Your United States senator or representative can send you booklets printed by the Government Printing Office, usually without cost. A list of these documents appears in a monthly catalog issued by the Superintendent of Documents, *Monthly Catalog of United States Government Publications*, Washington, DC 20402, available with an excellent search engine at

CHECKLIST

Interviews, Letters, Private Papers, Courthouse Documents

- Set your appointments in advance.
- Consult with experienced persons. If possible, talk to several people in order to weigh different opinions. Telephone and e-mail interviews are acceptable.
- Be courteous and on time for interviews.
- Be prepared with a set of focused, pertinent questions for initiating and conducting the interview.
- Handle private and public papers with great care.
- For accuracy, record interviews with a tape recorder (with permission of the person interviewed, of course).
- Get written permission before citing a person by name or quoting his or her exact words.
- Send helpful people a copy of your report along with a thank-you note.

http://www.access.gpo.gov/. In addition, you can gain access to the National Archives Building in Washington, D.C., or to one of the regional branches in Atlanta, Boston, Chicago, Denver, Fort Worth, Kansas City, Los Angeles, New York, Philadelphia, or Seattle. These archives contain court records and government documents that you can review in two books: *Guide to the National Archives of the United States* and *Select List of Publications of the National Archives and Record Service* (see http://www.archives.gov/). You can borrow some documents on microfilm if you consult the *Catalog of National Archives Microfilm Publications*.

The researcher should also make a bibliography entry to record the source of this table.

Clarksville/Montgomery County Economic Development Council. (2003).

  Population and demographics: Clarksville/Montgomery County,

  Tennessee. Retrieved January 16, 2004, from www.clarksville.tn.us

3b   Examining Audiovisual Materials, Television, and Radio

Important data can be found in audiovisual materials: films, filmstrips, music, phonograph recordings, slides, audiocassettes, and videocassettes. You will find these sources both on and off campus. Consult such guides as

CHECKLIST

Using Media Sources

- Watch closely the opening and closing credits to capture the necessary data for your bibliography entry. The format is explained on page 155.
- Your citations may refer to a performer, director, or narrator, depending on the focus of your study.
- As with the live interview, be scrupulously accurate in taking notes. It's best to write direct quotations because paraphrases of television commentary can unintentionally be distorted and biased.
- Plan your review of a media presentation, even to the point of preparing a set of criteria to help with your judgment or preparing a list of questions for which you want answers.

Educators Guide (film, filmstrips, and tapes), *Media Review Digest* (nonprint materials), *Video Source Book* (video catalog), *The Film File*, or *International Index to Recorded Poetry*. Television, with its many channels, such as the History Channel, offers invaluable data. With DVD or VCR, you can record a program for detailed examination. Again, write bibliography entries for any materials that contribute to your paper.

Fleischer, A. (2003, June 1). *Taking on the press* [Interview]. Atlanta: CNN.

3c Conducting a Survey

Surveys can produce current, first-hand data that you can tabulate and analyze. Use a formal survey only when you are experienced with tests and measurements as well as with statistical analysis or when your instructor will help you with the instrument. Be advised that most schools have a Human Subjects Committee that sets guidelines, draws up consent forms, and requires confidentiality or anonymity of participants for information gathering that might be intrusive. An informal survey gathered in the hallways of campus buildings lacks credibility in the research paper. Here are a few guidelines.

Developing a Questionnaire

Ask yourself these questions as you begin developing a questionnaire. Sample answers are provided.

What hypothesis are you examining?

Parental attitudes toward medication for ADHD.

Teacher attitudes toward medication for students with ADHD.

Why are you doing the evaluation?

> To learn teachers' ideas and beliefs about the value of medication as an effective means for working with ADHD students.

What do you hope to accomplish?

> To find information about the strengths and weaknesses among educators regarding the effectiveness of medication for students with ADHD.

Can you get the information you need from existing sources, which would make the survey unnecessary?

> No. This survey has not been performed previously, and it is applicable to the school system, parents, and students.

How can you clarify your objective?

> Using a Likert Scale or a yes/no questionnaire, decipher the ways that teachers feel medication is beneficial for students with ADHD.

What are you measuring? Select from this list:
Attitude
Knowledge
Skills
Goals and aspirations
Behavior
Perceptions

> This survey will measure teachers' attitudes and knowledge about the effectiveness of medication for ADHD.

Note: A sample can be statistically similar to a complete population if each participant represents the whole population in terms of age, sex, race, education, income, residence, and other factors. You might pull names from a hat, select every tenth person, or carefully select from groups by sex, race, and classification as freshman, sophomore, junior, senior, graduate student.

What is the population to be surveyed? Can you test a random sample rather than the entire population?

> The questionnaire will seek responses from teachers for grades K to 5 at four local elementary schools.

What method will you use to collect the data?
Mail
Telephone
E-mail
Personal interview

Personal distribution
Internet Web site (see pages 37–38)

> The survey will be personally distributed.

Will the collection be anonymous or confidential? Anonymous surveys do not ask for names of respondents, yet an e-mail survey may violate such anonymity. Confidential surveys include the names of respondents, but individual responses may not be shared and the confidentiality may not be violated. Destroy all identifying data after your report is completed.

> The survey will be confidential and anonymous; all records will be
>
> erased from the computers.

Will you need approval before administering the questionnaire? Your instructor's approval might be sufficient, but consult your college catalog for regulations on protection of subjects who participate in evaluation and research.

> I have approval from my professor and dean, approval from the
>
> university committee, and approval from the school system
>
> because the purpose of the survey is to determine the attitudes of
>
> teachers concerning the effectiveness of medication of ADHD.
>
> Program evaluation and the findings are intended for internal use.

Designing the Questionnaire
Giving directions to participants

Include these items:

A brief explanation of the questionnaire's purpose
Instructions on completing the survey
Directions on submitting the questionnaire (e.g., mail, e-mail, submit button, and so on)
Conditions of confidentiality

Wording the questions

Avoid slang, culture-specific, and technical words. Avoid words with connotations of bias that might influence the respondent. Avoid the word *and* to ensure that you ask only one question. Avoid the word *not* in questions requiring a yes or no answer. Keep multiple choice questions distinct and exclusive. Keep the questionnaire short and simple. Only ask questions whose answers are important to your research.

Writing a cover letter

Make a connection with the respondent. Introduce yourself and explain the importance of the survey. If the respondent will benefit from your research, tell them how so that he or she will take whatever time is needed to complete the survey. The cover letter should include these items:

The purpose of the study

The sponsor (such as the dean of admissions)

Reasons why the response is important

A promise of confidentiality explaining that responses will be anonymous and used in data analysis, not kept as individual records. Reassure the respondents of the data transfer security measures you have put into place

The deadline for returning the questionnaire

Informed consent, which is typically represented by the return of the form

Writing the questionnaire

Place the easiest and least controversial questions at the beginning of the survey. Try to arrange questions on the same subject matter together. Do not ask leading questions or make assumptions. Do not ask questions that require long, written answers, but do invite a brief commentary on the issues by the respondent. Include a comment section where respondents can personalize or explain their answers. Offer these options where appropriate: don't know, not applicable, none, other. Be consistent in the design. If the yes option is listed before the no option the first time, always show it that way.

Conducting a pilot study to test your design

Early in your work, test your questionnaire with a small group of students to get input on the language used, the clarity of the questions, and the potential for recovering pertinent data. A pilot is your test run to see if everything works before you build the complete version.

Designing the questions

The most frequently used question types are multiple choice, ratings, scales (agree/disagree, excellent/poor), and short-answer questions that allow either numeric or written answers. Examples are:

Multiple Choice:

Which television news program do you primarily watch?

1. CNN
2. ABC
3. CBS
4. NBC
5. FOX
6. Other

Rating Scales:

In terms of importance to you, please rate the university's electronic enrollment process. The scale is from 1, not important or valuable, to 5, very important and valuable.

Ease of access	1	2	3	4	5
Ease of navigation	1	2	3	4	5
Accuracy in listing course choices	1	2	3	4	5
Availability of courses with options	1	2	3	4	5

Agreement Scales:

These usually appear as agree/disagree or always/never. Note: Always include the "no opinion" option.

Are you satisfied with the university's electronic enrollment system? The scale is from 1, very dissatisfied, to 5, very satisfied.

1   2   3   4   5   no opinion

Questions Requiring Short Written Answers:

If you could do one thing to improve the university's enrollment system, what would it be?

Short-answer Questions:

Did you find the electronic enrollment system easy to use?   Yes   No
Did you build your course schedule successfully?   Yes   No

Writing Online Surveys

Internet surveys offer the possibility of collecting data in a short time from a large population, and the tabulation of results can be electronically tabulated. You create the questionnaire, place it online, recruit subjects, and let a software program, such as Microsoft Access, build a database. Your analysis of the data can begin within days.

Web-based data collection can be flexible, allowing randomization of question order and various skip patterns. In addition, gathering data online offers a relative degree of privacy and makes it easier for respondents to admit to their behavior, such as cheating on examinations, alcoholism, or unprotected sex.

To create a questionnaire for the Internet, use a Web page application such as Microsoft FrontPage or Macromedia DreamWeaver. You will need to read and follow the advice given in the tutorials about forms and hypertext buttons.

To send the forms, you can submit the questionnaire to members of a discussion group or send e-mail messages to a selected list of possible respondents whom you then direct to the Web site for the survey.

To collect the data from an Internet survey, you have three choices:

1. Have the completed survey sent directly to you via e-mail if it is brief.

2. Have the completed survey sent to a file controlled by software such as Microsoft Excel.

Note: For more information on these programs, go to the Web site at http://www.ablongman.com/lester.

3. Have the completed survey sent to a database controlled by software such as Microsoft Access.

Ethical guidelines require researchers to allow subjects to skip questions they do not wish to answer. Ask your respondents to answer each question, but include a response option for each item that allows the respondent to skip the item. Note this example:

Which type of graduation speaker do you prefer?

Politician
Professional or academic person
Successful graduate of the school
Other; please specify:
Skip this question

Your online questionnaire should include an option for withdrawal from the survey. If the respondent withdraws, discard all data from that subject.

For confidentiality, you should reassure respondents that you will not attempt to capture information they do not voluntarily provide. In addition, you might indicate you will save the e-mail addresses in a separate file from the responses so individual responses cannot be linked to a specific e-mail address. Also, remember that in most cases you may only guarantee confidentiality, not total anonymity.

Label your survey in the bibliography entry:

Electronic enrollment survey. (2004). Unpublished raw data. Knoxville:

University of Tennessee.

CHECKLIST

Conducting a Survey

- Keep the questionnaire short, clear, and focused on your topic.
- Write unbiased questions. Let your professor review the instrument before you use it.
- Ask subjects for a quick response to a scale (Choose A, B, or C), to rank responses (first choice, second choice, and so on), or to fill blanks.
- Arrange for an easy return of the questionnaire, even to the point of providing a self-addressed, stamped envelope.
- Retain e-mail responses until the project is complete, and then erase them from the computer.
- Provide a sample questionnaire and your tabulations in an appendix.
- Tabulate the results objectively. Even negative results that deny your hypothesis have value.

Unlike interview questions that elicit a response from one person or a couple, the questionnaire gathers multiple responses from many people, from twenty-five to several thousand. It should be designed for ease of tabulation, with results you can arrange in graphs and charts. If you want to build a table or graph from the results, see pages A-9 to A-10 for examples and instructions.

3d Conducting Experiments, Tests, and Observations

Empirical research, within and outside a laboratory, can determine why and how things exist, function, or interact. Your paper will explain your methods and findings in response to a hypothesis (see pages 18–23). An experiment thereby becomes primary evidence for your paper. Several methods can be used to collect data. We have discussed interviews (pages 26–28) and questionnaires (pages 33–37). Listed below are a few other methods. Consult with your instructor at all times with regard to your work and its design.

Observation

Observation is field research that occurs generally outside the lab in the field, which might be a child care center, a movie theater, a parking lot, or the counter of a fast food restaurant. The field is anywhere you can observe, count, and record behavior, patterns, and systems. It might include observing the thumb-sucking habits of infants, the eating disorders of fourteen-year-old girls, the self-discipline practiced by children on a playground, or students searching for a parking place on campus lots. We seldom notice the careful study conducted by retail merchandisers who want to know our buying habits or the analysis by a basketball coach on the shot selections by members of his team. Finding patterns in human behavior is the goal, and gathering data is a way of life for marketing firms, television networks, politicians—and, especially, behavioral researchers.

Most experiments and observations begin with a hypothesis (see pages 18–19), which is a statement assumed to be true for the purpose of investigation. Here is an example:

Academic success in the elementary grades increases with extra-

curricular activities, such as band, choir, athletics, yearbook, and art.

The hypothesis might be "The more active the student happens to be in extracurricular activities, the more teachers can expect success in the student's academic performance." However, two other words come into play: *variable* and *indicator.* Things subject to change are variables that must be indicated in some manner.

Variable	Indicator
Extracurricular activity	Participation in sports, band, choir, and so forth
Academic success	Grade point average

This researcher will study and observe the grade point average in correlation with the students' activities.

The study might be further advanced by the use of control and experimental groups. Thus, one set of students would be the control group and receive no stimulus, while the experimental group would be stimulated to participate actively in three or more extracurricular activities. The findings from scientific observation would eventually be the subject of the student's report.

In some situations, the researcher can begin observation without a hypothesis and let the results lead to conclusions.

Laboratory Experiments

If you collect your primary data in the laboratory, you must carefully design the equipment to meet the demands of the study. Your methods for recording information must be regimented to the point that another researcher could follow your steps and obtain identical results. Laboratory experiments are used extensively in the social sciences as well as the physical sciences and engineering fields. Your instructor will assign, design, and supervise your lab work.

Field Experiments

You might be asked to investigate a subject outside the laboratory but with controls for measuring the data.

- Observation and interviewing, as discussed earlier, are two types of field research.
- Ethnographies are studies of societies by anthropologists, such as a study to recreate the social climate of the Cherokee Indians in North Carolina or Georgia before the forced march to Oklahoma.
- Case studies usually involve participant observation to describe people in special social settings, such as a study of six families, each with a child diagnosed with autism.
- Action research investigates a specific problem that is localized, such as observing the behavior of smokers outside a classroom building, counting the number of drivers without seat belts locked, or keeping a diary or notebook on oral responses to a question.
- Documentary research requires you to read the literature and draw conclusions, not perform empirical research; for example, you would read documents written by the parents of children with autism.

3e Structuring Your Scientific Report

Generally, a report on an experiment or observation follows a format involving four distinct parts: introduction, method, results, discussion. Understanding these elements will help you design your final report.

Introduction to explain the design of your experiment:

- Present the point of the study.
- State the hypothesis and how it relates to the problem.
- Provide the theoretical implications of the study.
- Explain the manner in which this study relates to previously published work.

Method to describe what you did and how you conducted the study:

- Describe the subjects who participated, whether human or animal.
- Describe the equipment and how you used it.
- Summarize the procedure in execution of each stage of your work.

Results to report your findings:

- Summarize the data you collected.
- Provide the necessary statistical treatment of the findings with tables, graphs, and charts.
- Include findings that conflict with your hypothesis.

Discussion that explains the implications of your work:

- Evaluate the data and its relevance to the hypothesis.
- Interpret the findings as necessary.
- Discuss the implications of the findings.
- Qualify the results and limit them to your specific study.
- Make inferences from the results.

CHECKLIST

Conducting an Experiment or Observation

- Explain the purpose of your work.
- Express a clear hypothesis.
- Select the proper design for the study: lab experiment, observation, or the collection of raw data in the field.
- Include a review of the literature, if appropriate.
- Keep careful records and accurate data.
- Do not allow your expectations to influence your interpretation of the results.
- Negative or unexpected results have merit; present them in that light.
- Maintain respect for human and animal subjects. In that regard, you may find it necessary to get approval for your research from a governing board. Read your college's rules and regulations on any research that requires testing humans or animals.

Note: Consult the Lester Web site (http://www.ablongman.com/lester) for additional information, examples, and links to sites that discuss in greater detail the matters of experiment and observation.

Your experiment and the writing of the report will require the attention of your instructor. Seek his or her advice often. This model can also be used for a fully developed proposal.

YOUR RESEARCH PROJECT

1. Select an event involving human behavior and observe it for one week. Record your field notes in a double-entry format by using the left side of the page to record and the right side of the page to comment and reflect on what you observe. Afterward, write a brief paragraph discussing your findings and submit it to your instructor.

Record:

Response:

Day 1
10-minute session at the parking lot—three cars negotiating the lanes and two sitting, waiting for a slot to open.

Some drivers are restless and rush around in hopes of finding a parking space. Others seem resigned to a long wait.

Day 2
10-minute session at the parking lot—six cars rushing up and down the lanes and two cars sitting quietly at the end of two lanes.

I saw a hint of road rage as one student lost an opening to a car in front and began banging on the steering wheel.

Day 3
10-minute session at the parking lot—interviewed one of the students who parked and waited quietly for a slot.

I asked, "How long do you usually have to wait?" She said, "Sometimes 10 minutes, sometimes 30, but one eventually opens. I can study while I wait."

2. Look carefully for subjects in which research outside the library will contribute to your report. Determine the kind of field research that will serve your needs: correspondence? local records? the news media? a questionnaire? an observation? an experiment?

3. Write a preliminary questionnaire that will survey members of your class about their jobs and the number of hours worked that might be devoted to their studies. Work closely with your instructor to design an instrument that will affect your research and your findings. Submit your questionnaire to your instructor. Most instructors want to examine and approve any questionnaire you will submit to others and to approve the design of your experiment or observation.

4. Follow university guidelines for working with human subjects.

Blending Reference Material into Your Report

As you might expect, writing a research report carries with it certain obligations. You should read the literature on your subject, gather citations from the articles and books, and display the words of authorities prominently in your writing, especially in the introduction, where you must provide a brief history of the work that has been done in your area of study. APA style requires you to identify each source mentioned using the authority's last name, the year of publication, and page numbers to quotations. Of course, page numbers are not expected for lectures, news broadcasts, and most Internet sources. As a general policy, keep citations brief:

> Munon (2004) found that exposure duration affected eyewitness accuracy and confidence.

Remember, your readers will have full documentation to each source on the References page (see Chapter 11). However, make no entry on the References page for letters, e-mail, and informal interviews that cannot be recovered by other researchers. In those cases, give a more complete description of the source in your text with initials, surname, year, and the type of source:

> The chief investigator for the police department, W. M. Warren (2004), reported during a recent interview that his personnel had great difficulty in gathering effective witnesses for most trials.

10a Writing in the Proper Tense for Papers in the Social Sciences

Verb tense is an indicator that distinguishes papers written in APA style for the social sciences. Citations that refer to reports and articles by your sources require either the past tense or present perfect tense ("Jeffries *stipulated*" or "the work of Mills and Maguire *has demonstrated*"). However, this style does require present tense in two instances: (1) when you discuss the results (e.g., "the results confirm" or "the study indicates"), and (2) when you mention established knowledge (e.g., "the therapy offers some hope" or "salt contributes to hypertension"). Here's an example to show the differences in verb tense for a passage written in the humanities and one written in the social sciences.

Humanities style:	**Social sciences style:**
The scholarly issue at work here is the construction of reality. Cohen, Adoni, and Bantz label the construction a social process "in which human beings acts both as the creators and products of the social world" (34). These writers identify three categories (34–35).	The scholarly issue at work here is the construction of reality. Cohen, Adoni, and Bantz (2004) labeled the construction a social process "in which human beings act both as the creators and products of the social world" (p. 34). These writers have identified three categories.

The social science passage on the right shows the present tense used for generalizations and references to stable conditions, but it displays the present perfect tense or the past tense for sources cited (e.g., the sources *have tested* a hypothesis or the sources *reported* the results of a test). This next sentence uses tense correctly:

> The dangers of steroid use exists for every age group, even youngsters. Lloyd and Mercer (2003) reported on six incidents of liver damage to 14-year-old swimmers who used steroids. Since that time, several scientists have examined the connection between steroid use and liver damage (Boston, 2003; Randolph, 2002; Watson, 2003).

As shown in the example, use the present tense *(exists)* for established knowledge, the past tense *(reported)* for an action that has occurred, or the present perfect *(have examined)* for an action that began in the past and continues to the present. For example, "Grunfeld reported" (past tense) but "Responses of participants in the past six months have varied" (present perfect).

10b Using In-Text Citations in Your Reports

Use the following conventions for in-text citations:

- Cite last names only for sources listed on the References page.
- List author names in alphabetical order in the citation.
- Cite the year, within parentheses, immediately after the name of the author.
- Cite page numbers with a direct quotation but not with a paraphrase.
- Use *p.* or *pp.* before page numbers.

Citing Last Name Only and the Year of Publication

An in-text citation in social sciences style requires the last name of the author and the year of publication.

> Devlin (2003) and Watson (2004) have advanced the idea of combining the social sciences and mathematics to chart human behavior.

If you do not use the author's name in your text, place the name(s) within the parenthetical citation.

> Two studies have advanced the idea of combining the social sciences and mathematics to chart human behavior (Devlin, 2003; Watson, 2004).

If necessary, add initials to distinguish the person, especially if two people with the same last name are listed on the References page (e.g., G. W. Bush and G. H. Bush or E. Roosevelt and F. D. Roosevelt).

Providing a Page Number

If you quote the exact words of a source, provide a page number and use *p.* or *pp.* Place the page number in one of two places: after the year (2003, p. B4) or at the end of the quotation.

> George (2004) advanced the idea of "soft mathematics," which is the practice of "applying mathematics to study people's behavior" (p. B4).

Citing a Block of Material

Present a quotation of 40 words or more as a separate block, indented five spaces or 1/2 inch from the left margin. Because it is set off from the text in a distinctive block, do not enclose it with quotation marks. Do not indent the first line an extra five spaces; however, do indent the first line of any additional paragraphs that appear in the block an extra five spaces, that is, ten spaces from the left margin. Set parenthetical citations outside the last period.

Albert (2003) reported the following:

> Whenever these pathogenic organisms attack the human body and begin to multiply, the infection is set in motion. The host responds to this parasitic invasion with efforts to cleanse itself of the invading agents. When rejection efforts of the host become visible (fever, sneezing, congestion), the disease status exists. (pp. 314–315)

Citing a Work with More Than One Author

When one work has two or more authors, use *and* in the text but use *&* in the citation.

> Werner and Throckmorton (2003) offered statistics on the toxic
> levels of water samples from six rivers.

but

> It has been reported (Werner & Throckmorton, 2003) that toxic
> levels exceeded the maximum allowed each year since 1983.

For three to five authors, name them all in the first entry (e.g., Torgerson, Andrews, Smith, Lawrence, & Dunlap, 2003), but thereafter use *et al.* (e.g., Torgerson et al., 2003). For six or more authors, employ *et al.* in the first and in all subsequent instances (e.g., Fredericks et al., 2004).

Citing More Than One Work by an Author

Use small letters *(a, b, c)* to identify two or more works published in the same year by the same author—for example, (Thompson, 2004a) and (Thompson, 2004b). Then use 2004a and 2004b on your References page (see page 161 for an example). If additional items will clarify the citation for the reader, add them as necessary:

> Horton (2003; cf. Thomas, 2002a, p. 89, and 2002b, p. 426)
> suggested an intercorrelation of these testing devices. But after
> multiple-group analysis, Welston (2004, esp. p. 211) reached an
> opposite conclusion.

Citing Indirect Sources

Although it is desirable to use information from the original source, you may use a double reference to cite somebody quoted in a book or article—that is, you may use the original author(s) in the text and cite your source for the information in the parenthetical citation.

> In other research, Massie and Rosenthal (2002) studied home
> movies of children diagnosed with autism, but determining criteria
> proved difficult because of the differences in quality and dating of the
> available videotapes (cited in Osterling & Dawson, 2003, p. 248).

See also "Textbook, casebook, anthology" (page 151), for additional details about citing this type of source on the References page.

Citing from a Textbook or Anthology

If you make an in-text citation to an article or chapter of a textbook, case-book, or anthology for which many authors are listed, you should use the in-text citation to refer only to the person(s) you cite:

> One writer stressed that two out of every three new jobs in this decade will go to women (Rogers 2003).

The list of references will clarify the nature of this reference to Rogers (see "Textbook, casebook, anthology," page 151).

Citing Classical Works

If an ancient work has no date of publication, cite the author's name in the text followed by *n.d.* within parentheses.

> Sophocles (n.d.) saw psychic emotions as. . . .

Cite the year of any translation you have used, preceded by *trans.*, and give the date of the version used, followed by *version*.

> Plato (trans. 1963) offered a morality that. . . .
>
> Plato's *Phaedrus* (1982 version) explored. . . .

If you know the original date of publication, include it before the date of the translation or version you used.

> In his "The Poetic Principle," Poe (1850/1967) announced the doctrines upon which he built his poetry and fiction.

> Note: Entries on your References page need not cite major classical works and the Bible. Therefore, identify in your text the version used and the book, chapter, line, verse, or canto.

> In Exodus 24:3–4 Moses erected an altar and "twelve pillars according to the twelve tribes of Israel" (King James Version).
>
> The Epic of Gilgamesh demonstrated, in part, the search for everlasting life (Part 4).
>
> Homer (n.d.) took great efforts in describing the shield of Achilles (18:558–709).

Abbreviating Corporate Authors in the Text

Corporate authors may be abbreviated after a first, full reference:

> One source questioned the results of the use of aspirin for arthritis treatment in children (American Medical Association [AMA], 2003).

Thereafter, refer to the corporate author by initials: (AMA, 2003).

Citing an Anonymous Work

When no author is listed for a work, cite the title as part of the in-text citation (or use the first few words of the material).

> The cost per individual student has continued to rise rapidly as states cut funding and shift the expense to students and their parents (Money concerns, 2003, p. 2).

Citing Personal Communications

E-mail, telephone conversations, memos, and conversations do not provide recoverable data, so exclude them from your list of references. Thus, you should cite personal communications in the text only. In so doing, give the initials as well as the last name of the source, provide the date, and briefly describe the nature of the communication.

> M. C. Gaither (personal communication, August 24, 2003) described the symptoms of Wilson's disease.

Citing Internet Sources in Your Text

Material from electronic sources presents special problems. Currently, most Internet sources have no prescribed page numbers or numbered paragraphs. You cannot list a screen number because monitors differ. You cannot list the page numbers of a downloaded document because computer printers differ. Therefore, in most cases, do not list a page number or a paragraph number. Here are basic guidelines.

Omit a page or paragraph number. The marvelous feature of electronic text is that it is searchable, so your readers can find your quotation quickly with the Find feature. Suppose you have written the following:

> The UCLA Internet Report (2003) advised policy makers that "a better understanding of the impact of the Internet requires rigorous study."

A reader who wants to investigate further will find your complete citation in your References list. With the Internet address for the article and the Edit and Find features, the passage can be found quickly within the essay. That is much easier than counting through 46 paragraphs.

Provide a paragraph number. Some scholars who write on the Internet number their paragraphs. Therefore, if you find an article on the Internet that has numbered paragraphs, by all means supply that information in your citation.

> The Insurance Institute for Highway Safety (2003) has
> emphasized restraint first, saying, "A federal rule requiring special
> attachments to anchor infant and child restraints in vehicles is making
> installation easier, but not all child restraints fit easily in all
> vehicles" (par. 1).
> Recommendations for treating non-insulin-dependent diabetes
> mellitus (NIDDM), the most common type of diabetes, include a diet
> that is rich in carbohydrates, "predominantly from whole grains, fruit,
> vegetables, and low-fat milk" (Yang, 2003, par. 3).

Provide a page number. In a few instances, you will find page numbers buried within brackets here and there throughout an article. These refer to the page numbers of the printed version of the document. In these cases, you should cite the page just as you would a printed source. Here is the Internet source with the page numbers buried within the text to signal the break between page 17 and page 18:

> What is required is a careful reading of Chekhov's subtext, that elusive [pp17–18] literature that lingers in psychological nuances of the words, not the exact words themselves.—Ward, *Drama and Psychology,* 2001.

The page number may be included in the citation:

> One source has argued the merits of Chekhov's subtext and its
> "psychological nuances of the words" (Ward, 2001, p. 18).

In some instances, the Web site reproduces the original pagination, as in the case of JSTOR, which photocopies the original pages and makes them available electronically:

XL
SHAKESPEARE'S CONCEPTION OF *HAMLET*

What was Shakespeare's conception of *Hamlet?* That is the question. It is one which inevitably resolves itself into a reconstruction of the materials at his disposal, the dramatic problems with which he had to deal, and the means whereby he sought to satisfy contemporary dramatic taste. For such a reconstruction modern scholarship provides abundant information about both the theatrical practices and intellectual interests of the time and Shakespeare's habits as a craftsman. In particular should be noted his exceptional preoccupation with character portrayal and the scrupulous motivation of action; his conformity with changing theatrical fashion, yet at the same time his reluctance to pioneer in experiment; his sensitive, if sketchy, acquaintance with matters of contemporary interest; and his success as a skilled and inspired adapter rather than as an innovator. In the application of this knowledge two principles are fundamental. First, *Hamlet* must not be viewed as isolation, but in close conjunction with the theatrical environment which produced it. Second, Shakespeare must be recognized as primarily a practical playwright, a business man of the theater with obligations to fulfill, specific theatrical conditions to meet, and an audience to divert. For the rest, it is a pleasant exercise for the recreative imagination to try to think oneself into Shakespeare's mind, to face the problem of *Hamlet* as he faced it, and to trace the solution as he must have found it.

I

Shakespeare's *Hamlet* is a philosophical melodrama. Theatrically it is one of his most spectacular plays. For all its discursiveness it is crammed with action of the most sensational sort. Ghosts walk and cry "Revenge!" Murder is foully done. Conspirators plot and counterplot. Two characters go mad. A queen is terrified nearly to death. A play breaks up in a near-riot. An insurrection batters the palace gates. A brawl desecrates a suicide's grave. A duel explodes into murder and general butchery. There are poison, incest, war, and debauchery. This is not closet drama for the philosopher's study; it is blood and thunder for the popular stage.

Nevertheless, *Hamlet* is also one of Shakespeare's most thoughtful plays. Permeated with moralizing and philosophical speculation, it presents in its center character a most elaborate psychological study. As for the reader these are unquestionably the most enduring elements, so to the elucidation of these criticism has devoted most of its attention.

777

778 *Shakespeare's Conception of "Hamlet"*

Indeed, not infrequently is it implied that the play exists for the express purpose of expounding Shakespeare's views on life and death, or that the play is primarily a peg upon which to hang the character of Hamlet. Such a view, however, scarcely squares with the known practice of Shakespeare, or, for that matter, of any successful playwright. The one play of the period which openly advertised itself as a philosophical character study–Chapman's *Revenge of Bussy D'Ambois*–was an inglorious failure. Contrast with this the extraordinary popularity of *Hamlet*, and one may see how much of it depends upon the scrupulous subordination of those very philosophical elements which make Chapman's play so insufferably dull to the modern reader. To Shakespeare, doubtless, both character study and philosophical speculation were distinctly subsidiary to plot and stage business; and in the excised version, which must have been necessary for stage presentation, they probably interfered little with the more congenial business of swift melodrama.[1]

You may cite these page numbers because JSTOR photocopies the original publications.

Harold R. Walley 779

session with a few restricted preoccupations. The peculiarity of Hamlet's madness is that, no matter how insane his ravings may seem to his hearers, without exception they contain *double entendre* and make perfect sense from Hamlet's point of view. The method is substantially that which underlies the contemporaneous intellectual conceit; namely, the surprise association of apparently incongruous elements linked by a submerged chain of thought. Thus whatever madness Hamlet exhibits is an integral part of his own mental attitude.

This mental obsession, which issues in the evidences of Hamlet's supposed madness, is intimately connected with two other important features of the play. Hamlet is much concerned with his inability to carry forward his revenge. This delay is essential to the plot; that it is a delay for which Hamlet is himself responsible Shakespeare makes clear throughout.[2] Much, however, as Hamlet endeavors to understand the reason, he is incapable of explaining it to himself; it is an ingrained part

FIGURE 10.1 Sample page from JSTOR database

A citation to an article from the JSTOR database would include the page number:

Kandiyoti (1998) argued that "women strategize within a set of concrete constraints that reveal and define the blueprint of what I will term the *patriarchal bargain* of any given society . . . " (p. 275).

The citation on the References page would also include the pages:

Kandiyoti, D. (1998). Bargaining with patriarchy. *Gender and Society, 2*(3), 274–290.

Internet article

Commenting on the distinction between a Congressional calendar day and a legislative day, Dove (2003) stated that "a legislative day is the period of time following an adjournment of the Senate until another adjournment."

One source gave this cautionary notice: "Reports of abuses in the interrogation of suspected terrorists raise the question of how—or whether—we should limit the interrogation of a suspected terrorist when our national security may be at stake" (Parry & White, 2003, abstract).

HyperNews posting

Ochberg (2003) examined the use of algae in paper that "initially has a green tint to it, but unlike bleached paper which turns yellow with age, this algae paper becomes whiter with age."

Online magazine

BusinessWeek Online (2002) reported that the idea of peer-to-peer computing is a precursor to new Web applications.

Government document

The Web site *Thomas* (2003) outlined the amendments to the Homeland Security Act of 2002, which will implement the READICall emergency alert system.

Other Electronic Sources

E-mail

Personal communications such as e-mail, which others cannot retrieve, should be cited in the text only and not mentioned at all in the bibliography.

One technical writing instructor (March 8, 2003) has bemoaned the inability of hardware developers to maintain pace with the ingenuity of software developers. In his e-mail message, he indicated that educational institutions cannot keep pace with the hardware developers. Thus, "students nationwide suffer with antiquated equipment, even though it's only a few years old"(clemmerj@APSU.edu).

However, electronic discussion groups have gained legitimacy in recent years, so in your text you might wish to give an exact date and provide the e-mail address *only* if the citation has scholarly relevance and *only* if the group has made public the e-mail address with the expressed wish for correspondence.

Discussion group (listserv)

Postings available to others should be cited in the text and in the References page.

Blackmore (May 7, 2005) has identified the book *Echoes of Glory* for those interested in detailed battlefield maps of the American Civil War.

Funder (April 5, 2004) argued against the "judgmental process."

Posting to a newsgroup site

In an essay in *Electronic Antiquity,* Whitehead (2003) explored the issue of ancient Athenian oratory from the 420s to the 320s, including the opening or introduction of the speech:

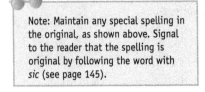

Note: Maintain any special spelling in the original, as shown above. Signal to the reader that the spelling is original by following the word with *sic* (see page 145).

Proem [sic] is the condition which a speaker needed to create at the beginning of his speech that would have been universally understood. He had to win his audience's goodwill.

FTP sites

Del Reyes (2003) demonstrated in the following graph that "enrollment in radiology programs of study has increased by 67% in the past ten years" (p. 54).

CD-ROM

Grolier's Multimedia Encyclopedia (2003) explained that in recent decades huge swaths of the rain forest have been toppled; as the trees disappeared, so, too, did the flora and fauna that thrived under their canopy.

10c Punctuating Citations Properly and Consistently

Keep page citations outside quotation marks but inside the final period, as shown here:

> Smith (2004) argued, "The benefits of cloning far exceed any
> harm that might occur" (p. 34).

If there is a page citation to a paraphrase, which is not required, the period follows the page citation.

> Smith (2004) argued that cloning will bring benefits to medical
> science that will outweigh any disadvantages within the field (p. 34).

See page 133 on placing the page citation with a block quotation.

Commas and Periods

Place commas and periods inside quotation marks unless the page citation intervenes. The example below shows (1) how to put the mark inside the quotation marks, (2) how to interrupt a quotation to insert the speaker, (3) how to use single quotation marks within the regular quotation marks, and (4) how to place the period after a page citation.

> "Modern advertising," said Rachel Murphy (2004), "not only
> creates a marketplace, it determines values." She added, "I resist the
> advertiser's argument that they 'awaken, not create desires'" (p. 192).

Sometimes you may need to change the closing period to a comma. Suppose you decide to quote this sentence: "Scientific cloning poses no threat to the human species." If you start your sentence with the quotation, you must change the period to a comma, as shown:

> "Scientific cloning poses no threat to the human species,"
> declared Wineberg (2004) in a recent article (p. 357).

However, retain question marks or exclamation marks, and no comma is required:

> "Does scientific cloning really pose a threat to the human
> species?" wondered one scientist (Durham, 2004, p. 546).

Let's look at other examples. Consider this original material:

> The Russians had obviously anticipated neither the quick discovery of the bases nor the quick imposition of the quarantine. Their diplomats across the world were displaying all the symptoms of improvisation, as if they had been told nothing of the placement of the missiles and had received no instructions what to say about them.

—Arthur M. Schlesinger, Jr., *A Thousand Days,* (New York: Houghton, 1965), 820.

Punctuate citations from this source in one of the following methods.

"The Russians," wrote Schlesinger (1965), "had obviously anticipated neither the quick discovery of the [missile] bases nor the quick imposition of the quarantine" (p. 820).

Schlesinger (1965) noted, "Their diplomats across the world were displaying all the symptoms of improvisation . . . " (p. 820).

Schlesinger (1965) observed that the Russian failure to anticipate an American discovery of Cuban missiles caused "their diplomats across the world" to improvise answers as "if they had been told nothing of the placement of the missiles . . . " (p. 820).

Note that the last example correctly changes the capital *T* of *their* to lowercase to match the grammar of the restructured sentence, and it does not use ellipsis points before *if* because the phrase flows smoothly into the text.

Semicolons and Colons

Both semicolons and colons go outside the quotation marks, as illustrated in the following examples:

Zigler (2004) admitted that "the extended family is now rare in contemporary society"; however, he stressed the greatest loss as the "wisdom and daily support of older, more experienced family members" (p. 42).

Sutton-Smith (2004) said, "Adults don't worry whether their toys are educational" (p. 64); nevertheless, parents want to keep their children in a learning mode.

The example immediately above shows how to place the page citation after a quotation and before a semicolon. The next example shows a clause following the colon that could stand alone as a complete sentence, so it begins with a capital letter.

Zigler (2004) lamented the demise of the "extended family": The family suffers by loss of the "wisdom and daily support of older, more experienced family members" (p. 42).

If the word group following the colon cannot stand alone as a sentence, do not capitalize the first word after the colon.

> Zigler (2004) lamented the demise of the "extended family" for this primary reason: the loss of the "wisdom and support of older, more experienced family members" (p. 42).

Question Marks and Exclamation Marks

When a question mark or an exclamation mark serves as part of the quotation, keep it inside the quotation mark. Put the page citation with the year to avoid a conflict with the punctuation mark.

> Thompson (2004, p. 16) passionately shouted to union members, "We can bring order into our lives even though we face hostility from every quarter!"
>
> "We face hostility from every quarter!" declared the union leader.

Question marks may appear inside the closing quotation mark when they are part of the original quotation; otherwise, they go outside.

> The philosopher Bremmer (2004, p. 16) asks, "How should we order our lives?"

but

> Did Brackenridge (2004) say that we might encounter "hostility from every quarter" (p. 16)?

Single Quotation Marks

When a quotation appears within another quotation, use single quotation marks with the shorter one.

> George Loffler (2004, p. 32) confirmed that "the unconscious carries the best of human thought and gives man great dignity, but it also has the dark side so that we cry, in the words of Shakespeare's Macbeth, 'Hence, horrible shadow! Unreal mockery, hence.'"

Remember that the period always goes inside the quotation marks unless the page citation intervenes, as shown below:

> George Loffler (2004) confirmed that "the unconscious carries the best of human thought and gives man great dignity, but it also has the dark side so that we cry, in the words of Shakespeare's Macbeth, 'Hence, horrible shadow! Unreal mockery, hence'" (p. 32).

10d Altering Some Capital Letters and Lowercase Letters

Social sciences style permits you to change some initial capital letters to lowercase letters when you incorporate them into your text, and on occasion to change lowercase letters to capital letters.

Change Some Initial Capital Letters to Small Letters

If you change a sentence to quote only a subordinate clause or a phrase, you integrate the words into your sentence; thus, the first letter of the quotation should be small *even though it was a capital letter in the original:*

> E. Roosevelt (1937) warned her audience that "you will have to rise above considerations which are narrow and partisan" (p. 45).

Compare to "E. Roosevelt warned, "You will. . . ."

> Plath (1945) surprised her readers with unusual similes, as in "love set you going like a fat gold watch" (p. 432).

The original line reads: "Love set you going like a fat gold watch."

Change Some Small Letters to Capitals

Change a small letter to a capital letter within a separated citation—that is, if a quotation that is only part of a sentence in the original forms a complete sentence as quoted, the initial lowercase letter may be changed to a capital where your introductory structure permits it. For example, in the next quotation note that the word *the* is in lower case.

> "Men can never lead if they are afraid, for the leader who is afraid will never be followed" (Roosevelt, 1937, p. 43).

Notice next how the word *the* may be changed to a capital letter:

Eleanor Roosevelt (1937) wisely observed, "The leader who is afraid will never be followed" (p. 43).

10e Editing a Quotation with [*sic*], Ellipsis Points, and Brackets

You are permitted to include additional information in a quotation under certain circumstances. You must use brackets around material you insert, and you must use ellipsis if you delete any part of an entire sentence.

Use [*sic*] to Signal a Mistake in a Quotation

When a quotation has a questionable spelling or word usage, let your reader know that you are quoting exactly and that the structure is not your error. The word *sic* ("thus," "so," "in this manner") is placed in brackets immediately after the word in question. In the next example, the student writer makes clear that the year *1964* was the error of Lovell. The assassination occurred in 1963.

Lovell (2004) said, "John F. Kennedy, assassinated in November of 1964 [*sic*], became overnight an immortal figure of courage and dignity in the hearts of most Americans" (p. 92).

The word *sic* is not an abbreviation and therefore takes no period. Because of its Latin roots, it is usually set in italics. Do not overuse the device. In a linguistics study, for example, it is unnecessary to call attention to every variant:

Whan that Aprille with his shoures sote
The droghte of Marche hath perced to the rote.

Chaucer

Use Brackets to Enclose Interpolation, Corrections, Explanations, Translations, or Comments within Quoted Matter

Use square brackets, not parentheses, to clarify a statement:

E. Roosevelt (1936) warned, "You [the Democratic delegates] will have to rise above considerations which are narrow and partisan" (p. 367).

Use the brackets, without ellipsis, to correct the grammar within an abridged quotation:

ORIGINAL:	"Eleanor Roosevelt, who served in the United Nations after FDR's death, gained international attention, especially as a champion of the impoverished people around the globe."—Orin Roberts, 2003, p. 15
ABRIDGED:	"Eleanor Roosevelt [became] a champion of the impoverished people around the globe," reported Orin Roberts (2003, p. 15).

Use brackets to note any addition or change you make in the quotation:

E. Roosevelt (1943) observed, "You gain *strength, courage, and confidence* [my emphasis] by every experience in which you really look fear in the face"; then she added, "You must do the thing you think you cannot" (p. 342).

Lovell (2004) said, "John F. Kennedy, assassinated in November of [1963], became overnight an immortal figure of courage and dignity in the hearts of most Americans" (p. 92).

Compare the citation of Lovell, above, with the one on page 145 that retains the wrong date and marks it with *sic*.

Use brackets to substitute a proper name for a pronoun, such as *she*:

Roberts (2003, p. 7) added, "We all know [Roosevelt] implored us into action by saying 'look fear in the face.'"

Note: Use parentheses to enclose the comments or explanations that fall outside the quotation, as shown in this example:
Boughman (46) and other experts have child care providers to "instruct their employees on responding *wisely* to medical emergencies with CPR and other lifesaving techniques" (emphasis added).

Use Ellipsis Points to Omit Portions of a Quotation

An ellipsis shows an omission of a word, phrase, line, paragraph, or more from a quoted passage. The ellipsis is marked with points, not asterisks, printed on the line like periods, separated from each other by a space and from the text by a space. Three points indicate an omission within a quoted sentence.

ORIGINAL:	"Success in marriage depends on being able, when you get over being in love, to really love," advised Eleanor Roosevelt, who added, "You never know anyone until you marry them."
ELLIPSIS:	"Success in marriage depends on being able . . . to really love," advised Eleanor Roosevelt (1937), who added, "You never know anyone until you marry them" (p. 45).

When the ellipsis occurs at the end of a sentence and what remains is still grammatically complete, use a period followed by three spaced points.

ORIGINAL:	Osburn observed, "The final years of Eleanor Roosevelt's life were filled with public service to the needy and the private love of her family in travels around the world that always brought her back to the New York mansion" (p. 23).
ELLIPSIS:	Osburn (2000, p. 23) observed, "The final years of Eleanor Roosevelt's life were filled with public service to the needy and the private love of her family. . . ."

Three spaced dots without the period show the omission of a quoted sentence that is purposely and grammatically incomplete:

> Everybody knows that the "Gettysburg Address" begins with the line, "Four score and seven years ago . . . " But who can recite the entire speech?

Note: Consult a grammar handbook for issues beyond what is discussed here.

YOUR RESEARCH PROJECT

1. Make a critical journey through your draft with one purpose: to examine your handling of the sources. Have you introduced them clearly so the reader will know when the borrowing began? Have you provided last name

and year for each citation? Have you placed quotation marks at the beginning and the end of borrowed phrases as well as borrowed sentences? Have you provided a page number for quoted matter as appropriate?

2. If you have used any Internet sources, look at them again to see if the paragraphs on the Internet site are numbered. If so, use the paragraph numbers at the end of your citation(s); if not, use no numbers—not the page numbers on a computer printout and not paragraph numbers if you must count them.

3. If you have used a table, graph, figure, or photograph, be sure you have labeled it correctly (see pages A-9–A-10 for examples).

4. Did you keep verb tenses in the correct form—past tense or present perfect tense for citations and present tense for discussing results and making a conclusion? Compare your work with the instructions in section 10a.

11 Preparing the References List

When you write a final document for your instructor in APA style, place an entry for each of your sources in an alphabetical list using the hanging indention form shown below.

> Kharif, O. (2003, June 11). The net: Now, folks can't live without it.
>
> *BusinessWeek Online.* Retrieved June 18, 2003, from
>
> http://www.businessweek.com/technology/content/jun2003/
>
> tc20030610_1865_tc104.htm

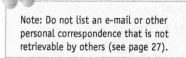

Note: Do not use a period at the end of the URL.

The default style as explained in Section 11a applies to research reports written in APA style for the social sciences:

Education	Home Economics	Physical Education	Political Science
Psychology	Social Work	Sociology	Women's Studies

11a Preparing the List of References

At the end of your paper, create a References page to list the sources you cite in the paper, in footnotes, in figures and illustrations, and in an appendix. Alphabetize the entries and double-space throughout.

Note: Do not list an e-mail or other personal correspondence that is not retrievable by others (see page 27).

Type the first line of each entry flush left, and indent succeeding lines five spaces. You may italicize or underscore the names of books, periodicals, and volume numbers. List the author with surname first and initials only for given names. Include the year of publication within parentheses, followed by the title of a book or journal, italicized or underscored. Capitalize only the first word of the title and the first word of any subtitle; do capitalize proper nouns. Finish with the publication data, as demonstrated in the following examples.

Books

Turlington, C. (2003). <u>Living yoga: Creating a life practice.</u> New York: Hyperion.

For books, close the citation with the place of publication and the name of the publisher. In the publisher's name you may omit the words *Publishing, Company,* and *Inc.,* but otherwise give the full name: Florida State University Press; Pearson Longman; HarperCollins.

> Note: If you underline the titles, be sure to underline any punctuation marks at the end of titles and volume numbers.

Two authors

List chronologically, not alphabetically, two or more works by the same author—for example, Fitzgerald's 2003 publication would precede a 2004 publication.

Fitzgerald, R. A. (2003). *Psychological persuasion in marriage.*

Fitzgerald, R. A. (2004). *Marriage, emotions, and surrender.*

References with the same author in the same year are alphabetized and marked with lowercase letters *(a, b, c)* immediately after the date:

Murphy, T. B. (2004a). *Addressing preschool childcare needs.*

Murphy, T. B. (2004b). *Marketing a revolutionary reading program.*

Entries of a single author precede multiple-author entries beginning with the same surname without regard for the dates:

Martin, D. C. (2003). *Principles of sociology.*

Martin, D. C., & Smith, A. F. (2001). *Handbook to sociology.*

References with the same first author and different second or third authors should be alphabetized by the surname of the second author:

Bacon, D. E., & Smithson, C. A. (2004). <u>A primer in political science.</u>

Bacon, D. E., & Williamson, T. (2003). <u>The nuances of political power.</u>

Part of a book

List author(s), date, chapter or section title, editor (with name in normal order) preceded by *In* and followed by *(Ed.)* or *(Eds.),* the name of the book (underscored or italicized), page numbers to the specific section of the book cited (placed in parentheses), place of publication, and publisher.

Graham, K. (2003). The male bashing stereotype. In P. Elbow & P. Belanoff (Eds.), *Being a writer* (pp. 249–254). New York: McGraw Hill.

If no author is listed, begin with the title of the article.

Obadiah. (1999). In C. Wellington (Ed.), *Who was who in the Bible* (p. 245). Nashville: Nelson.

Textbook, casebook, anthology

Make a primary reference to the anthology:

VanderMey, R., Meyer, V., Van Rys, J., Kemper, D., & Sebranek, P. (Eds.) (2004). *The college writer*. Boston: Houghton Mifflin.

You have several options for identifying individual sources drawn from the anthology. First, you can cite each author with a cross-reference to the VanderMey book.

Bulthuis, J. (2002). Education through application. In VanderMey et al., p. 271.

Loeb, P. R. (1999). Soul of a citizen: Living with conviction in a cynical time. In VanderMey et al., pp. 287-289.

Turner, L. (2002). The media and the ethics of cloning. In VanderMey et al., pp. 323-327.

Note: These entries should be placed in alphabetical order with all others on the reference page so that cross-references may appear before or after the primary source. The year cited should be that in which the cited work was published, not the anthology itself; such information is usually found in a headnote, footnote, or list of credits at the front or back of the anthology.

An alternative to the style shown above is to provide a double reference in your text by naming the authority cited and, within parentheses, the source, as shown below. Only VanderMey et al. would be listed on the References page.

Turner (2002) examined the media's rather dubious role in examining the ethics of cloning (as cited in VanderMey et al., 2004).

Note: Full information on Turner is *not* provided with this method.

Finally, you may prefer to provide a complete entry for each of the authors cited from the casebook, in which case you do not need a separate entry to VanderMey:

Bulthuis, J. (2002). Education through application. In R. VanderMey, V. Meyer, J. Van Rys, D. Kemper, & P. Sebranek (Eds.), (2004), *The college writer* (p. 271). Boston: Houghton Mifflin.

Loeb, P. R. (1999). Soul of a citizen: Living with conviction in a cynical time. In R. VanderMey, V. Meyer, J. Van Rys, D. Kemper, & P. Sebranek (Eds.), (2004), *The college writer* (pp. 287–289). Boston: Houghton Mifflin.

Turner, L. (2002). The media and the ethics of cloning. In R.
VanderMey, V. Meyer, J. Van Rys, D. Kemper, & P. Sebranek (Eds.),
(2004), *The college writer* (pp. 323–327). Boston: Houghton
Mifflin.

Encyclopedia or dictionary

To cite an entry:

Foley, A. F. (2004). Cognitive psychology. In *Encarta 2004 encyclopedia
standard* [CD]. Redmond, WA: Microsoft.

To cite the entire work:

Vogt, P. (1999). *Dictionary of statistics & methodology: A nontechnical
guide for the social sciences*. Thousand Oaks, CA: Sage.

Book with corporate author

American Medical Association. (2003). *American medical association
complete medical encyclopedia*. New York: Random House.

Brochure or booklet

Mathis, R. (2002). *Human resource management: Student resource guide*
(10th ed.) [Brochure]. Washington, DC: Thompson.

Edition

Acredolo, P., Goodwyn, S., & Abrams, D. (2002). *Baby signs* (Rev. ed.).
Boston: McGraw.

Chapter in one volume of a series

Fuchs, A., & Milar, K. S. (2000). Psychology as a science. In I. B.
Weiner (Series Ed.) & D. K. Freidman (Vol. Ed.). (2003). *Handbook
of psychology: Vol. 1. History of psychology* (2nd ed, pp. 1–20).
New York: Wiley.

Numbered report

Raveis, V. H. (2003). *Aging families and breast cancer:
Multigenerational issues* (NTIS Rep. No. ADA418090). New York:
Columbia University.

Proceedings

> Kvale, S. (2000). *The church, the factory, and the market: Scenarios for psychology in a postmodern age.* Paper presented at the proceedings of the International Congress of Psychology. Stockholm, Sweden.

If the presentation is published as an article in a journal or a chapter in a book, provide publication data:

> Kvale, S. (2003). *The church, the factory, and the market: Scenarios for psychology in a postmodern age.* Paper presented at the International Congress of Psychology, Stockholm, Sweden. In *Theory and Psychology, 13,* 579–603.

Periodicals
Journal

List author(s), year, title of the article without quotation marks and with only the first word (and any proper nouns) capitalized, name of the journal underscored or italicized and with all major words capitalized, volume number underscored or italicized, and inclusive page numbers *not* preceded by *p.* or *pp.*

> Smiler, A. P., Gagne, D. D., & Stine-Morrow, E. A. L. (2003). Aging, memory load, and resource allocation during reading. *Psychology and Aging, 18,* 203–209.

Article retrieved from ERIC, InfoTrac, Silverplatter, Proquest, or other library servers

> Wakschlag, L. S., & Leventhal, B. L. (1996). Consultation with young autistic children and their families. *Journal of the American Academy of Child and Adolescent Psychiatry, 35,* 963–965. Retrieved August 8, 2003, from *Expanded Academic Index* database.

Magazine

List author, the date of publication (year, month without abbreviation, and the specific day for magazines published weekly and fortnightly [every two weeks]), title of the article without quotation marks and with only the first word capitalized, name of the magazine underlined with all major words capitalized, the volume number if it is readily available, and inclusive page numbers preceded by *p.* or *pp.* if you do not provide the volume number. If a magazine prints the article on discontinuous pages, include all page numbers.

> Creedon, Jeremiah. (2003, May/June). The greening of Tony Soprano.
>
> *Utne, 14,* 73–77.
>
> Harman, T. D. (2003, August). The unchanging plan. *Civil War Times,*
>
> 43–47, 52.

Newspaper

List author, date (year, month, and day), and title of the article with only first word and proper nouns capitalized, the complete name of newspaper in capitals and underlined or italicized, and the section number of letter with all inclusive and discontinuous page numbers.

> Haynes, T. (2003, June 10). Saving the Columbia. *Boston Globe,* pp.
>
> C12–13, C24.

Abstract of a published article

> Tasker, F. L. (1992). Anti-marriage attitudes and motivations to marry
>
> amongst adolescents with divorced parents. [Abstract]. *Journal of*
>
> *Divorce & Remarriage, 18,* 105–120.

Abstract of an unpublished work

> Gandhi, J. (2003). Political institutions under dictatorship [Abstract].
>
> New York: New York University.

Abstract retrieved from Infotrac, Silverplatter, Proquest, or other servers

> Gryeh, J. H., et al. (2000). Patterns of adjustment among children of
>
> battered women. *Journal of Consulting and Clinical Psychology, 68,*
>
> 84–94. Abstract retrieved August 15, 2004 from *PsycINFO*
>
> database.

Review of a book

> Sharpe, K. (2003, Summer). The whole world in your hands [Review of
>
> the book *World Atlas of Biodiversity*]. *Nature Conservancy,* 86.

Review article

Review articles are devoted to an examination of the literature on a subject, not just a review of one book.

Tindale, R. (2003). Self-harm and domestic violence. *Emergency Nurse,*

11, 7.

Report

Gorman, L.(2003). Why pay more? Simple insurance reform would save

Coloradoans millions (No. 2003-2). Golden, CO: Independence

Institute.

Nonprint material

If the source is not printed, insert a description of the product within brackets.

Ford, B., & Ford, S. (Producers). (2003). *Child Care Reading Programs.*

[Videotape]. Brentwood, CA: Images in Motion.

Howe, C. (Speaker). (2004, March 25). *Relationships: The Path to self-*

discovery [Cassette Recording]. Orlando: Howe Press.

Excel 2003 [Computer software]. (2003). Redmond, WA: Microsoft.

Remember that sources that cannot be recovered by others (e.g., some e-mail messages, personal interviews, unpublished letters, and private papers) should be described in your text but not included as an entry in the References list. For example, write into your text this type of description:

I. Barstow (2003, May 22) submitted to an interview with the

author in Chattanooga, Tennessee, on the role of palm reading in

predicting a person's future.

To maintain the anonymity of the source, write this in-text citation:

In an anonymous interview (2003, April 6) in Chattanooga,

Tennessee, an alleged medium revealed several interesting aspects of

palm reading as a predictor of a subject's future behavior.

Electronic Sources

When citing electronic sources in the References section of your paper, provide the following information if it is available:

1. Author/editor last name, followed by a comma, given-name initials, and a period.
2. Year of publication, followed by a comma, then month and day for magazines and newspapers, within parentheses, followed by a period.
3. Title of the article, not within quotations and not underscored, wil first word and proper nouns capitalized, followed by the total numl

paragraphs within brackets only if that information is provided. You do not need to count the paragraphs yourself; in fact, it is better that you do not. This is also the place to describe the work within brackets, as with [Abstract] or [Letter to the editor].

4. Name of the book, journal, or complete work, underscored or italicized, if one is listed.
5. Volume number, if listed, underscored or italicized.
6. Page numbers only if you have that data from a printed version of the journal or magazine. If the periodical has no volume number, use *p.* or *pp.* before the numbers; if the journal has a volume number, omit *p.* or *pp.*
7. The word *Retrieved,* followed by the date of access, followed by the URL. URLs can be quite long, but you must provide the full data so other researchers can find the source.

Abstract of an online article

Townsend, J. W. (2003). Reproductive behavior in the context of global

population. *American Psychologist, 58.* Abstract retrieved October

13, 2003, from http://www.apa.org/journals/amp/303ab.html#2

Article from an online journal

Clune, A. C. (2002). Mental disorder and its cause. *Psycoloquy, 13*(18).

Retrieved September 23, 2003, from

http://psycprints.ecs.soton.ac.uk/archive/00000210/

Article from a printed journal reproduced online

Many articles online are reproduced in the Portable Document Format (PDF files) by Adobe Reader. These electronic pages are the exact duplicates of their print versions, so if you view an article in its electronic form and are confident that the electronic form is identical to the printed version, add within brackets *Electronic version.* This notation allows you to omit the URL. Your clue is the appearance of the original pages with the original page numbers.

White, A. M., Jamieson-Drake, D. W., & Swartzwelder, H. S. (2002).

Prevalence and correlates of alcohol-induced blackouts among

college students: Results of an e-mail survey [Electronic version].

Journal of American College Health, 51, 117–131.

However, give the URL and date of access of any article that is not an exact reproduction with original page numbers. Most electronic articles do not have page numbers and do not look like a reproduction. Be aware that in many instances with InfoTrac and other servers, you may choose a PDF version or a text version. The next example shows how to cite the text version:

White, A. M., Jamieson-Drake, D. W., & Swartzwelder, H. S. (2002).

>Prevalence and correlates of alcohol-induced blackouts among

>college students: Results of an e-mail survey. *Journal of American*

>*College Health, 51.* Retrieved July 2, 2004, from

>http://morris.lib.apsu.edu:2062/itw/infomark/177/153/52565w2.htm

Article from a library database

University libraries, as well as public libraries, feature servers that supply articles in large databases, such as PsycInfo, ERIC, and netLibrary. Use the examples below as models that give the date of your retrieval, the name of the database, and—only if readily available—the item number within parentheses. You need not cite the URL. If you cite only from an abstract, mention that fact in your reference entry (see the Kang entry below).

Coleman, L., & Coleman, J. (2002). The measurement of puberty: A

>review. *Journal of Adolescence, 25.* Retrieved April 2, 2004, from

>ERIC database (EJ65060).

Firestone, D. (2000, August 10). The south comes of age on religion

>and politics. *New York Times.* Retrieved November 24, 2004, from

>UMI-ProQuest database.

Kang, H. S. (2002). What is missing in interlanguage: Acquisition of

>determiners by Korean learners of English. *Working Papers in*

>*Educational Linguistics, 18.* Abstract retrieved April 2, 2004, from

>ERIC database.

Article from a printed magazine reproduced online

If original pagination is listed with a PDF reproduction, use this form:

Creedon, Jeremiah. (2003, May/June). The greening of Tony Soprano

>[Electronic version]. *Utne, 4,* 15–19.

If original pagination is not listed, use this form:

Hanner, N. (2003, February 10). Demystifying the adoption option: Was

>taking in my brother-in-law's kids a noble act? I quickly realized

>the answer is beside the point. *Newsweek.* Retrieved July 2, 2004,

>from http://web7.infotrac.galegroup.com

Article from an online magazine, no author listed

Children make every day special. (2004, February 3). *Capper's.*

>Retrieved July 2, 2004, from http://web7.infotrac.galegroup.com

Article from an online newspaper

Because online newspapers have their own archival files with a search engine, a reference to the Web site is often sufficient:

Zaino, J. S. Learning a little discipline. (2003, June 12). *Chronicle of Higher Education.* Retrieved June 12, 2003, from http://chronicle.com

Otherwise, provide the URL:

Ippolito, M. (2003, June 12). Delta Moon rising locally. *Atlanta Journal-Constitution Online.* Retrieved June 12, 2003, from http://www.accessatlanta.com/hp/content/entertainment/features/ 0603/12delta.html

Article from an Internet-only newsletter

Tau, M. (2000, August 16). Data-jacking prevention for the psychologist. *Telehealth News.* Retrieved July 18, 2003, from http://telehealth.net/articles/datajacking.html

Compact disc

Encyclopedias, music, movies, and instructional matter are often stored on compact diskettes; use this form:

African American history: Abolitionist movement. (2003). In *Encarta 2004 encyclopedia standard* [CD]. Redmond, WA: Microsoft.

Miller, A. (2003). What is the Power of Attorney? In *Family Lawyer* [CD]. Novato, CA: Broderbund.

Bulletins and government documents

Murphy, F. L. (2003). What you don't know can hurt you. Preventive Health Center. Retrieved October 19, 2003, from http://www.mdphc.com/education/fiber.html

U.S. Cong. House. (2003, January 7). Unlawful Internet gambling funding prohibition act. House Resolution 21. Retrieved September 18, 2003, from http://thomas.loc.gov/cgibin/query/ D?c108:2:./temp/~c108k7golG::

Document, no date

National Broadband Task Force. (n.d.). *An action plan for achieving basic broadband access by 2004.* Retrieved October 17, 2003, from

http://broadband.gc.ca/Broadband-document/english/

recommendation.htm

Document, section, or chapter

Benton Foundation. (2003). *What is the initiative's purpose in 21st*

century skills initiative? (sec. 1). Retrieved June 25, 2004, from

http://www.benton.org/initiatives/skillsinitiative.html#Q1

Document, no author identified, no date

Begin the reference with the title of the document if the author of the document is not identified.

GVU's 10th WWW user survey. (n.d.). Retrieved September 11, 2003,

from http://www.gvu.gatech.edu/user_surveys/survey-1998-10/

Document from a university, available on a private organization's Web site

University of Illinois at Chicago, Health Research and Policy Centers.

(2000). *Partners with tobacco use research centers: Advancing*

transdisciplinary science and policy studies. Retrieved September

9, 2003, from the Robert Wood Johnson Foundation Web site at

http://www.rwjf.org/programs/npoDetail.jsp?id=TRC

Message posted to an online discussion group or forum

Lettevall, E. (2003, January 7). Analysis of small population size.

Retrieved July 18, 2003, from Population Discussion Group at

http://canuck.dnr.cornell.edu/HyperNews/get/marked/marked/289/

1.html

Message posted to an electronic mailing list

Cheramy, R. (2004, April 18). Inexpensive and easy site hosting.

Message posted to Fogo mailing list, archived at http://

impressive.net/archives/fogo/20030418170059.GA23011@bougan.org

Newsgroup message

Burke, G. V. (2003, November 5). Narrative bibliography [Msg. 33].

Message posted to jvmacmillan@mail.csu.edu

Symposium report, abstract

Eisenfeld, B. 2003, October 19). *Tutorial: CRM 101: The basics.* Paper

presented at the Gartner Symposium ITxpo, Orlando, Florida.

Abstract retrieved October 22, 2004, from

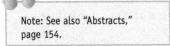

Note: See also "Abstracts,"
page 154.

http://www.gartner.com/2_events/

symposium/2003/asset_46841.jsp

Usenet, Telnet, FTP message

Haas, H. (2004, August 5). Link checker that works with cold fusion

[Msg. 34]. Message posted to impressive.net/archives/fogo/

200000805113615.AI4381

Virtual conference, Report

A virtual conference occurs entirely online, so there is no geographic location. Treat a conference report as a book.

Verhey, S. D., Stefanides, S., & Pinkart, H. C. *Geonomics and education:*

An undergraduate genome project. Paper presented at the Second

Virtual Conference on Genomics and Bioinformatics. Retrieved

October 1, 2004, from http//www.ndsu.nodak.edu/

virtual-genomics/Proc_VCGB2002.pdf

11b Presenting the References Page

Every scientific report requires a References page that alphabetically lists each source cited in the paper. The next example shows the references for a student paper on the social and political implications of ancient warfare. Additional examples of the References page are shown on pages 173, 183, and 199.

References

Adams, M. (1998). The 'Good War' myth and the cult of nostalgia. *The*

Midwest Quarterly, 40. Retrieved May 23, 2004, from InfoTrac

database.

Cooper, L. D. (1999). *Rousseau, nature, and the problem of the good*

life. University Park: Pennsylvania State University Press.

Ferrill, A. (n.d.) Neolithic warfare. Frontline Educational Foundation. Retrieved May 22, 2004, from http://eserver.org/history/neolithic-war.txt

Hanson, V. D. (2002). War will be war: No matter the era, no matter the weapons, and the same old hell. *National Review, 54.* Retrieved May 22, 2004, from *InfoTrac* database.

Harder, B. (2002, April 29). Ancient Peru torture deaths: Sacrifices or war crimes? *National Geographic News.* Retrieved May 20, 2004, from http://news.nationalgeographic.com/ news/2002/ 04/0425_020426_mochekillings.html

Jones, P. (2003). Ancient and modern. *Spectator, 291.* Retrieved May 23, 2004, from *InfoTrac* database.

Kagan, D. (1997). History's largest lessons. Interview by Fredric Smoler. *American Heritage, 48.* Retrieved May 20, 2004, from *InfoTrac* database.

LeBlanc, S. A. (2003a). *Constant battles: The myth of the peaceful, noble savage.* New York: St. Martin's Press.

LeBlanc, S. A. (2003b, May/June). Prehistory of warfare. *Archaeology, 17,* 34–42.

Parsell, D. L. (2002, March 21). City occupied by Inca discovered on Andean peak in Peru. *National Geographic News.* Retrieved May 19, 2004, from http:// news.nationalgeographic.com/news/2002/03/ 0314_0318_vilcabamba.html

Shy, J. (1993). The cultural approach to the history of war. *The Journal of Military History, 57.* Retrieved May 20, 2004, from *InfoTrac* database.

Thorpe, N. (2000). Origins of war: Mesolithic conflict in Europe. *British Archaeology, 52.* Retrieved May 28, 2004, from http://www.birtarch.ac.uk/ba/ba52/ba52feat.html.

Webster, D. (1999). Ancient Maya warfare. In K. Raaflaub & N. Rosenstein (Eds.), *War and society in the ancient and medieval worlds* (pp. 246–340). Cambridge, MA: Center for Hellenic Studies.

Yates, R. (1999). Early China. In K. Raaflaub & N. Rosenstein (Eds.), *War and society in the ancient and medieval worlds* (pp. 216–246). Cambridge, MA: Center for Hellenic Studies.

YOUR RESEARCH PROJECT

Submit to your instructor the initial draft of your References list. The instructor's response will indicate the quality of your work and its precision. You may have time to revise it carefully before final submission of your report.

13 Report of an Empirical Study

Empirical research requires you to conduct original research in the field or lab. It means designing a questionnaire for conducting a survey or interviewing subjects in person or by e-mail. It can also mean manipulating or stimulating a nest of laboratory rats, testing the manner in which elementary teachers administer examinations, or observing the behavior of automobile drivers at a busy intersection. Thus, empirical research is hands-on field or lab investigation, and you should understand its implications for work in the social sciences. As a student, you must work closely with your instructor to (1) plan a proposal, (2) conduct the research, and (3) write the report.

Note: Your instructor may request only the proposal, in which you explain a hypothesis and the manner in which a study might be conducted, even though you will not actually conduct the research (see pages 19–24 and 186–190 for an example of such a proposal).

Typically, the report of an empirical study in APA style has four major elements:

1. The report identifies a problem or issue and expresses a hypothesis that requires investigation and testing.
2. The report describes the design and methodology of the research, explaining the subjects, procedures, and tools employed.
3. The report describes in detail the results of the investigation or test. Here you display the data you collected and the findings you discovered, even if the results contradict your hypothesis or presuppositions. These findings are displayed in this section without editorial comment, which is reserved for the Discussion section.
4. The report comments on the findings and examines their implications in light of the hypothesis that launched the study. Thus, a Discussion section explains, interprets, and analyzes the work reported in the results section.

Each of these four parts is a vital element of your research and the polished report, as explained below.

13a Writing the Introduction to a Report on Empirical Research

The Introduction names your theory to explain the general nature of your project, the rationale for conducting the investigation, and suggestions about what might be found or what results are expected. For example, you might wish to study the peer responses to self-cutting by secondary school adolescents—that is, how do friends respond when a fellow student appears with unexplained cuts on an arm or leg? The interviews and written survey become the primary vehicles for conducting the research. In another example, a student might investigate the implications of marriages arranged, in part, by online dating. The research might determine the effect of Internet activity on the private lives of participants. You can read this type of introduction on pages 179–180.

An effective introduction also provides a review of the literature on the topic in order to establish the study's veracity as scholarly research.

Thus, the Introduction should:

- Introduce a theory addressing a problem that can be examined by testing in the field or the laboratory.
- Explain how you addressed the problem by a hypothesis to be proved or disproved as your research explores it.
- Relate your work to other research in this area with a review of the literature.
- Suggest briefly the possible implications, keeping in mind that the Discussion section will explore these findings fully.

13b Writing the Method Section of the Report on Empirical Research

The Method section describes the investigation to answer several questions:

What was tested?
Who participated, human or animal?
Where was the field work accomplished?
What was the apparatus (or equipment) and how did you use it?

In other cases, the Method section explores your use of a control group and an experimental group along with your methods for stimulating the experimental group. It can also explain your methods for conducting a survey with a questionnaire or for gathering information by e-mail responses. The Method section summarizes the procedure and execution of each stage of your investigation. An appendix is the appropriate place to display a copy of a questionnaire, test questions, and similar forms used to collect data.

Thus, the Method section should:

- Explain the design of the study so others can see clearly how you conducted the work.
- Give sufficient information so that other researchers in the lab or field can duplicate your work.
- Identify the subjects, show how they are representative of the population under study, and explain how they were selected and assigned to a group.
- Describe your apparatus for conducting the study—laboratory equipment, questionnaire, a classroom with a viewing window, and so forth.
- Explain the procedure by giving a step-by-step description of the process, from initial instructions to the participants to details on how an experimental group was manipulated or a test was performed.

13c Writing the Results Section of the Report on Empirical Research

This section provides the data discovered by your investigation—charts, graphs, statistics, tables, and general data to substantiate your work. It reports in detail but without editorial comment because your interpretation is reserved for the Discussion section. You should display your findings in detail even if the results contradict your hypothesis or presuppositions. Individual scores should not be included but placed in an appendix where interested readers can examine the statistics and tabulations. Consult with the instructor for accuracy in the statistical analysis.

Thus, the Results section should:

- Provide a summary of the data collected.
- Supply graphs, charts, and figures to illustrate the findings.
- Present statistical tables that tabulate the results in meaningful patterns.
- Keep the Results presentation objective without discussion of the study's implications.

13d Writing the Discussion Section of the Report on Empirical Research

In this section, you must discuss the implications of the study and its findings. Here you interpret and evaluate the results with commentary. Explain how the test supported or failed to support the hypothesis. You can verify the validity of the results yet acknowledge any failures or variations you encountered.

The discussion can, and often does, explain applications to be pursued and areas demanding further research and analysis. This section is the place to comment on the importance of your research, delineating how it extends the current work in the field by adding another data set to illuminate the problem or issue.

Thus, the Discussion section should:

- Explain how the results of the study yield implications with regard to your original hypothesis.
- Discuss how the findings support or fail to support the hypothesis.
- Comment on the discoveries and explain how the findings might be applied in addressing the theory underlying the work.
- Identify implications for future research in this area.

13e Writing the Title Page, Abstract, References, and Appendix

Each of your papers opens with a title page followed on the next page by an abstract. The title page gives essential information, and the abstract overviews the study. These two pages may be the only ones read by readers who examine an abstract to decide on reading or skipping the complete report. Therefore,

- The *title page* gives the official title of the paper, the byline of the writer, his or her academic affiliation, and a running head that appears on every page with a page number.
- The *abstract* establishes clearly the theory on which the whole work is based, the hypothesis under experimentation, the methods used, the findings, and the implications drawn from the testing. In just a few words, from 50 to 200, it provides an accurate and self-contained description of the problem. It explains the topic and problem, the purpose of the study, the kind of evidence gathered, the experimental method, the findings, the implications, and issues for additional research or theoretical study.
- The *References* page(s) provides the bibliography of sources cited in the paper, in tables and graphs, and in content notes. Pages 173, 183, and 199 provide detailed examples of Reference pages, and pages 149-162 provide an explanation of these forms.
- An *appendix* furnishes research material that contributed to the study but was not essential to the content of the paper itself. This information—tests, experiments, interviews, surveys, questionnaires, and so forth—may or may not serve the reader. See pages 184-185 for an example.

13f Sample Report of Empirical Research

The student paper that follows, written in APA style, provides an example of one student's investigation into Internet romance—that is, the effect of online matchmaking services such as Match.com. She examines this hypothesis: Online dating services provide, among other things, an opportunity for people to meet, chat, and reveal things about themselves yet, like ancient matriarchs, set the criteria for determining a good match.

ARRANGED MARRIAGES: THE REVIVAL IS ONLINE   Running head

Arranged Marriages: The Revival Is Online   Title
Valerie Nesbitt-Hall   Byline
Sociology 2020, Austin Peay State University   Affiliation

Abstract

Computer matchmaking was investigated to examine the theoretical implications of marriages arranged in part by online dating. The goal was to determine the effect of Internet activity on the private lives of the participants. One researcher started with a theory that arranged marriages exist from a variety of procedures, but the researcher can use a hypothesis to support or refute by experimentation and observation of one issue. Thus, a case study that interviewed an affected coupled determined social and psychological implications. The social implications might affect the workplace as well as the private lives of the men and women who are active in chat rooms and dating services. The psychological implications involve hesitation in romance procedures, but they suggest the possibility for discovering a true and lasting love.

Arranged Marriages: The Revival Is Online

Arranged marriages display a theory, but with a twist. Online dating services provide today, among other things, an opportunity for people to meet, chat, reveal things about themselves, and—as one source has expressed it—"play the role of patriarchal grandfathers, searching for good matches based

Establish the topic along with social and/or psychological issues that will be examined

on any number of criteria that you select" (Razdan, 2003, p. 71). In addition, hundreds of Internet groups draw people together by the millions, so computer matchmaking has social implications that psychologists examine carefully. This study examined the implications of marriages arranged by online dating to test this hypothesis: Online dating revised ancient matchmaking by the patriarchs and matriarchs of the family.

Statistics vary greatly on the amount of activity. Sources show the figure is in the millions, and that is substantial. *People Weekly* (2004) reported that 50 million Americans were registered online, and that figure climbs considerably each year. People have visited, many have found a mate, and some have even married. Match.com and America Online's dating areas credit themselves for hundreds of marriages that began as personal online messages. Can it be called a social revolution? Some have said "yes" to that question because about one-fifth of all singles in the country are online, prearranging their meetings and their lives, assuring themselves a better match than an evening's trip to a local nightclub. For example, Cooper (2002) argued that online dating has the potential to lower the nation's divorce rate. Kass (2003) identified the "distanced nearness" of a chat room that "encourages self-revelation while maintaining personal boundaries" (cited in Razdan, 2003, p. 71). Fein and Schneider (2002) insisted that many arranged marriages, by parents or by cyberspace, have produced enduring love because of a deliberation performed in rational moments before moments of passionate impulse.

With the divorce rate at 50 percent, marriage has become a roll of the dice, so some experts agreed that online dating reverts to the prearranged meetings of two young people identified as compatible by economic, political, religious, and social reasons.

Meanwhile, persons online can enjoy a distance, even hiding their real names to enjoy "an intimate but protected (cyber)space" (Kass, 2003, cited in Razdan, p. 71). Participants

A theoretical study depends heavily upon the literature, which must be cited in correct APA form.

Arranged Marriages 5

online have erected and maintained personal fences of privacy but at the same time revealed private feelings that they might never express in face-to-face meetings.

Method

An e-mail technique for collecting evidence was used. It featured a case study in which the subjects were interviewed with regard to their online romance.

Subjects

The subjects of the interview preferred to remain anonymous; they were Stephen of Scotland and Jennifer of the United States. This research uncovered a match that resulted in marriage.

Procedure

The subjects were interviewed on cyber romance by e-mail correspondence. The interview as recorded appears in the Appendix, pp. 10–11, and is described next as a case study.

Case Study

Research uncovered a match that resulted in marriage. The two subjects, Jennifer and Stephen, were interviewed on the matter of cyber romance. What follows is a brief summary of the interview, which is on file. The couple met online in September of 1996 in a chat room, not on a matching service. Stephen initiated the first contact, and they chatted anonymously for nine months before Jennifer initiated an exchange of phone numbers, addresses, and photographs. Stephen initiated the first meeting in person after 11 months, inviting Jennifer to travel from the United States to Glasgow, Scotland. Seven months later they married; it was 1.5 years from the time they met at the Internet newsgroup.

When asked if online romance protected her privacy and gave her time to prearrange things, Jennifer answered in the affirmative with emphasis. When asked who was more aggressive

Center major headings

in pushing forward the romance, Stephen said it was a mutual thing. Both agreed that when they finally met in person, they really knew the other person—spiritually, emotionally, and intellectually. The matter of different nationalities also played a role on two fronts—immigration matters and the concern of Jennifer's parents that she would fly to Scotland to see someone she had never met.

When asked if the relationship had been excellent to this point, both replied with affirmative answers. When asked if they would recommend online dating to others who are seeking mates, Stephen and Jennifer said, yes, under the right circumstances— "be cautious and take your time." Thus, online dating in this instance was successful.

It should be noted that the people who participate in online romance run the whole range of human subjects. Millions now consider meeting someone over the Internet is like phoning them or sending a fax. It has become an everyday thing to send dozens of e-mails, so the next logical step would be finding romance on the Internet.

Procedure

Stephen and Jennifer received a set of questions as an e-mail attachment. They answered each question, as shown in the Appendix, pages 10–11. Procedures to access a matching partner are varied, yet each has one thing in common—to bring two compatible people together on the Web, where they can e-mail each other, participate in IM chats, send attachments of favorite songs or personal photographs, and eventually exchange real names, phone numbers, and addresses. Newsgroups work in a similar fashion with back-and-forth discussion, even argument, about a variety of topics.

Discussion

In conclusion, the world of online romance is growing at a staggering rate with millions signing on each year, with thousands finding happiness, and with thousands more finding sexual chaos and dangerous liaisons. Yet little research is being done in this area. My search of the literature produced a surprisingly limited number of journal articles. Various sources have discussed methods of helping clients, even to the point of counseling in cyberspace itself, which would establish professional relationships online. Schneider and Weiss (2001) describe it but offer little psychoanalysis. Cooper (2002) has an excellent collection of articles in his guidebook for clinicians. Counseling needs to be in place for persons who substitute fantasy sex online for a true relationship. However, numerous case studies also show that online romance can produce healthy relationships and successful marriages (Brooks, 2003; Cha, 2003; Fein, 2002; Nussbaum, 2002; and Young, et al., 2002).

References

Brooks, L. (2003, February 13). The love business. *The Guardian* (London), p. 6. Retrieved April 8, 2003, from InfoTrac database.

Cha, A. E. (2003, May 4). ISO Romance? Online matchmakers put love to the test. *Washington Post*, p. A01. Retrieved April 9, 2003, from Lexis-Nexis database.

Cooper, A. (Ed.). (2002). *Sex and the Internet: A guide book for clinicians*. New York: Brunner-Routledge.

Fein, E., & Schneider, S. (2002). The rules for online dating. New York: Pocket Books.

Nussbaum, E. (2002, December 15). The year in ideas: Online personals are cool. *New York Times*, Sec. 6, p. 106. Retrieved April 8, 2003, from http://www.nytimes.com

Razdan, A. (2003, May-June). What's love got to do with it? *Utne*, pp.69-71.

Schneider, J., & Weiss, R. (2001). *Cybersex exposed: Simple fantasy or obsession?* Center City, MN: Hazelden.

Young, K., Griffin, S., Shelley, E., Cooper, A., O'Mara, J., & Buchanan, J. (2002). Online infidelity: A new dimension in couple relationships with implications for evaluation and treatment. *Sexual Addiction and Compulsivity, 7,* 59–74. Abstract retrieved April 4, 2003, from InfoTrac database.

Appendix

Following is the set of 12 questions and the answers by Stephen and Jennifer:

1. When did you first meet online?

   Answer: September of 1996

2. What prompted you to try an online matching service?

   Answer: We didn't really try online matching services. We chatted in a chat room, became friends there, and met in person later.

3. Who initiated the first contact?

   Answer: Stephen initiated the first online chat.

4. How long into the relationship did you correspond by e-mail before one of you gave an address and/or phone number? Who did it first, Steve or Jennifer?

   Answer: We chatted and corresponded by e-mail for nine months before Jennifer shared her phone number.

5. How long into the relationship did you go before sharing photographs?

   Answer: At nine months we began to share written correspondence and photographs.

6. Who initiated the first meeting in person? Where did you meet? How long were you into the relationship before you met in person?

Arranged Marriages 11

Answer: Stephen first requested the meeting, and Jennifer flew from the States to Glasgow, Scotland. This was about a year into the relationship.

7. How much time elapsed between your first online discovery of each other and your marriage?

Answer: One and a half years after our first chat we were married.

8. Did you feel that online romance enabled you to prearrange things and protect your privacy before meeting in person?

Answer: Yes, we were cautious and at times reluctant to continue, but we kept coming back to each other online until we knew the other well enough to trust in the relationship. Once we got offline into what we might call real-time dating, the love blossomed quickly.

9. Did you feel, when you finally met in person, that you really knew the other person spiritually? emotionally? intellectually?

Answer: Yes.

10. Not to put you on the spot, but do you feel as a couple that the relationship has been excellent to this point?

Answer: Yes, super.

11. Has the difference in nationalities been a problem?

Answer: Yes, but only in relation to sorting out immigration matters. Also, Jennifer's parents were concerned that she was going to another country to see someone she had never met.

12. Finally, would you recommend online matching services or chat rooms to others who are seeking mates?

Answer: Yes, in the right circumstances. We were lucky; others might not be.

13g Writing the Proposal for Conducting Empirical Research

In some instances, instructors might require a proposal for empirical research but not the actual research. In other words, your grade will be based only on the proposal—its presentation of the problem, its review of the literature on the topic, and its design of a method for conducting the research. The general design of a proposal, like the finished report, should conform to the following guidelines. The *introduction* should:

- Establish a problem or topic worthy of examination.
- Provide background information, including a review of literature on the subject.
- Give the purpose and rationale for the study, including the hypothesis that serves as the motivation for the experiment.

The *body* of the proposal for empirical research should:

- Provide a Methods section for explaining how you will design the study with regard to subject, apparatus, and procedure.
- Offer a Results section for listing any potential findings of the study.

The *conclusion* of a proposal for empirical research should:

- Suggest implications to be drawn from the possible findings in relation to the hypothesis.
- Offer suggestions for additional research by others.

Effects of Communication Skills 1

Proposal: The Effects of Communication

Skills on Development of Interpersonal Relationships

Julie A. Strasshofer

Department of Psychology

Austin Peay State University

May 4, 2004

Effects of Communication Skills 2

Abstract

Marital and premarital counselors have used communication skills training on a regular basis to enhance a couple's relationship. This study explores the theory that communication training can affect an adolescent's ability to develop constructive relationships with friends and family members. Hypothesis: In-class instruction to students to express themselves and listen to others will improve their relationships as measured by a revised version of the Interpersonal Relations Questionnaire (IRQ). The discussion explores the expected results of this study.

Effects of Communication Skills 3

The Effects of Communication Skills

on the Development of Interpersonal Relationships

The ability of a student to relate with others in personal relationships, as opposed to public, has been an important aspect of classroom training. The breakdown of the American family has led society into crime, violence, and a decay in moral values. Feindler and Starr (2003) stated: "Teaching children and adolescents to recognize how they feel when they are angry and what pushes their buttons enables them to make better choices about how they express their anger" (p. 158).

Mongrain and Vettese (2003) argued that young women are often ambivalent in their emotional expression, which "entails less congruent communication" and "less positivity in close relationships" (abstract). Black (2002) showed that young women rated lower than young men in withdrawal and higher than the men in communication skills during a test of their conflict resolution in conversations with their best friends. Since the family structure depends highly upon the relationship of husband and wife, a breach in that relationship can destroy the family unit. Thus, teaching communication skills to married couples before problems arise can reduce marital distress.

This concept has carried over into the realm of premarital counseling. Numerous churches extending across the denominations have come to require premarital counseling weighed heavily with communication skills in order to prevent distressed marriages and to decrease divorce rates.

Effects of Communication Skills 4

Other types of close relationships include those of parent-child, sibling-sibling, and same-sex friendships. The ability of a person to relate with others in social and intimate settings begins when children interact with others by observation and instruction. Even though this acquisition of knowledge steadily increases in childhood, many young adults are not sufficiently prepared to deal with the types of social interaction they face as they proceed through adolescence and young adulthood. Since communication has an important role in relationships and since relationships have such an impact on society, then the effects of training adolescents in communication skills should be further examined.

This study will test the hypothesis that training high school students in the applied use of communication skills will enable these students to develop healthy and constructive interpersonal relationships as measured by a revised version of the Interpersonal Relations Questionnaire (IRQ). They will have a definition of their opinions, develop accurate expression of these options, and build a courteous reception to the opinions and emotions of others.

Method

Subjects

The subjects will consist of high school students in grades 10, 11, and 12. They will be selected from a local high school through contact with the principal by letter. Only a school that has a mandatory Health and Wellness class will be accepted because interpersonal relationship is a relevant issue to the mental and emotional well-being of students. Two classes from the school will be allowed for a control group and a treatment group.

Instrumentation

Characteristics of the students' interpersonal relationship will be measured by using a test based on the standard IRQ. This test measures personal adjustment in adolescents aged 12 to 15 and will be adjusted for 16- to 18-year-olds.

Effects of Communication Skills 5

An open-ended questionnaire will also be developed to inquire about the perceived quality of past and present relationships by the students. It will question these items:

- Average length of past and present relationships.
- Satisfaction of communication in family and friendly relationships.
- The ability to solve conflicts verbally.
- The awareness in his or her ability to communicate since taking the course.

Procedure

Communication skills will be taught to one class for six weeks, preferably when the students return from Christmas break. This will allow the students time to develop relationships during the school year prior to skill training and also allow time after the training, but before the school year ends, so that students might notice tendency changes in their relationships.

The skills taught will stress the definition and expression of feelings and opinions, along with listening techniques. These skills will be focused toward those strategies used in a variety of interpersonal relationships as administered by an instructor. The students will once again take the IRQ, and the open-end questionnaire will be administered to all students at the completion of the school year.

Results

The IRQ pretest and posttest scores will be compared, and open-ended questionnaires will be examined for pattern changes and perceived changes in relationship quality. The results between the treatment and non-treatment group will be compared in order to examine whether any changes or trends could be related to normal growth. The results might also be compared to the IRQ results in the attempt to expose any sensitivity created by pretesting.

Effects of Communication Skills 6

Discussion

If the results of this study actually do show a positive correlation between communication skills and interpersonal relationships in the students tested, then consideration should be given to refining this technique and using it in Wellness classes in an attempt to prepare adolescents for their growth into young adults.

Effects of Communication Skills 7

References

Black, K. A. (2002). Gender differences in adolescents' behavior during conflict resolution tasks with best friends. *Women and Language, 25.* Abstract retrieved March 7, 2004, from InfoTrac database.

Feindler, E. L., & Starr, K. E. (2003). From steaming mad to staying cool: A constructive approach to anger control. [Electronic version]. *Reclaiming Children and Youth, 12,* 158–161.

Mongrain, M., & Vettese, L. C. (2003). Conflict over emotional expression: Implications for interpersonal communication. *Personality & Social Psychology Bulletin, 29.* Abstract retrieved March 7, 2004, from the InfoTrac database.

YOUR RESEARCH PROJECT

1. Write a report on your empirical research. Conform to the standards established in this chapter and the preceding sections of the text. Submit your report to your instructor.

2. As an alternative, write a proposal for empirical research, as demonstrated in this chapter on pages 186–190. Submit the proposal to your instructor.

The review of literature is an educational activity that trains you in the investigation of sources. It does not require empirical research, but it does involve theory—that is, you examine the theoretical basis for each article in order to describe the work and compare it with others. Accordingly, the literature review written in APA style has several goals:

1. The review discovers conflicts, contradictions, and variables, for you show how several scholars, under differing circumstances, examined the issues. It compares the key theories in one small area of research.

2. It shows gaps in the research to pinpoint areas worthy of additional study. Along the way, it explains the ramifications of the problem to show how each article contributes another aspect of the problem and solution.

3. The literature review classifies current research to show relationships. Thus, it should not be a chronological listing of the sources, nor should each paragraph be devoted to a single source. The articles that address the same issue should be grouped to show the various positions. Some will agree on an answer while others disagree, and immediately you have two classifications.

4. The review of literature, as shown on pages 194–200, can be a short paper of its own or part of the introduction to your theoretical study or your report of empirical research.

5. Your review serves other researchers who might be interested in the topic and who want to know how other scholars have addressed the problem.

14a Choosing a Topic

Three factors affect the selection of an effective topic for review purposes: relevance, currency, and a narrow focus.

First, choose a topic of interest to you, if you have that option. For example, you may know a person with an addiction to drugs or another who suffers with depression. Examining such topics has relevance to your life and will keep you interested.

Second, select a subject of current interest so you can find articles published in recent years. Glance at a few magazines and journals to see what the experts are writing about, and use an electronic search engine to find articles.

For example, entering the topic "cutters" in the PsycINFO search engine will produce 30 to 40 current articles on this subject of adolescents who are purposely cutting themselves.

Third, you can begin with a broad subject, such as hypnosis, abortion, same-sex marriage, and so forth, but you will soon need to narrow the topic to a specific issue. The topic "hypnosis," for example, will show over 12,000 articles in the PsycINFO database. Try narrowing it to "hypnosis and addictions" or, even tighter, "hypnosis and smoking." The search engine also allows you to narrow the search to recent articles of the last five or ten years. See pages 58–61 for more information on conducting searches.

14b   Reading the Articles

Give each article a careful, critical reading. In particular, look for differences and similarities in the theoretical outlook of the writers, which will enable you to classify the articles, such as those that examine peer response, those that advocate pharmacological remedies, and those that promote parental intervention. The classifications should become evident as you move from one article to the next. Make notes that summarize, paraphrase, or quote the authors, for these materials will form the basis of your review. You must be able to explain what the various writers are saying in defense of their theoretical positions.

> Note: See Chapter 7, "Responding to the Evidence," pages 94–104, for complete details on the techniques for examining the literature.

14c   Writing the Literature Review

The length of your review depends primarily on the number of articles you have included, which may number from six to seven or as many as 25, depending on the assignment, the subject, and available articles.

Introduction

The introduction establishes the theme, theory, or research question you review. All articles should then, of course, address the central issue, which you have narrowed as much as possible. Not *abortion* but *grief responses in women following abortion* and not *gender bias* but *gender bias toward African-American women.*

If you wish, the introduction is a good place to trace the history of research in the subject because the body of your review will comment on *recent* works.

The introduction describes the organization of the paper. In the case of a controversy, show how you describe research that supports one side and then the other. If you have three classifications of critical approaches, explain them briefly, as with *bias in the workplace, bias in the schools,* and *bias in the courts.* Thus, the introduction of the review should:

- Identify the problem or subject to be reviewed.
- Explain its currency and its significance.
- Briefly describe the organization of the essay.

Body

The body of the review traces the various issues, and explains for each the articles that pertain to it. Under your classifications, you compare and evaluate the studies to address each article's contribution to research on the subject. You should identify and describe each article in detail, especially to explain how the work contributes to the overall design of research on the subject.

Depend heavily on paraphrase to describe what each author or set of authors has advanced. Reserve direct quotations for statements that are truly germane to the issues.

In each major section of your review, you should compare the research projects of various scientists and discuss the implications of each. Your comparisons of the sources will advance your reader's understanding of the central issues. For example, you might compare:

- Hypotheses advanced by various writers.
- Assumptions drawn from the research by the writers.
- Theories that have been tested.
- The designs or methods used for the research.
- The results of the research.
- The writers' interpretations of their findings.

Every literature review must find its own way, and yours will fall into place as you read, analyze, and compare the various approaches to the problem or question at hand. Be courageous enough to evaluate the research, not just describe it. In that way, your paper becomes a critical review, not merely an objective description of articles. Only by evaluation can you make the essay your own.

Thus, the body of the review should:

- Provide a systematic analysis of each article.
- Compare the articles that fall within a specific classification.
- Discuss the relevance of the findings by each piece of research.
- Comment on the apparent significance of the results.

Conclusion

The conclusion of the review should explain again the significance of the subject under review. It can also give a general overview of the prevailing theories you examined in the body. Of vital importance is your discussion of the implications drawn from your examination of several research reports. You might wish to defend one theory, and you might also suggest additional research work to launch in pursuit of more answers to the problem or question.

Thus, the conclusion of the literature review should:

- Discuss the implications of the findings.
- Make judgments as appropriate.
- Evaluate the relative merits of the various works of research.
- Defend one theory.
- Suggest additional research.

14d Sample Literature Review

The paper that follows classifies several articles on gender communication under a progression of headings: the issues, the causes (both environmental and biological), the consequences for both men and women, and possible solutions. You also should arrange the sources to fit your selected categories or to fit your preliminary outline, and, like Kaci Holz in the paper below, use centered heads and side heads to identify the sections of your APA-style paper.

Gender Communication 1

GENDER COMMUNICATION: A REVIEW OF THE LITERATURE

Kaci Holz

Women's Studies 2040

April 23, 2004

Gender Communication 2

Gender Communication: A Review of the Literature

Several theories have existed about different male and female communication styles. These ideas have been categorized below to establish the issues, to show causes for communication failures, to describe the consequences for both men and women, and to discuss the implications.

The Issues

Tannen (1990) identified basic gender patterns or stereotypes. She said men participate in conversations to establish "a hierarchical social order" (*You Just Don't Understand,* p. 24), while women most often participate in conversations to establish "a network of connections" (p. 25).

Gender Communication 3

She distinguished between the way women use "rapport-talk" and the way men use "report-talk" (p. 74).

In similar fashion, Basow and Rubenfeld (2003) explored in detail the sex roles and how they determine and often control the speech of each gender. They noticed that "women may engage in 'troubles talk' to enhance communication; men may avoid such talk to enhance autonomy and dominance" (p. 186).

In addition, Yancey (1993) has asserted that men and women "use conversation for quite different purposes" (p. 71). He provided a 'no' answer to the question in his title, "Do Men and Women Speak the Same Language?" He claimed that women converse to develop and maintain connections, while men converse to claim their position in the hierarchy they see around them. Yancey asserted that women are less likely to speak publicly than are men because women often perceive such speaking as putting oneself on display. A man, on the other hand, is usually comfortable with speaking publicly because that is how he establishes his status among others. Similarly, masculine people are "less likely than androgynous individuals to feel grateful for advice" (Basow & Rubenfeld, p. 186). In similar fashion, Woods (2002) claimed that "male communication is characterized by assertion, independence, competitiveness, and confidence [while] female communication is characterized by deference, inclusivity, collaboration, and cooperation" (p. 440). This list of differences described why men and women have such opposing communication styles.

In another book, Tannen (1998) addressed the issue that boys, or men, "are more likely to take an oppositional stance toward other people and the world" and "are more likely to find opposition entertaining—to enjoy watching a good fight, or having one" (*The Argument Culture*, p. 166). Girls try to avoid fights.

Causes

Two different theories suggest causes for gender differences.

Environmental Causes. James and Cinelli (2003) made this observation: "The way men and women are raised contributes to differences in conversation and communication . . . " (p. 41). Another author, Witt (1997), in "Parental Influence on Children's Socialization to Gender Roles," discussed the various findings that support the idea that parents have a great influence on their children during the development of their self-concept. Witt stated, "Children learn at a very early age what it means to be a boy or a girl in our society" (p. 253) and added that parents "[dress] infants in gender-specific colors, [give] gender-differentiated toys, and [expect] different behavior from boys and girls" (p. 254).

Yancey (1993) noticed a cultural gap, defining culture as "shared meaning" (p. 68). He said, "Some problems come about because one spouse enters marriage with a different set of 'shared meanings' than the other" (p. 69). The cultural gap affects the children. Yancey also talked about the "Battle of the Sexes" as seen in conflict between men and women. Reverting back to his 'childhood gender pattern' theory, Yancey claimed, "Men, who grew up in a hierarchical environment, are accustomed to conflict. Women, concerned more with relationship and connection, prefer the role of peacemaker" (p. 71).

Like Yancey, Tannen (1990) also addressed the fact that men and women often come from different worlds and different influences. She argued, "Even if they grow up in the same neighborhood, on the same block, or in the same house, girls and boys grow up in different worlds of words" (*You Just Don't Understand*, p. 43).

Gender Communication 5

Biological Causes. Though Tannen (1990) addressed the
environmental issue in her early research, she has also
considered the biological issue in her book *The Argument Culture*
(1998). Tannen observed, "Surely a biological component plays a
part in the greater use of antagonism among men, but cultural
influence can override biological inheritance" (*Argument*, p.
205). She summed up the nature versus nurture issue by saying,
"the patterns that typify women's and men's styles of opposition
and conflict are the result of both biology and culture" (p. 207).

Glass (1992) addressed the issue that different hormones
found in men and women's bodies make them act differently and
therefore communicate differently. She also discussed how brain
development has been found to relate to sex differences.

Mann (1997) said, "Most experts now believe that what happens
to boys and girls is a complex interaction between slight biological
differences and tremendously powerful social forces that begin to
manifest themselves the minute the parents find out whether they
are going to have a boy or a girl" (cited in McCluskey, p. 6).

Consequences of Gender Differences

Now that we have looked at different styles of gender
communication and possible causes of gender differences, let us
look at the possible results. M. Weiner-Davis (1996), author of
Divorce Busting, said to this point, "Ignorance about the
differences in gender communication has been a major
contributor to divorce" (cited in Warren, p. 106).

Through various studies, Tannen has concluded that men
and women have different purposes for engaging in
communication. In the open forum that Tannen and Bly (1993)
gave in New York, Tannen (on videotape) explained the different
ways men and women handle communication throughout the day.
She explained that a man constantly talks during his workday in

order to impress those around him and to establish his status in the office. At home, he wants peace and quiet. On the other hand, a woman is constantly cautious and guarded about what she says during her workday. Women try hard to avoid confrontation and avoid offending anyone with their language. So when a woman comes home from work, she expects to be able to talk freely without having to guard her words. The consequence? The woman expects conversation, but the man is tired of talking.

Implications

Answers for better gender communication seem elusive. What can be done about this apparent gap in communication between genders? In an article published in *Leadership,* Arthurs (2002) suggested that women should make an attempt to understand the male model of communication and that men should make an attempt to understand the female model of communication.

However, in an article entitled "Speaking Across the Gender Gap," Cohen (2003) mentioned that experts didn't think it would be helpful to teach men to communicate more like women or for women to communicate more like men. This attempt would prove unproductive because it would go against what men and women have been taught since birth. Rather than change the genders to be more like one another, we could simply try to "understand" each other better.

In addition, Weaver (1995) made this observation: "The idea that women should translate their experiences into the male code in order to express themselves effectively . . . is an outmoded, inconsistent, subservient notion that should no longer be given credibility in modern society" (p. 439). Weaver suggested three behavioral patterns we can change:

1. Change the norm by which leadership success is judged.

2. Redefine what we mean by power.

Gender Communication 7

3. Become more sensitive to the places and times when
   inequity and inequality occur (p. 439).

Similarly, Yancey offered advice to help combat "cross-cultural" fights. He suggested:

1. Identify your fighting style.

2. Agree on rules of engagement.

3. Identify the real issue behind the conflict (p. 71).

McCluskey (1997) argued that men and women need honest
communication that shows respect, and they must "manage
conflict in a way that maintains the relationship and gets the job
done" (p. 5). McCluskey said, "To improve relationships and
interactions between men and women, we must acknowledge the
differences that do exist, understand how they develop, and
discard dogma about what are the 'right' roles of women and
men" (p. 5).

The most obvious implication is that differences exist in
the way men and women communicate, whether they are caused
by biological and/or environmental factors. We can consider the
possible causes, the consequences, and possible solutions. Using
this knowledge, further research should more accurately interpret
communication between the genders.

Gender Communication 8

References

Arthurs, J. (2002, Winter). He said, she heard: Any time you
  speak to both men and women, you're facing cross-cultural
  communication. *Leadership, 23.1,* 49.

Basow, S. A., & Rubenfeld, K. (2003). Troubles talk: Effects
  of gender and gender typing. *Sex Roles: A Journal
  of Research*. Retrieved April 24, 2003, from
  http://web5.infotrac.galegroup.com/search

Cohen, D. (1991). Speaking across the gender gap. *New Scientist 131,*
  36. Retrieved September 28, 2003, from *InfoTrac* database.

Gender Communication 9

Deborah Tannen and Robert Bly: Men and women talking
   together. (1993). [Videocassette]. New York: Mystic
   Fire Video.

Glass, L. (1992). *He says, she says: Closing the communication*
   gap between the sexes. New York: G.P. Putnam's Sons.

James, T., & Cinelli, B. (2003). Exploring gender-based
   communication styles. *Journal of School Health, 73,* 41–61.

McCluskey, K. C. (1997). Gender at work. *Public Management,*
   79(5), 5–10.

Tannen, D. (1990). *You just don't understand: Women and men in*
   conversation. New York: Ballantine.

Tannen, D. (1998). *The argument culture: Moving from debate to*
   dialogue. New York: Random House.

Warren, A. (1996, March). How to get him to listen. *Ladies' Home*
   Journal, 113, 106.

Weaver, R. L. (1995). Leadership for the future: A new set of
   priorities. *Vital Speeches of the Day, 61,* 438–441.

Witt, S. D. (1997). Parental influence on children's socialization
   to gender roles. *Adolescence. 32,* 253–264.

Woods, J. T. (2002). *Gendered lives.* San Francisco: Wadsworth.

Yancey, P. (1993). Do men and women speak the same language?
   Marriage Partnership, 10, 68–73.

YOUR RESEARCH PROJECT

1. Write a review article that evaluates at least four sources on a topic of your choice. Conform to the standards established in this chapter. Submit the review article to your instructor.

2. As an alternative, write a review of one article and submit it to your instructor.